THE WORLD ENCYCLOPEDIA OF
FISH AND SHELLFISH

THE WORLD ENCYCLOPEDIA OF
FISH AND SHELLFISH

KATE WHITEMAN

HERMES
HOUSE

This edition published by
Hermes House
an imprint of
Anness Publishing Limited
Hermes House
88-89 Blackfriars Road
London SE1 8HA

A CIP catalogue record for this book is available from the British Library

ISBN 1-84309-620-X

Publisher: Joanna Lorenz
Executive Editor: Linda Fraser
Copy Editor: Jenni Fleetwood
Indexer: Hilary Bird
Designer: Nigel Partridge
Photography: William Lingwood, assisted by Vanessa Davies
Food for Photography: Sunil Vijayakar, assisted by Tonia Hedley (recipes) and
Annabel Ford (reference section)

Printed and bound in Singapore

© Anness Publishing Limited 2000
Updated © 2002
1 3 5 7 9 10 8 6 4 2

NOTES

For all recipes, quantities are given in both metric and imperial measures and, where
appropriate, measures are also given in standard cups and spoons. Follow one set, but
not a mixture because they are not interchangeable.

Standard spoon and cup measures are level.
1 tsp = 5ml, 1 tbsp = 15ml, 1 cup = 250ml/8fl oz

Australian standard tablespoons are 20ml. Australian readers should use 3 tsp in place
of 1 tbsp for measuring small quantities of gelatine, cornflour, salt etc.
Medium eggs are used unless otherwise stated.

CONTENTS

INTRODUCTION

Since man evolved as a hunter-gatherer, the world's rivers, lakes and seas have served as a limitless larder, providing a bountiful supply of fish and seafood almost infinite in its variety. From tiny streams to brackish ponds to great oceans, all waters yield some kind of fish and shellfish, almost all of them edible, although in many cases you might not guess this from their outward appearance.

Although for many years fish was undervalued in the western world, particularly in areas far from the coast, its importance as a highly nutritious and delicious food is now universally recognized. As controversial farming methods make many important foods such as meat, dairy produce and cereals less attractive than they once were, fish has really come into its own as a healthy alternative.

There is no doubt that fish is good for you. All fish and seafood is low in fat and high in proteins, minerals and vitamins; oily fish can actually improve your health by lowering cholesterol levels and unclogging arteries. The Japanese, whose diet consists largely of spanking fresh raw fish, have the lowest incidence of heart disease in the world.

Good health is only one of many reasons to eat fish, however. When properly prepared and cooked, it can be among the most delicious foods imaginable. Unfortunately, too many of us were brought up on institutional offerings of heavily-breaded deep-fried scampi, or unpalatable, overcooked or watery fish, whose delicate flavour was

Below: In many areas good fish stalls, like this one in Venice, Italy, are becoming increasingly hard to find.

Right: Octopus and baby squid on sale at Tsukiji fish market in Tokyo.

often rendered tasteless, or masked with floury sauces. Well-cooked fish is quite another matter, however. Really fresh fish needs little cooking or embellishment and most takes very little time to prepare, a huge bonus for the modern cook whose time is often very limited. It is easy to rustle up the most elegant fish dish in under half an hour.

Every fish and shellfish has its own unique flavour, offering something for all tastes. It is unlikely that there is a recipe for a piscatorial pudding, but fish and shellfish can feature in every other part of a meal, including appetizers, main courses, salads and savouries.

It is hard to understand why fish has been undervalued for so long. Perhaps it has something to do with the fact

that it was traditionally eaten on fast days, as a substitute for meat, so is associated with self-denial and penance. In times of plenty, easily-obtainable seafoods, such as salmon and oysters, were regarded as foods fit only for the poor. Medieval apprentices complained bitterly and refused to eat oysters more than three times a week. Bland, easily-digested white fish was perceived as invalid food and rejected by those with more robust constitutions.

Probably the main reason for eschewing fish, however, was lack of understanding of how to prepare it. Skinning, filleting, scaling and shelling all seemed like rather hard work. Nowadays, despite the demise of many fishmongers, there is no need to do all the hard work yourself. Just visit your local supermarket and choose ready-prepared fish or, better still, follow the instructions given in this book, which will guide you through the complexities of handling and preparing all kinds of fish and shellfish.

Fish and shellfish are rewarding to cook and extremely versatile. Although some types have become scarce through over-fishing, and therefore very expensive, the price of others has plummeted, thanks to advances in fish farming. Salmon, for example, has come full circle. Once despised as being too common, its subsequent rarity made it one of the most expensive and

sought-after fish. Now, once again, it has become one of the cheapest types of fish available. Be wary, however, of buying very cheap farmed fish. Careless farming results in poor quality specimens. Poor fish farming can also promote diseases, which may spread to other sea creatures in their natural habitat. Consumers must not repeat the mistakes of the past, when demand for ever-cheaper meat and other foods had disastrous consequences in terms of health and ecology. Fish and shellfish are superb natural foods and should remain so. That said, well-managed fish and shellfish farms produce healthy specimens and help counteract the disastrous effects of over-fishing of wild stocks.

The variety of edible underwater creatures is staggering. I often wonder which intrepid (or desperately hungry) soul was the first to imagine that a hideous lumpfish, malevolent eel or multi-limbed octopus might serve as a snack, or spot the potential in a spider crab, sea urchin or slimy sea cucumber for providing a palatable meal. Imagine what pleasures we might have missed had our ancestors been repelled by the appearance of such strange creatures. With a few poisonous exceptions, almost everything that swims, crawls, scuttles or merely lurks in the water can supply us with food.

One of the greatest pleasures when travelling is to visit the local fish market and see the dazzling array of brightly coloured fresh fish and seafood set out on the stalls. However strange their shapes and forms, all have a unique beauty and character. Modern methods of fishing and transportation have made sea creatures from all over the world accessible to adventurous cooks, so allow yourself the pleasure of experimenting and enjoy the infinite variety of textures, flavours and colours of the fruits of the sea.

KATE WHITEMAN

Right: There are fish and shellfish from all over the world on sale on this stall at an indoor market in the Champagne region of France.

EQUIPMENT

Although it is perfectly possible to prepare and cook fish without special equipment, there are a few items which make the process much easier. Some such as the fish kettle take up quite a lot of storage space; other gadgets, such as the fish scaler, are quite tiny, but all will prove invaluable for fish and shellfish cookery.

KNIVES, SCISSORS AND SCALERS

Chef's knife

A large heavy knife with a 20–25cm/ 8–10in blade is essential for cutting fish steaks and splitting open crustaceans such as crayfish and lobster.

Filleting knife

For filleting and skinning fish, you will need a sharp knife with a flexible blade, which is at least 15cm/ 6in long. This type of knife can also be used for opening some kinds of shellfish. It is essential to keep a filleting knife razor sharp.

Oyster knife

This short, stubby knife – sometimes called a shucker – has a wide, two-edged blade to help prise open the shells of oysters and other bivalves. Make sure that it has a safety guard above the handle to protect your hands.

Kitchen scissors

A sturdy, sharp pair of scissors that have a serrated edge are needed for cutting off fins and trimming tails.

Fish scaler

Resembling a small, rough grater, a fish scaler makes short work of a task that few relish.

Below: Fish scalers

Below: Chef's knife

Below: Filleting knife

Below: Scissors

PANS

Fish kettle

Long and deep, with rounded edges, this attractive utensil has a handle at either end, and a tightly-fitting lid. Inside is a perforated rack or grid on which to lay the fish. This, too, has handles, and enables the cook to lift out the fish without breaking it. Most modern fish kettles are made of stainless steel, but they also come in aluminium, enamelled steel and copper with a tin-plated interior. Fish kettles are used on the hob and are invaluable for cooking whole large fish, such as salmon and sea trout. Fish kettles can also be used for steaming other foods.

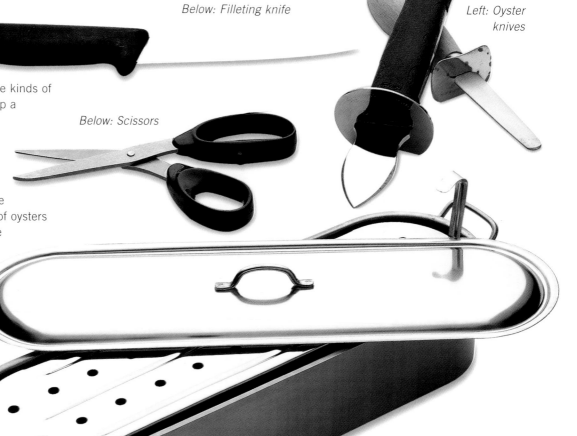

Left: Oyster knives

Above: A fish kettle takes up a lot of storage space in the kitchen, but if you want to cook whole fish, such as salmon, it is well worth buying.

Right: Oval
frying pan

Right: Griddle
pan

Right: Chinese bamboo
steamers

Above: Stainless steel steamers

Oval frying pan

Such a simple idea, but intensely practical, this large pan enables you to cook whole fish flat instead of bending them to fit a round pan and spoiling their shape.

Griddle pan

A ribbed cast-iron griddle pan is ideal for searing and grilling fish. They can be round, oval or rectangular. Some of the large griddles need to be used over two electric rings or gas burners on top of a stove.

Steamer

If you steam food frequently, a stainless steel steamer set is a good investment. They have a lidded, deep outer pan and a perforated inner basket. Choose the widest type that you can find. Chinese bamboo steaming baskets are an economical alternative. They come in a variety of sizes, from very small dim sum baskets to very wide baskets that are about 35cm/14in across. Chinese steaming baskets can be stacked one on top of each other so that several layers of food can be cooked at one time. Cheapest of all is a small, collapsible, perforated steamer, which unfolds like a flower to fit any pan.

Above: A single-handled wok can be used for steaming and deep-frying as well as stir-frying.

Below: Double-sided hinged rack

Above: Barbecue grilling rack for whole large fish

Wok

A 35cm/14in wok with a lid will be large enough to cope with most types of fish and will prove invaluable in the kitchen. There's no need to reserve this piece of equipment for stir-frying; a wok also makes an effective steamer and can also be used for deep-frying.

SPECIALIST ITEMS

Barbecue grilling rack

A hinged rack in the shape of a fish makes cooking – and turning – a single large fish relatively easy. Also available are shaped racks designed to hold 6–12 sardines. These can be rectangular or round. More useful for general purposes is a double-sided hinged grill rack. These can be square or rectangular and have long handles so that several steaks or small fish can be barbecued and turned over simultaneously. However, the flat sides do tend to squash the delicate flesh of some fish. Always oil grilling racks before use to prevent the fish from sticking to them.

Smoker

The cheapest home-smoker is a lidded metal box with a rack to hold the fish. Smoke produced by placing dampened aromatic wood chippings or herbs on the coals gives extra flavour. More convenient (and much more expensive) are electric smokers. Stove-top models can be used indoors.

Below: Sardine rack

Left: Fish smoker

Right: Fish slices

Right: Fish lifters

Above: Lobster pick and crackers

OTHER USEFUL UTENSILS

Fish lifter

Resembling an elongated fish slice, the curved and perforated turner is useful for flipping over whole fish during cooking without breaking them.

Fish slices

Two fish slices with sturdy yet flexible blades will make easy work of turning most fish.

Lobster pick

Choose a pick with a two-pronged fork at the end to extract the flesh from lobster and crab legs.

Lobster crackers

If you eat a lot of lobster or crab, these are well worth having. Lobster crackers look like hinged nutcrackers (often made in the shape of lobster claws) with ridges on the inside to give a good grip. Crackerjack nutcrackers are equally effective.

Mallet

A wooden mallet is useful for cracking crustacean claws and for batting out fish escalopes.

Pins

Use dressmakers' pins with round heads to extract winkles and whelks from their shells. For safety's sake, stick them in a cork when not using, so that the sharp ends cannot prick the unwary.

Tweezers

Use these to extract small bones and pin bones from fish fillets.

Right: Tweezers and pins

BUYING AND PREPARING FISH

Fish is only worth buying if it is absolutely fresh, and it is best if you eat it on the day you buy it. Fresh fish have shiny skin with a metallic glint and they are covered with a transparent mucus that becomes opaque when the fish is old and stale. The eyes should be clear, bright and slightly bulging. The flesh should feel firm and springy when you press it lightly with your finger; if it feels limp and your finger leaves an indentation, the fish is past its best. Stale fish has an unpleasant "fishy" smell, the skin looks dull, dryish and unattractive and the eyes are sunken.

The best test of freshness for whole fish is to open up the gills; they should be a clear red or rosy colour, not a dull brown. Look for a firm tail and plentiful, shiny close-fitting scales. A fish which has been dead for an unacceptable length of time, or which has not been properly kept, will shed its scales all over the counter. Seafish should have a pleasant odour, redolent of seaweed; freshwater fish should smell of waterweeds. There should never be more than a hint of a "fishy" smell.

Ready-prepared white fish fillets, steaks and cutlets should be neatly trimmed, with moist, firm, translucent flesh. If you must buy frozen fish, make sure that it is frozen solid, with no sign of thawing, and that the packaging is not damaged.

When buying fish, shop with an open mind and be prepared to purchase whatever looks freshest and best on the day. If you want a specific type of fish, it is best to ask the fishmonger in advance so that it can be bought fresh from the market for you. It pays to develop a relationship with one particular fishmonger – if you show that you are really interested in what you are buying, you are sure to get a much better standard of service.

An accommodating fishmonger will gut and clean your fish for you and even scale, skin and fillet it. It is not unreasonable to expect this service, but it does take time. At busy periods, therefore, be prepared to place an order and come back later to collect it. However, if you do have to prepare fish

yourself, don't despair; it is really not difficult, given a sharp, flexible knife and a little dexterity.

Quantities

Allow about 175g/6oz fish fillet, cutlets or steaks per serving for a main course. There is a lot of wastage in whole fish, so allow at least 300g/11oz per person if buying fish this way.

Storing fish

Fresh fish should be eaten as soon as possible after purchase, but most types can be kept in the fridge for a day or overnight if necessary. Remove the wrapping or packaging and rinse the fish in very cold water. Pat dry with kitchen paper and place on a plate. Cover with clear film and store at the bottom of the fridge.

Frozen fish

Although fresh fish is much nicer than frozen, for practical reasons it is not always possible to buy it, and on some occasions frozen fish may be your only option. Of course, you cannot apply the usual tests for freshness – prodding, smelling and judging the colour – so it is important to buy frozen fish from a reputable shop with a quick turnover. Transport it in a freezer bag if possible and get it home and into your own freezer without delay. White fish can be kept in the freezer for three months and oily fish for two months.

Commercially frozen fish is frozen extremely rapidly and at a lower temperature than can be attained by the average domestic freezer. This preserves the delicate texture of the flesh. It is not advisable to freeze fish at home, but if you must, it should be kept at –18°C/0°F or below.

Thawing fish

If possible, thaw frozen fish overnight in the fridge. If you need it in a hurry, microwave the fish on the defrost setting. Separate the pieces as soon as they are thawed enough and spread out in an even layer. Remove from the microwave while still slightly icy; if fish is over-thawed it will become dry.

ROUND FISH

Scaling

Smooth-skinned round fish such as trout and mackerel do not need scaling. For others, such as sea bass and mullet, it is vital.

First, trim off all the fins with a strong pair of scissors. Take care with the dorsal fins on the back, as they can have sharp spines. Work in the sink, preferably under running water, or the scales will fly all over your kitchen. Otherwise you can cover the fish with a damp cloth to catch the scales. Ideally, you should use a proper fish scaler to do the job, but the back of a round-bladed knife will do almost as well. Always scale fish before filleting if you are going to cook it with the skin on.

1 Wash the fish under cold water. Cut off the three fins that run along the stomach, and the dorsal fins on the back, using strong, sharp scissors.

2 Hold the fish firmly by the tail (a cloth will give a better grip). Using a fish scaler or the back of a knife, and working from tail to head, scrape against the lie of the scales to remove them. Wash the fish again to detach any clinging scales.

Braising

This is another excellent cooking method for whole fish or large fillets.

1 Butter a flameproof dish and make a thick bed of thinly sliced or shredded vegetables, such as a mixture of carrots, onions, fennel and celery.

2 Place the fish on top and pour on enough white or red wine and/or fish or chicken stock to come nearly halfway up the fish.

3 Scatter over 15ml/1 tbsp of fresh chopped herbs, cover with buttered greaseproof paper and bring to the boil. Braise the fish at a low temperature on top of the stove or in a preheated oven at 180°C/350°F/Gas 4, allowing about 20 minutes for a 1kg/2¼lb fish; 10–15 minutes for large fillets.

Fish stock

For many recipes, a good fish stock is essential. It is very simple to make. White fish bones and trimmings make the best stock. Ask the fishmonger for these whenever you buy fish; even if you cannot make stock that day, you can freeze them for later use. To make about 1 litre/1¾ pints/4 cups stock, you will need 1kg/2¼lb white fish bones, heads and trimmings.

1 Wash the fish heads thoroughly and remove the gills. Chop the heads and bones if necessary. Put them in a large saucepan.

2 Coarsely chop the white part of 1 leek (or ½ fennel bulb), 1 onion and 1 celery stick. Add these to the fish heads and bones in the pan.

3 Add 150ml/¼ pint/⅔ cup dry white wine. Toss in 6 white peppercorns and a bouquet garni, add 1 litre/ 1¾ pints/4 cups water.

4 Bring to the boil, lower the heat and simmer for 20 minutes (not more, or the flavour will become unpleasant). Strain through a muslin-lined sieve.

Frying

Shallow-frying or pan-frying

For this popular method, pieces of fish (fillets, steaks or cutlets) or small whole fish are cooked in a little fat in a shallow pan to caramelize and colour the outside. This can either be a prelude to another cooking method or the fish can be fully cooked in the pan. Before frying, the fish can be coated with flour, breadcrumbs or oatmeal. Plain fish can be fried without fat using a non-stick pan, but it will have to be cooked carefully to prevent drying out.

Frying in butter gives the best flavour, but it burns easily, so should be combined with a small amount of oil. Alternatively, use clarified butter or just oil. Heat the fat in the pan until very hot, put in the fish and seal briefly on both sides. Lower the heat and cook the fish gently until done. If the pieces of fish are large or the recipe is more complex it may be necessary to finish cooking in a moderate oven.

Deep-frying

Because fish is delicate, it must be coated in flour or some kind of batter before being deep-fried. This seals in the flavoursome juices, so that the fish is deliciously crisp on the outside and moist inside. Most fish is suitable for deep-frying, from tiny whitebait to large chunky fillets.

Use plenty of oil and make sure that it is really hot (180–190°C/350–375°F) before putting in the fish. Use an electric deep-fryer, or test by carefully dropping a cube of bread into the hot oil; if it browns within 30 seconds, the oil is hot enough. Larger pieces of fish should be cooked at a slightly lower temperature than small pieces like goujons. This allows the heat to penetrate to the centre before the outside burns. Do not cook too many pieces of fish at the same time, or the temperature of the oil will drop. Oil used for frying fish should never be used for any other purpose, as it will inevitably impart a fishy flavour.

1 Heat the oil in a deep-fryer to 180°C/350°F. Dip the fish in seasoned flour, add to the oil and cook until golden.

2 Drain the fish on a double thickness of kitchen paper before serving.

Goujons of sole or plaice

The name goujon comes from the French for gudgeon, which are small fresh water fish that are often served crisply fried. Goujons are strips of fish, usually sole or plaice; which are deep-fried and served with tartare sauce. Goujons are the perfect way to persuade children to eat fish, especially if you let them eat them with their fingers.

SERVES FOUR

INGREDIENTS
  8 sole or plaice fillets
  120ml/4fl oz/½ cup milk
  50g/2oz/1 cup plain flour
  vegetable oil, for deep-frying
  salt and ground black pepper

1 Skin the fish fillets and cut them into 7.5 x 2.5cm/3 x 1in strips. Season the milk with a little salt and pepper. Pour it into a shallow bowl, and place the plain flour in another bowl or spread it out on a plate.

2 Dip the fish strips first into the milk, then into the flour. Shake off the excess flour.

3 Fill a large saucepan one-third full with vegetable oil. Heat to about 185°C/360°F or until a small cube of bread dropped into the oil turns brown in 30 seconds.

4 Carefully lower the fish strips into the hot oil, adding 4 or 5 at a time. Fry for about 3 minutes, turning them occasionally using a slotted spoon, until the strips rise to the surface and turn golden brown in colour.

5 Lift out each piece of cooked fish with a slotted spoon and drain them on a double thickness of kitchen paper. Keep the cooked goujons hot in the oven while you cook successive batches.

Stir-frying

This quick-cooking Oriental method is perfect for fish, prawns and squid.

1 Cut fish or squid into bite-size strips; leave prawn tails whole, with the tail shells intact. Toss in a little cornflour to prevent them falling apart as they cook.

2 Heat a little oil in a wok over a very high heat, add a few pieces of fish or shellfish and stir-fry for a few moments.

Searing

This method is best for thickish fillets that have not been skinned or small whole fish such as sardines and red mullet.

1 Smear the base of a heavy frying pan or griddle with a little oil and heat until smoking. Lightly brush both sides of the fish with oil and put it into the hot pan.

2 Sear for a couple of minutes, until the skin is golden brown, then turn the fish over and cook on the other side.

Grilling and Barbecuing

Fish steaks, thick fillets and relatively small whole fish, such as sardines, red mullet or trout, can be grilled or barbecued, as can crustaceans. The grill should be preheated to a very high heat so that the fish juices are sealed in quickly. Griddle pans are better than overhead grills, but either will do. Grilling on the barbecue can be a little more tricky, as bastes or marinades used to keep the fish moist can drip on to the coals and cause flare-ups.

All grilled fish will benefit from being marinated for 1 hour in a mixture of oil and lemon juice before being cooked. If the fish is to be cooked whole, make several slashes down to the bone on either side to ensure that the fish cooks quickly and evenly. Brush the grill rack and fish with oil to prevent sticking. Thin fillets need only be grilled on one side. Do not use a grill rack. Brush the grill pan with oil. Place it under the grill until hot, then pass both sides of the fish through the oil before grilling on one side only; the underside will cook at the same time.

Microwaving

Fish can be cooked successfully in a microwave oven. As long as you do not overcook it, it will emerge moist and full of flavour. Always cover the fish with clear film. Microwave it on full power (100%) for the shortest possible time, as recommended in your handbook, then give it a resting period to allow it to finish cooking by residual heat. Cooking time depends on the thickness and density of the fish. The following are general guidelines for 500g/1¼lb fish, but test before the end of the given time to check that the flesh is still succulent.

Whole round fish, thick fillets, steaks and cutlets: cook for 4–5 minutes, then leave to stand for 5 minutes.

Flat fish, thin fillets: cook for 3–4 minutes, then rest for 3–4 minutes.

Fish with denser flesh (shark, tuna, monkfish, skate etc): cook for 6–7 minutes: allow to stand for 5 minutes.

Cook fillets in a single layer, thinner parts towards the centre, or tuck a thin tail end underneath a thicker portion.

Fish can also be microwaved whole, provided that they will fit in the oven. Slash the skin in several places to prevent it from splitting. Turn the fish over halfway through cooking.

Poaching

Cooking in a stock or court-bouillon brings out the flavour of fresh fish.

1 A whole fish can be poached in a fish kettle, provided it is not too large, while portions are best placed in a single layer in a shallow heatproof dish.

2 Cover with cold court-bouillon or stock, add a few herbs and flavourings.

3 Lay some buttered or greaseproof paper on top and heat until the liquid just starts to tremble. At this point, thin pieces of fish may be done. Continue to cook thicker pieces at a bare simmer either on top of the stove or in the oven, until the flesh is just opaque. For 1kg/ 2¼lb fish allow 7–8 minutes. To serve the fish cold, leave it to cool in the poaching liquid.

Butter sauce for poached fish

Poached fish needs very little enhancement other than a simple sauce that has been made from the poaching liquid.

1 Remove the cooked fish from the poaching liquid and keep it hot while you make the sauce.

2 Strain the liquid into a saucepan and place it over a medium heat. Simmer gently until the liquid has reduced by half.

3 Whisk in some cold diced butter or a little double cream to make a smooth, velvety sauce. Season to taste. Pour the sauce over the fish and serve.

Roasting

This is more usually associated with meat, but it is an excellent method of cooking whole fish and "meaty" cuts, such as monkfish tails or swordfish steaks. The oven should be preheated to very hot – 230°C/450°F/Gas 8 – with the roasting tin inside. The fish will then be seared by the heat of the tin and the juices will not escape.

Drizzle a little olive oil over the fish before roasting. For extra flavour, roast it on a bed of rosemary, fennel or Mediterranean vegetables.

Smoking

Although most of the smoked fish we buy has been commercially smoked, it is easy to smoke your own, adding a new dimension to bland tastes.

Hot smoking

This method cooks and smokes the food at the same time, using a special smoker filled with fragrant hardwood chips (hickory and oak are popular), which give the fish a delicious flavour. Domestic smokers are quite small and very easy to use. Some can be used indoors, but on the whole they are best suited to outdoor use, where the smoke can dissipate easily. For large quantities you can use a kettle barbecue. Heat the wood chips to 80–85°C/176–185°F, place the fish on the rack, put on the lid and smoke until the fish looks like pale burnished wood.

Cold smoking

This method cures but does not cook the fish. It must first be salted in dry salt or brine, then hung up to drip dry before smoking at 30–35°C/86–95°F.

Tea smoking

This Chinese method of smoking is usually used for duck, but imparts a wonderful flavour to oily fish such as mackerel and tuna, and seafood such as scallops, mussels and prawns.

1 Line a wok with foil and sprinkle in 30ml/2 tbsp each of raw long grain rice, sugar and aromatic tea leaves.

2 Place a wire rack on top of the wok and then arrange the fish in a single layer on the rack. Cover the wok with a lid or more foil and cook over a very high heat until you see smoke.

3 Lower the heat slightly (some smoke should still escape from the wok) and cook until the fish is done. A mackerel fillet takes 8–10 minutes, large prawns 5–7 minutes.

Steaming

Many people assume that steaming will result in bland, flavourless fish. Far from it; this method of cooking enhances the natural flavour and the fish remains moist and retains its shape, even if you overcook it.

Steaming is the healthiest way of cooking fish. It uses no fat and because the fish is not in contact with the cooking liquid, fewer valuable nutrients are lost.

1 Half-fill the base pan of a steamer with water and bring it to the boil. Place the fish in a single layer in the steamer basket, leaving room to enable the steam to circulate freely.

2 Lower the fish into the steamer, making sure that the insert stands well clear of the boiling water.

3 Lay a sheet of greaseproof paper over the surface of the fish, then cover the pan tightly with a lid or foil and steam until the fish is just cooked through.

4 Fish cooks very quickly in a steamer, but take care that the level of the water does not fall too low. Check once or twice during cooking and keep a kettle of boiling water on hand to top it up.

Alternative steamers

There are plenty of purpose-made steamers on the market, which range from the hugely expensive stainless steel models to modest Chinese bamboo baskets. However, you can easily improvise with a saucepan, any perforated container (a colander or sieve, for example) and some foil. Make sure that the saucepan is large enough to hold several inches of water.

Whatever the type of steamer, remember that the golden rule of steaming is not to allow the boiling liquid to touch the steamer basket or the fish or shellfish.

A Chinese bamboo steamer, which can be used in a wok or on top of a large saucepan, is ideal for steaming fish. If you like, arrange the fish on a bed of aromatic flavourings, such as lemon or lime slices and sprigs of herbs. Alternatively, before adding the fish or shellfish, you can place finely shredded vegetables, seaweed or samphire in the base of the steamer to give extra flavour.

Buying, Preparing and Cooking Shellfish

The term "shellfish" is loosely applied to seafood other than fish. Strictly speaking, it means aquatic invertebrates with shells or shell-like carapaces. This includes the crustaceans – lobsters, crabs, prawns and similar creatures – as well as some molluscs, such as clams, mussels and oysters. For convenience, however, the category extends to other molluscs too, such as the cephalopods (octopus, squid and cuttlefish) and less well known sea creatures such as sea urchins.

When discussing shellfish, it is impossible to divorce preparation and cooking techniques, since one is bound up so closely with the other. Lobsters and crabs, for instance, are cooked live; mussels are opened and cooked in one simple process.

Crustaceans and molluscs need very little cooking to enhance their already superb flavour. Indeed, many molluscs can be eaten raw, provided they are extremely fresh and come from unpolluted waters. Crustaceans of all types must be cooked; unlike fish, the larger specimens can be boiled. Many of the methods used for cooking fish are suitable for shellfish, particularly poaching, frying, grilling and steaming.

CRUSTACEANS

Lobsters and crabs

Buying

Live lobsters or crabs should smell very fresh and still be lively and aggressive when picked up. The tails of lobsters should spring back sharply when they are opened out. Crabs should feel heavy for their size, but you should make sure this is not because there is water inside the shell. Shake them – any sloshing sounds are a bad sign. The shell should neither be soft nor should it contain any cracks or holes.

Lobsters in particular command a high price, which reflects the effort involved in catching them. It is a good idea to check that lobsters and crabs have both claws, as one may often be lost in a fight. If a claw is missing, make sure the price is reduced accordingly.

Preparing and cooking a live lobster

1 The most humane way to kill a live lobster is to render it unconscious by placing it in a freezerproof dish or tray and covering it with crushed ice. Alternatively, put the lobster in the freezer for 2 hours.

2 When the lobster is very cold and no longer moving, place it on a chopping board and drive the tip of a large, sharp heavy knife or a very strong skewer through the centre of the cross on its head. According to the experts, death is instantaneous.

3 If you can't face stabbing the lobster, put it in a large pan of cold, heavily salted water and bring slowly to the boil. The lobster will expire before the water boils.

4 Alternatively, you can add the comatose lobster to a large pan of boiling water. Plunge it in head first and immediately clamp on the lid. Bring the water back to the boil.

5 Lower the heat and simmer the lobster gently for about 15 minutes for the first 450g/1lb and then allow 10 minutes more for each subsequent 450g/1lb, up to a maximum of 40 minutes.

6 When cooked, the lobster will turn a deep brick red. Drain off the water and leave to cool, if not eating hot.

If cooking two or more lobsters in the same pan, wait until the water comes back to the boil before adding the second one. More than two lobsters should be cooked separately.

Always buy cooked lobsters or crabs from a reputable supplier who cooks them fresh every day. The colour should be vibrant and the crustaceans should feel heavy for their size. Cooked lobsters should have their tails tightly curled under their bodies; avoid specimens with floppy tails, which may have been dead when they were cooked.

Quantities

When calculating how much you should buy, allow about 450g/1lb per person.

Storing

For practical reasons you will wish to cook live lobsters or crabs on the day you buy them, unless you fancy having a little nipper inhabiting your bath.

If you cannot pop them straight into the pot, live crustaceans can be wrapped in wet newspaper or covered in a very damp dish towel and kept in the coldest part of the fridge. If you intend the crustaceans to be unconscious when you kill them, you may want to put them in the freezer for a couple of hours or submerge them in crushed ice.

Removing the meat from a boiled lobster

1 Lay the lobster on its back and twist off the large legs and claws.

2 Carefully crack open the claws with a wooden mallet or the back of a heavy knife and remove the meat, keeping the pieces as large as possible. Scoop out the meat from the legs with a lobster pick or the handle of a small teaspoon.

3 On a chopping board, stretch out the body of the lobster so that its tail is extended. Turn it on to its back and, holding it firmly with one hand, use a sharp, heavy knife to cut the lobster neatly in half along its entire length.

4 Discard the whitish sac and the feathery gills from the head and the grey-black intestinal thread that runs down the tail.

5 Carefully remove all the meat from each half of the tail – it should come out in one piece.

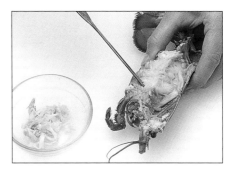

6 Keep the greenish tomalley (liver) and the coral (roe), which are delicious. This roe is only to be found in the female or "hen" lobsters. Like the tomalley, it is usually added to a sauce. The creamy flesh close to the shell can also be scraped out and used in a sauce.

Grilling lobster

Preheat the grill to high. Boil the lobster for 3 minutes only, then drain, split in half lengthways and clean.

Lay the halves cut side up in a grill pan, brush generously with melted butter and grill for about 10 minutes, spooning on more melted butter halfway through.

If the lobster has already been killed by stabbing, it can be split in half and grilled for about 12 minutes without being parboiled first.

Barbecuing lobster

Prepare the lobster as for grilling. Brush the cut sides with butter seasoned with garlic or cayenne pepper. Grill cut side down over moderately hot coals for about 5 minutes, then turn the halves over and grill them on the shell for 5 minutes more. Turn the lobster halves over once more, brush the flesh with more melted butter and grill flesh side down for 3–4 minutes more.

Preparing a live crab

To kill a crab humanely, chill it by submerging it in ice, or leave it in the freezer for a couple of hours until it is comatose (see Preparing and cooking a live lobster, page 24). When the crab is no longer moving, lay it on its back on a chopping board, lift up the tail flap and look for a small hole at the base of a distinct groove. Drive an awl or sturdy skewer into this hole, then carefully push the skewer between the mouth plates between the eyes. The crab is now ready for cooking.

Alternatively, if stabbing a crab does not appeal to you, the live crab can be killed and cooked simultaneously. There are two ways of doing this. Either plunge the crustacean into a large pan of boiling salted water, bring the water back to the boil and cook for 10–12 minutes; or place it in a pan of cold salted water and bring it slowly to the boil. The latter method is reckoned to be the more humane, because the crab becomes sleepy as the temperature rises and succumbs well before the water reaches boiling point. Either way, calculate the cooking time from the moment that the water boils, and do not boil the crab for more than 12 minutes, whatever its size.

Removing the meat from a cooked crab

1 Lay the cooked crab on its back on a large chopping board. Hold the crab firmly with one hand and break off the tail flap. Twist off both the claws and the legs.

2 Stand the crab on its head and insert a heavy knife between the body and shell. Twist the knife firmly to separate them so that you can lift the honeycomb body out.

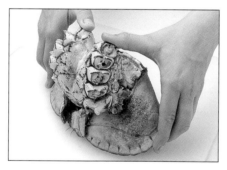

3 Alternatively, hold the crab firmly and use your thumbs to ease the body out of the shell.

4 Remove and discard the feathery, grey gills (these are unattractively but descriptively known as "dead men's fingers"), which are attached to either side of the body.

5 Press down on the top shell to detach the spongy stomach sac – this is found directly behind the mouth. Cut the honeycomb body into quarters with a large heavy knife.

6 Carefully pick out the white meat, using a skewer.

7 Use a teaspoon to scoop out all the creamy brown meat from the back shell, then scoop out the thin solid brown meat from inside the flaps.

8 Crack open the claws and legs with a mallet (or use the back of a heavy knife), then remove the claw meat in the largest possible pieces. Pick or scrape out the leg meat with a lobster pick or a skewer. The smallest legs can be kept whole and used to make a delicious shellfish stock.

Prawns, Shrimps, Langoustines and Crayfish

Buying

Prawns and shrimps are not sold alive, but crayfish must be, as their flesh deteriorates quickly after death and they can become poisonous. All fresh raw prawns and shrimps should have crisp, firm shells and a fresh smell. Do not buy them if they smell of ammonia. If you cannot obtain fresh prawns or shrimps, buy frozen. Transport them in a freezer bag and get them into your freezer as quickly as possible. Do not buy frozen prawns or shrimps that have been thawed – they may have been lying about for some time.

Quantities

If you buy them with the shells on, allow about 300g/11oz prawns or shrimps per serving. Some crustaceans – Dublin Bay prawns, for example – tend to be sold shelled, without the heads. If you buy Dublin Bay prawns in the shell, remember that there will be a lot of wastage (up to 80 per cent) so buy a generous amount. Keep the shells to flavour sauces, stocks and soups.

Storing

Fresh prawns and shrimps should be eaten as soon as possible after purchase. Crayfish are the exception. These freshwater crustaceans – including the Australian yabby – are none too fussy about what they eat, so it is best to purge them after capture or purchase. Place them in a large bowl, cover with a very damp dish towel and leave in the coldest part of the fridge for 24 hours.

Poaching langoustines or prawns

Raw langoustines or prawns are best poached in sea water. Failing that, use a well-flavoured *nage* (fish stock) or heavily salted water. Bring the poaching liquid to the boil in a large deep saucepan, drop in the crustaceans and simmer for only a minute or two, depending on their size. Do not overcook the shellfish, or the delicate flesh will become tough.

Peeling and deveining raw prawns

Raw prawns and large shrimps are often peeled before cooking, Raw prawns must have their intestinal tracts removed before cooking, a process that is known as "deveining". It is not necessary to devein shrimps.

1 Pull off the head and legs from each prawn or shrimp, then carefully peel off the body shell with your fingers. Leave on the tail "fan" if you wish.

2 To remove the intestinal vein from prawns, make a shallow incision down the centre of the curved back of the prawn using a small sharp knife, cutting all the way from the tail to the head.

3 Carefully pick out the thin black vein that runs the length of the prawn with the tip of the knife and discard.

Grilling or barbecuing langoustines or large prawns

This method is also suitable for crayfish. The shellfish can be raw or cooked.

1 Preheat the grill or barbecue to hot. Butterfly the shellfish by laying them on their backs and splitting them in half lengthways, without cutting right through to the back shell.

2 Open the shellfish out like a book and brush the cut sides all over with a mixture of olive oil and lemon juice.

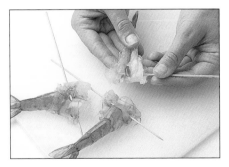

3 Lay the shellfish in a grill pan or on the barbecue rack. Grill for 2–3 minutes on each side; cooked shellfish for about half this time. To ensure they keep their shape, you could thread the butterflied langoustines or prawns on to skewers before grilling them.

Peeling cooked prawns, langoustines and crayfish

1 Twist off the heads and, in the case of langoustines, the claws.

2 Squeeze the shellfish along their length and pull off the shell and the legs with your fingers.

3 To keep the tail fan, carefully peel off the last piece of body shell, otherwise, squeeze the end of the tail and remove.

Fantail or phoenix prawns
This way of serving prawns comes from China. The cooked prawns, with their bright red tails, are supposed to resemble the legendary phoenix, which in China is a symbol of dignity and good luck. Large prawns are used.

1 Remove the heads from the prawns and peel away most of the body shell with your fingers. Leave a little of the shell to keep the tail "fan" intact.

2 Make a long shallow incision in the back of each prawn and remove the black intestinal cord with the point of the knife.

3 Hold the prepared prawns by the tails and dip them lightly in a little seasoned cornflour, and then in a frothy batter before deep frying them in hot oil until the tails, which are free from batter, turn red.

Potted Shrimps
These are very simple to make and will keep for several days. If possible, use fresh, not frozen, brown shrimps. They are a bore to peel, but worth the effort. Serve with buttered brown bread or toast and lemon wedges.

SERVES FOUR

INGREDIENTS
   350g/12oz butter
   225g/8oz cooked peeled shrimps, defrosted if frozen
   1 bay leaf
   1 large blade of mace or 2.5ml/ $^{1}/_{2}$ tsp ground mace
   ground black pepper and cayenne pepper

1 Melt 250g/9oz of the butter in a small pan. Add the shrimps, bay leaf, mace and seasoning. Heat gently until hot, then discard the bayleaf and mace. Divide the shrimps between four ramekins and leave to set.

2 Clarify the remaining butter, by placing it in a small saucepan and heating gently over a low heat until melted and foaming. Strain through a muslin-lined sieve into a small bowl, leaving the milky solids at the bottom of the pan.

3 Spoon the clarified butter over the potted shrimps, making sure they are completely covered. When cool, transfer the ramekins to the fridge and chill for up to 2–3 days until ready to serve.

MOLLUSCS

Bivalves (mussels, clams, oysters and scallops)

Buying

Like other types of shellfish, molluscs deteriorate rapidly, so you must make sure that they are alive when you cook them. Scallops are an exception, as they are often sold already opened and cleaned. Bivalves such as mussels, clams and oysters should contain plenty of sea water and feel heavy for their size. Do not buy any that have broken shells. If the shells gape, give them a sharp tap on a hard surface. They should snap shut immediately; if they don't, do not buy them as they will either be dead or moribund.

Quantities

When buying mussels, clams or similar shellfish, allow about 450g/1lb per person, as the shells make up much of the weight. Four or five scallops will serve one person as a main course.

Storing

Mussels, clams and other bivalves must be eaten within one day of purchase, but will hold briefly when kept in the fridge. Tip them into a large bowl, cover with a damp cloth and keep them in the coldest part of the fridge (at 2°C/36°F) until ready to use. Some people advocate sprinkling them with porridge oats and leaving them overnight to fatten up. Oysters can be kept for a couple of days, thanks to the sea water contained in their shells. Store them cupped side down. Never store shellfish in fresh water, or they will die. Ready-frozen bivalves should not be kept in the freezer for more than 2 months.

Preparing

Scrub bivalves under cold running water, using a stiff brush to remove any sand or dirt. Open the shellfish over a bowl to catch the delicious juice. This will be gritty, so must be strained before being used in a sauce or stock. Cockles usually contain a lot of sand. They will expel this if left overnight in a bucket of clean sea water or salted water.

Cleaning mussels

1 Wash the mussels in plenty of cold water, scrubbing them well. Scrape off any barnacles with a knife.

2 Give any open mussels a sharp tap; discard any that fail to close.

3 Pull out and discard the fibrous "beard" that sprouts between the two halves of the shell.

Moules Marinière

1 Chop 1 onion and 2 shallots. Put in a large saucepan with 25g/1oz/ 2 tbsp butter and cook over low heat until translucent.

2 Add 300ml/½ pint/1¼ cups white wine, a bay leaf and a sprig of fresh thyme. Bring to the boil. Add 2kg/4½lb cleaned mussels, cover the pan tightly and steam over a high heat for 2 minutes. Shake the pan vigorously and steam for 2 minutes more. Shake again and steam until all the mussels have opened. Discard any closed ones.

3 Stir in 30ml/2 tbsp chopped parsley and serve at once.

Steaming mussels

This method opens and cooks the shellfish all at once. It is also suitable for clams, cockles and razor-shells.

1 Put a few splashes of white wine into a wide saucepan. Add some finely chopped onion and chopped fresh herbs if you like and bring to the boil.

2 Add the mussels, cover the pan and shake over a high heat for 2–3 minutes. Remove the mussels that have opened.

3 Replace the lid and shake the pan over a high heat for another minute or so. By this time all the mussels that are going to open should have done so; discard any that remain closed.

4 Strain the cooking liquid through a muslin-lined sieve.

5 The cooking liquid can be reheated and used as a thin sauce, or heated until it has reduced by about half. For a richer sauce, stir in a little cream.

6 The mussels can be eaten as they are, or the top shell can be removed and the mussel served on the half shell. Alternatively, they can be grilled, but take care not to overcook them.

Grilling mussels and clams

Steam open the molluscs and remove the top shell. Arrange in their half shells in a single layer on a baking tray. Spoon over a little melted butter that has been flavoured with chopped garlic and parsley. Top with fresh breadcrumbs, sprinkle with a little more melted butter and cook under a hot grill until golden brown and bubbling.

Opening clams and razor-shells

The easiest way to open clams or razor-shells is by steaming them, in the same way as you do for mussels. However, this method is not suitable if the clams are going to be eaten raw like oysters.

1 Protect your hand with a clean dish towel, then cup the clam in your palm, holding it firmly. Work over a bowl to catch the juices.

2 Insert a sharp pointed knife between the shells. Run the knife away from you to open the clam, twisting it to force the shells apart.

3 Cut through the hinge muscle, then use a spoon to scoop out the muscle on the bottom shell. This part of the mollusc should be discarded.

Opening small clams in the microwave

1 Thin-shelled molluscs like small clams can be opened in the microwave. Place them in a large bowl and cook on full power for about 2 minutes.

2 Remove the open molluscs and repeat the process until all have opened. Do not try to open large clams, oysters or scallops this way, as the thick shells will absorb the microwaves and cook the molluscs before they open.

Opening scallops in the oven

The easiest way to open scallops is to place them rounded side down on a baking sheet and place them in an oven preheated to 160°C/325°F/Gas 3 for a few moments until they gape sufficiently for you to complete the job by hand.

1 Spread the scallops in a single layer on a baking sheet. Heat them until they gape, then remove them from the oven.

2 Grasp a scallop in a clean dish towel, flat side up. Using a long, flexible knife, run the blade along the inner surface of the flat shell to cut through the muscle that holds the shells together. This done, ease the shells apart completely.

3 Lift off the top shell. Pull out and discard the black intestinal sac and the yellowish frilly membrane.

4 Cut the white scallop and orange coral from the bottom shell and wash briefly under cold running water. Remove and discard the white ligament attached to the scallop flesh.

Cooking scallops

Scallop flesh is very delicate and needs barely any cooking; an overcooked scallop loses its flavour and becomes extremely rubbery. Small scallops need to be cooked only for a few seconds; larger ones take a minute or two.

Scallops can be pan-fried, steamed, poached and baked au gratin. They are also delicious grilled.

Wrap scallops in thin strips of streaky bacon or pancetta before grilling them to protect the delicate texture and add extra flavour.

Opening oysters

You really do need a special oyster knife if you are to open – or shuck – oysters successfully. If you haven't got one, use a strong knife with a short, blunt blade.

1 Scrub the shells under cold running water. Wrap one hand in a clean dish towel and hold the oyster with the cupped shell down and the narrow hinged end towards you.

2 Push the point of the knife into the small gap in the hinge and twist it to and fro between the shells until the hinge breaks. Lever open the top shell.

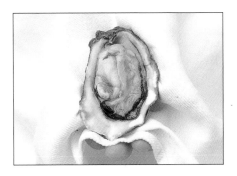

3 Slide the knife along the inner edges of the top shell and sever the muscle that joins the oyster to the shell. Lift off the top shell, leaving the oyster in its juices in the bottom shell.

Cooking oysters

Oysters are best eaten raw with just a squeeze of lemon or a dash of Tabasco sauce. If you prefer to cook them, do so very briefly. They can be poached or steamed for a minute or two and served with a white wine sauce; grilled like mussels or clams; deep-fried in cornmeal batter; or added to meat, fish or shellfish pies or casseroles.

Gastropods (winkles, whelks and abalone)

Small gastropods such as winkles, whelks and limpets need little preparation other than a quick rinse under cold running water. They are removed from the shell after cooking, either with a small fork or, in the case of winkles, with a dressmaker's pin. Larger gastropods, such as abalone (or their cousins, the ormers) and conch, must be removed from the shell and beaten vigorously to tenderize them before cooking. In some fishmarkets, especially those in California, tenderized abalone is sold in slices.

Cooking abalone or ormers

There are two schools of thought when it comes to cooking abalone. One claims the best way is to marinate the flesh, then cook it briefly in butter; the other claims that if abalone is to be truly tender, it needs long, slow cooking. Both methods work equally well, but only if the abalone has been thoroughly beaten first.

Boiling winkles or whelks

Ideally, these tasty shellfish should be boiled in sea water, so if you gather them yourself, take home a bucket of water in which to cook them. Otherwise, use heavily salted water. Bring this to the boil in a pan, add the winkles or whelks and simmer for about 5 minutes for winkles; 10 minutes for whelks.

To test whether winkles or whelks are ready, use a fork or dressmaker's pin to remove the body from the shell. It should come out easily. If not, cook for a little longer, but do not overcook, or the winkles will become brittle and the whelks tough.

Cephalopods (octopus, squid, cuttlefish)

Buying

You may have seen Mediterranean fishermen flailing freshly caught octopus against the rocks to tenderize them. It is said that they need to be beaten at least a hundred times before they become palatable. Fortunately for the consumer large octopus are usually sold already prepared, so we are spared this unpleasant task. Small octopuses can be dealt with in much the same way as squid, but even they have tough flesh which needs to be beaten with a wooden mallet before being cooked.

Most fishmongers and supermarkets now sell ready-cleaned squid, but cuttlefish are more usually sold whole. Both are easy to clean, and are prepared in similar ways. When buying fresh squid, look for specimens that smell fresh and salty, have good colour and are slippery. Avoid squid with broken outer skins, or from which the ink has leaked.

Quantities

The amount of octopus or squid that will be required will depend on how substantial a sauce you are going to serve. As a general guide, 1kg/2¼lb octopus, squid or cuttlefish will be more than ample for six people.

Storing

As for fish.

Cleaning and preparing octopus

1 Cut the tentacles off the octopus and remove the beak and eyes. Cut off the head where it joins the body and discard it. Turn the body inside out and discard the entrails.

2 Pound the body and tentacles with a mallet until tender, then place in boiling water and simmer very gently for at least 1 hour or until tender. Serve with a flavoursome sauce.

Baby Octopus and Red Wine Stew

Baby octopuses are tender and delicious, particularly cooked in a stew with the robust flavours of red wine and oregano. Unlike large octopuses, they need no tenderizing before cooking.

SERVES FOUR

INGREDIENTS
  900g/2lb baby octopuses
  450g/1lb onions, sliced
  2 bay leaves
  60ml/4 tbsp olive oil
  4 garlic cloves, crushed
  450g/1lb tomatoes, peeled
    and sliced
  15ml/1 tbsp each chopped fresh
    oregano and parsley
  salt and ground black pepper

Put the octopuses in a saucepan of simmering water with a quarter of the sliced onion and the bay leaves. Cook gently for 1 hour. Drain the octopuses and cut into bite-size pieces. Discard the heads. Heat the olive oil in a saucepan, add the remaining onions and the garlic cloves and fry for 3 minutes. Add the tomatoes and herbs, season with salt and pepper and cook, stirring, for about 5 minutes until pulpy, then cover the pan with a lid and cook very gently for 1½ hours.

Cleaning and preparing squid

1 Rinse the squid thoroughly under cold running water. Holding the body firmly in one hand, grasp the tentacles at the base with the other, and gently but firmly pull the head away from the body. As you do this the soft yellowish entrails will come away.

2 Use a sharp knife to cut off the tentacles from the head of the squid. Reserve the tentacles but discard the hard beak in the middle.

Squid ink
This can be used as a wonderful flavouring and colouring for home-made pasta and risotto, or to make a sauce. Having removed the ink sac, put it in a small bowl. Pierce it with the tip of a knife to release the thick, granular ink. Dilute this with a little water and stir until smooth. Use the ink right away, or freeze for later use.

There is ink in an octopus too. It is found in the liver and is very strongly flavoured. Like squid ink, it should be diluted in water before being used.

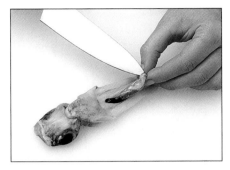

3 Remove and reserve the ink sac, then discard the head.

4 Peel the purplish-grey membrane away from the body.

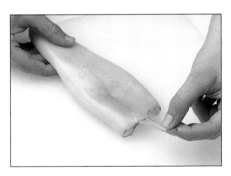

5 Pull out the "quill". Wash the body under cold running water.

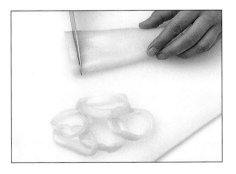

6 Cut the body, flaps and tentacles to the required size.

Cooking squid

Squid is often cut into rings and deep-fried. It can also be stewed, stuffed and baked, or sliced and stir-fried.

1 For stir-frying, slit the body from top to bottom and turn it inside out. Flatten it and score the inside lightly with a knife to make a criss-cross pattern.

2 Cut each piece lengthways into ribbons. These will curl when stir-fried.

Cleaning and preparing cuttlefish

Cut off the tentacles and remove the beak from the cuttlefish. Along the length of the body you will see the dark line of the cuttle bone. Cut along this line and remove the cuttle bone. Prepare in the same way as squid. The body is usually left whole.

Sea urchins
There are several edible varieties of sea urchin. They are particularly popular in France, where they are served raw, or lightly cooked in salted water and eaten like boiled eggs. The tops are sliced off and fingers of bread are then dipped into the coral flesh.

A CATALOGUE OF FISH AND SHELLFISH

The almost infinite variety of edible sea and freshwater fish has always been an inspiration to cooks, who love them for their fresh flavour, versatility and nutritious qualities. There is a host of delicious shellfish, each with its own unique flavour and all evoking the unmistakable tang of the sea. Once, we were limited to eating only fish and shellfish from local waters, but now, thanks to modern transportation methods, a whole new world of exciting species is available to cooks. This chapter is designed to help you to identify the fish and shellfish you may find on the fishmonger's slab and to give you an indication of how it can be cooked.

SEAFISH

There are two main categories of seafish: round and flat. Those that live on or near the sea bed are known as demersal fish. Flat fish are demersal fish, spending most of their time sitting on the sea bed and doing very little swimming. Consequently they have delicate white flesh with little muscle tone. The nutritious oil of "white" fish is concentrated in the liver.

In "oily" fish, this oil is dispersed throughout the flesh. Oily fish tend to swim in shoals near the surface of the sea; they are known as pelagic fish.

ROUND WHITE FISH

THE SEA BASS AND GROUPER FAMILY

This large and important family of fish is known as *perciformes* because they all share some of the characteristics of perch. They have at least some spiny fins, a V-shaped tail and pectoral fins set high on the body. The pelvic fins have one spiny ray each.

Various species of perciformes are found in the Indian and Pacific oceans and the Caribbean, and also in Mediterranean and Atlantic waters.

Right: Sea bass

Sea bass *(Dicentrarchus labrax)*

One of the finest of all fish, sea bass are as good to look at as they are to eat. They have an elegant, sleek shape rather like a salmon, and a beautiful silvery body with a darker back and a white belly. They can grow to a length of 90cm/36in and weigh up to 7kg/15½lb, although the average weight is 1–3kg/2¼–6½lb.

Habitat Sea bass are voracious predators that live in small shoals close to rocky coasts in Great Britain and the Mediterranean. They can also be found in salt water lakes and large river estuaries. They can be caught in traps or trawled, but the best are line-caught. Because sea bass are in such demand, wild fish have become prohibitively expensive. They can, however, be farmed successfully, and there are sea bass farms all over the Mediterranean.

Other names The French for sea bass is *bar*; due to their ferocity, they are also known as *loup de mer* (sea wolf). In Italian, they are *spigola* or *branzino*; their Spanish name is *lubina*.

Buying Sea bass are available all year round, as whole fish or as fillets. They are best in spring and early summer, before they spawn. Line-caught, wild sea bass have the finest texture and flavour, but farmed fish are an acceptable and much cheaper alternative. Look for bright, silvery skin and clear eyes. Allow about 200g/7oz per serving.

Cooking Sea bass have very few small bones and fine, firm flesh that holds its shape well during cooking. They are versatile fish with a delicate flavour and can be cooked by almost any method – grilled, baked, braised, poached, shallow or stir-fried or steamed over seaweed or samphire. A whole poached sea bass, skinned and served cold with mayonnaise, makes a marvellous party dish. Plainly cooked sea bass can be served with any number of sauces, from *beurre blanc* to fresh tomato coulis and Oriental sesame dressing. A classic French dish is *bar au fenouil*; grilled sea bass served on a bed of fennel twigs flamed with Pernod.

Scaling sea bass

The skin of sea bass is excellent to eat and it becomes deliciously crisp when grilled or pan-fried. It does, however, have very hard scales, so it is essential to scale sea bass before cooking. Ask your fishmonger to do this, or follow the instructions in the section on Buying and Preparing Fish.

Sea bass are highly prized in China, where they are braised with ginger and spring onions, while the Japanese slice the flesh wafer-thin and use it raw for *sashimi*.

Alternatives Few fish can equal sea bass for flavour, but good substitutes in most recipes are grey mullet, sea bream, grouper and John Dory.

Other varieties

Dicentrus punctatus (speckled bass) takes its Latin name from the small black spots on its back and sides. It is found mainly in the southern Mediterranean and is very similar to sea bass. Two other varieties come from North America and southern seas; striped bass and black bass. Both are excellent fish, but neither tastes quite so fine as sea bass.

Stone bass/Wreckfish *(Polyprion americanum)*

This ugly cousin of the sea bass lives in deep Atlantic waters, often amid wrecked ships at the bottom of the sea, which is how it came by its alternative name. This makes it difficult to catch; it can only be line-fished at a depth of more than 150m/500ft, so it is seldom found in shops and markets. Its Italian name is *cernia di fondale* (bass from the deep). It has dark skin and large, bony fins and the end of its tail is straight, not V-shaped like the tails of other types of bass.

Cooking If you do find stone bass for sale, it is likely to be as fillets or steaks, which can be cooked in the same way as any other white fish.

Comber *(Serranus)*

These smaller members of the grouper family have reddish or brownish skin with wide vertical markings. *Serranus scriba* is so called because its markings are said to resemble scribbles.

Cooking Comber have delicious firm white flesh. The whole fish can be poached, steamed, braised or baked. Fillets and steaks can be grilled, pan-fried or steamed.

THE SEA BREAM FAMILY

There are approximately two hundred species of sea bream, some of which, unusually for seafish, are vegetarian. They have tall, compact bodies and slightly snub noses.

Habitat Sea bream are found in all warm and temperate coastal waters, including the Atlantic, up to the Bay of Biscay.

Above: Sea bass fillets

Gilt-head bream *(Sparus aurata)*

This beautiful fish is considered the finest of all sea bream. It has silver scales, a gold spot on each cheek and a golden crescent in the middle of its head from which it takes its name. Its dense, juicy white flesh has been highly prized for thousands of years; the ancient Greeks and Romans considered it a fish fit for feasting and it was sacred to Aphrodite, the goddess of love. One wonders what she would have made of the fact that gilt-head breams are hermaphrodite, starting as male and becoming female as they mature.

Other names Gilt-heads are also known as royal bream. Sometimes in English they are called *daurade* (also spelt *dorade*), as in French. The Italian name is *orata*, the Spanish is *dorada*.

Buying Gilt-heads grow to a length of 60cm/24in and can weigh up to 3kg/6½lb. They are sold whole or as fillets. There is a high percentage of wastage, which makes this quite an expensive fish. Nowadays, gilt-heads are farmed successfully in the Mediterranean, which makes them a little less costly. Fresh gilt-head bream should have bright, shiny scales.

Cooking All bream have numerous wide scales that must be removed before cooking, or the diner will experience a most unpleasant mouthful. Whole gilt-head bream can be treated like sea bass or sole – baked, grilled, poached,

steamed in seaweed or braised. The flesh should be scored in several places on both sides before the fish is grilled or baked whole, to ensure even cooking. The dense flesh is robust enough to withstand spicy or aromatic flavours. A classic French dish is *daurade rôtie*, where the fish is covered with alternate strips of pork fat or streaky bacon and anchovy fillets, then wrapped in greaseproof paper and baked.

Gilt-head fillets can be pan-fried, grilled or baked. Very fresh fish can be used raw to make *sashimi*.

Red bream *(Pagellus bogaraveo)*

This tall rosy-red fish has a pronounced black spot above the pectoral fin on each shoulder. It grows to about 50cm/20in and is usually sold already filleted. Red bream lives deep in the sea and feeds on crustaceans and molluscs, which make it particularly tasty. It is found in northern European waters, but swims southwards in winter to spawn, and is a much sought after fish in Spain and Portugal.

Other names Young red bream have small blue spots on their backs and are sometimes known as blue-spotted bream. In French, red bream is rather rudely called *dorade commune* (common bream); the Italians call it *pagro*, *pagello* or *occhialone*, meaning "big eye". The Spaniards call it *besugo*.

Cooking Extremely fresh red bream can be eaten raw as *sashimi*. Whole fish and fillets should be cooked in the same way as snapper, bass or red mullet.

Black bream *(Spondyliosoma cantharus)*

This large bream is sometimes found in the North Sea. It is actually dark grey, with beautiful golden stripes running from head to tail. Unlike the gilt-head, it is unisexual and monogamous. Like gilt-head bream, it can be baked, grilled, poached, steamed in seaweed, or braised. The flavour and texture are similar but not as fine.

Ray's bream *(Brama brama)*

These large shoaling fish live in depths of 100m/328ft and below, but come up to the surface in summer, sometimes with tragic consequences, as the eponymous John Ray found when he discovered huge quantities of the fish stranded on the coast of Britain in the 17th century. Ray's bream are brownish-grey, with firm flesh and a good flavour. They should be cooked in the same way as other bream.

Dentex *(Dentex dentex)*

These relatives of the sea bream are particularly popular in Mediterranean countries, in whose waters they are found. They are also found to a lesser extent in the East Atlantic. Their colour varies with their age; young dentex are grey, changing first to reddish pink, then to a beautiful steel blue with a sprinkling of dark spots.

Above, from front: gilt-head bream, red bream and black bream

Other names *Denté* in French, *dentice* in Italian and *dentón* in Spanish.
Cooking Although dentex can grow up to 1m/39in in length, they are best eaten when about 30cm/12in long. Fish this size can be grilled whole or baked with herbs. Larger specimens should be cut into steaks and grilled or fried.

Porgy *(Pagrus pagrus)*

The eponymous hero of Porgy and Bess took his name from these rosy-tinted North American relatives of the bass, variations of which are also found in the Atlantic coastal waters around Africa. Porgies grow to a length of up to 75cm/30in and can be cooked whole or as steaks – baked, grilled, poached, steamed, or braised, using any of the recipes for bream.

Unusual species of bream
Among the many varieties of bream, there are a number whose names describe their appearance. The **two-banded bream**, a fish which makes very good eating, has two distinct vertical black bands fore and aft.
Annular bream, which is the smallest of its group, has a dark ring round its tail, as does **saddled bream**, while **sheepshead bream** has an upturned snout.
The small varieties, such as annular bream and saddled bream, are used for making soup.
A classic Tuscan dish, *sarago e parago*, uses two different kinds of small bream, boned and stuffed with raw ham and rosemary, then grilled over a wood fire.

THE COD FAMILY

This large family of fish includes haddock, hake, ling, whiting and many other related species of white-fleshed fish. Most of them come from the Atlantic and other cold northerly waters, although hake is found in the warmer Mediterranean and is very popular with the Spaniards and Portuguese.

Cod *(Gadus morruha)*

Long, torpedo-shaped fish with vibrant yellowish-brown mottled skin and a whitish belly, cod have a large head with a snub nose, a protruding upper jaw and a whiskery barbel on the chin which acts as a sensor as they search for food on the sea bed. They can live to over twenty years and grow to a length of 6m/20ft (weighing up to 50kg/110lb), although such specimens are sadly rare and most commercially fished cod weigh between 3 and 8kg/6½ and 17½lb.

Habitat Cod prefer to live in cold water with a high salt content. They hatch in huge numbers (a single female can lay up to five million eggs) close to the surface of the water, but gravitate down to the sea bed where they feed on crustaceans, molluscs and worms. Large cod also feed on smaller fish. Cod can be caught in trawler nets or line-caught. Trawled fish are often damaged in the nets.

For years, cod was so plentiful that it was regarded as an inferior fish, fit only to be fried with chips or masked with an unpleasant floury white sauce. All too often, its succulent, flaky white flesh was overcooked, making it watery or dry. Today, overfishing has depleted stocks so much that now it has become relatively scarce and therefore more highly appreciated. As the great French chef Auguste Escoffier predicted in the 19th century: "If cod were less common, it would be held in as high esteem as salmon;" (at that time, regarded as the king of fish) "for, when it is really fresh and of good quality, the delicacy and delicious flavour of its flesh admit of its ranking among the finest of fish".

Other names In France, fresh cod is called *cabillaud*. In Italy, it is *merluzzo* and in Spain, *bacalao* (which can also mean salt cod).

Buying Cod is most commonly trawled or netted, but it can also be line-caught. The first two methods can damage the delicate flesh, so try to buy the superior line-caught fish if possible.

When buying a whole small cod or codling, the skin should be shiny and clear. There is a lot of wastage in whole cod, which makes these fish very expensive, so they are more usually sold as steaks and fillets. Shoulder steaks have the finest flavour. Try to buy thick cuts from the shoulder or middle of the fish and always check that the flesh is very white. Never buy cod with discoloured patches on the flesh. The fresher the fish, the firmer and flakier the flesh will be.

Cooking Cod holds its texture well and can be cooked in many different ways, but it is vitally important not to overcook it. The flavour is robust enough to take quite strong and spicy flavours. Whole fish can be poached in a court-bouillon and served cold with mayonnaise, green sauce or tartare sauce. Cod can also be baked or roasted in the oven or braised in white wine.

Above: Cod fillet and steaks

Most cooking methods are suitable for cod fillets and steaks, except for grilling, which can destroy the flaky texture. They can be poached, steamed, braised in tomato sauce or topped with a crust of breadcrumbs and herbs and baked. They are also delicious floured and sautéed, or coated with batter and deep-fried. Cod makes an excellent substitute for more exotic fish in curries. A classic English dish is poached cod with parsley sauce. Fresh and smoked cod fillets can be used to make fish cakes, croquettes, fish pies, salads and mousses.

Cod can be salted or dried (see Dried and Salted Fish). The roe is often smoked and used to make *taramasalata*. Frozen cod is usually frozen at sea to retain freshness and flavour, but is never as good as fresh fish. It is available as steaks, fillets, breaded cuts and fish fingers. The liver produces cod liver oil, which tastes disgusting but is good for you.

Alternatives Any firm-fleshed white fish can be substituted for cod, including flat fish such as brill, halibut and turbot.

Above: Cod

Above: Haddock

Coley *(Pollachius virens)*

Traditionally regarded as cod's poor relation, fit only for feeding to the cat, coley has unappealing greyish flesh, which is responsible for its low price. Long and slim, the fish has a protruding lower jaw and no barbel. The skin on the back is dark grey, lightening to mottled yellow on the sides and almost white on the belly. Coley generally weigh 5–10kg/11–22lb, but smaller fish do appear on the fishmonger's slab.

Habitat Coley live in huge shoals in both deep waters and near the surface. They prefer cold, very salty water. They are voracious predators who prey on herring and have cannabalistic tendencies.

Other names Coley are also known as saithe, coalfish and pollock (not to be confused with pollack). In French, they are *lieu noir*, in Italian *merluzzo nero* and in Spanish *abadejo*.

Buying Coley are sometimes sold whole, weighing 1–4kg/2¼–8¾lb, but are more usually sold as steaks, cutlets and fillets. The unattractive grey flesh looks off-putting, but whitens during cooking. It should feel firm to the touch. Coley must be extremely fresh, or the flesh will become woolly and unpleasant.

Cooking Coley is less fine than cod in texture and flavour. Rubbing the greyish flesh with lemon juice helps to whiten it, but the colour can also be masked by coating the fish in batter or using it in a fish pie, casserole or fish cakes. It will withstand robust flavours and can be baked, braised, grilled or fried. Smoked coley has an excellent flavour, but is seldom available commercially. It is worth trying if you have a home smoker.

Alternatives Haddock, cod or any firm-fleshed white fish can be used instead of coley.

Haddock *(Melanogrammus aeglefinus)*

These are generally smaller than cod, growing up to 1m/39in long and weighing 1–2kg/2¼–4½lb. They have dark brownish-grey skin with a black lateral line and a black spot above the pectoral fin (purportedly the thumb print of St. Peter). Their eyes are large and prominent. They live close to the sea bed and prefer water with a high salt content.

Haddock is often considered to be interchangeable with cod, but its white flesh has a more delicate flavour and a softer, less flaky texture.

Habitat Haddock are shoaling fish which live at the bottom of cold northern seas in Europe and North America. They feed on molluscs, worms and other small fish and spawn in the coldest, saltiest water they can find, off the coast of Norway and the Faroes, for example.

Other names In North America, haddock are known as scrod. In French, the fish is called *aiglefin* (from the Latin name). Confusingly, the French for smoked haddock is *haddock*. In Italian, haddock is *asinello*; in Spanish it is *eglefino*.

Buying Fresh haddock is at its best in winter and early spring, when the cold has firmed up the flesh. You may find whole small haddock (weighing 450g–2kg/1–4½ lb) at the fishmonger's, but the fish is usually sold as fillets. Before you buy, prod the flesh to make sure that it is firm.

Cooking Fresh haddock is a versatile fish, which can be cooked in the same way as cod. When cooking whole haddock, leave the skin on to hold the delicate flesh together.

Haddock is the perfect fish for deep-frying and it makes wonderful fish and chips. It also makes excellent fish lasagne and pie, especially when the fresh fish is mixed with an equal quantity of smoked haddock.

Below: Haddock fillets

Hake *(Merluccius merluccius)*

This most elegant member of the cod family is a long, slim fish with two spiny dorsal fins, bulging eyes and a protruding lower jaw without a barbel. The head and back are dark steely grey and the belly is silvery white. The inside of the mouth and gills is black. A mature fish can grow up to 1m/39in, but the average length is 30–50cm/12–20in.

Habitat Hake are found in most temperate and cold waters. By day, they live near the sea bed, but at night they move to the surface to hunt oily fish such as herrings, mackerel and sprats.

Other names The French have several names for hake: *merlu*, *colin* and *merluchon* (small immature fish). The Spanish call it *merluza*. In Italian, it is *nasello*. In North America, hake is often known as ling or whiting, although it is far superior to the European whiting.

Buying Due to overfishing, hake are becoming quite scarce and expensive. Hake can be trawled or caught on long lines. Try to buy line-caught fish, which has a better texture. Hake must be very fresh, or it becomes flabby. The flesh has a pinkish tinge; it will always feel soft to the touch, but should never feel limp. Whole fish should have bright eyes and smell of the sea.

When calculating how much hake to buy, allow for 40 per cent wastage for whole fish. Keep the head, as it makes particularly delicious soup or fish stock.

Hake is usually sold as cutlets or steaks. Those cut from near the head have the best flavour. The fish has few bones, and these are easy to remove. Avoid buying fillets, as they tend to disintegrate during cooking.

Cooking Whole hake can be poached, baked or braised in wine, lemon juice and fresh herbs or tomato sauce. Like all fish, it should never be overcooked. Steaks can be grilled, coated in egg and breadcrumbs and deep-fried, or sautéed in olive oil and garlic. They can also be layered with potatoes and onions, or with tomatoes and cheese

Above: Ling

and baked *au gratin*. Light buttery sauces go well with hake, as does caper sauce. Shellfish such as mussels and clams are perfect partners. A popular Spanish hors d'oeuvre is *escabeche* – marinated hake served cold.

Alternatives Haddock or cod can be substituted for hake in any recipe.

Other varieties North American silver hake is a small, streamlined fish with an excellent flavour. Varieties of hake are also found in the warmer waters of South America and southern Africa, but don't taste as good as northern hake.

Ling *(Molva molva)*

This fish has a long, slender greenish-brown body with a silver lateral stripe, no scales and a barbel on the lower jaw. It is the largest relative of the cod, growing to a length of 1.8m/6ft.

Habitat Common ling live in the Atlantic, often in proximity to rocks, where they feed on round and flat fish, small octopus and crustaceans. A smaller relative is found in the Mediterranean.

Other names Mediterranean ling are sometimes known as blue ling. They have larger eyes and a shorter barbel than common ling, and are esteemed for their superior flavour. Both varieties are known as *lingue* in French, *molva occhiona* in Italian and *maruca* in Spanish. Rock ling are available in Australia. In Scandinavian countries, ling is salted, dried and sold as *lutfisk* or *klipfisk* (see Dried and Salted Fish).

Buying As with all fish, the best ling are line-caught. You may find small whole ling on the fishmonger's slab, but the fish is more commonly sold as fillets or middle-cut cutlets. Ling is available most of the year, except in high summer.

Cooking Ling has firm flesh with a fairly good flavour and is sometimes substituted for monkfish. Whole fish can be baked or braised, or made into casseroles, soups and curries. Fillets and cutlets can be grilled or pan-fried, and served with a flavoursome sauce.

Alternatives Any member of the cod family can be substituted. For a more extravagant substitute, use monkfish or conger eel.

Pollack *(Pollachius pollachius)*

These attractive fish have steely grey backs and greenish-yellow bodies with a curved lateral line. They have a protruding lower jaw and no barbel. Pollack are smaller than cod, growing to a length of less than 1m/39in.

Habitat Pollack can live in shoals near the surface of the sea, where they feed on sprats and herrings, or close to the bottom where they eat deep-sea prawns and sand-eels.

Other names Its yellow colour gives pollack the name of *lieu jaune* in French, *merluzzo giallo* in Italian and *abadejo* in Spanish.

Buying Pollack are at their best in autumn and winter. They are usually sold as fillets, cutlets or steaks. If you need a whole fish, look for a superior line-caught specimen.

Above: Hake

Cooking Pollack has a drier texture and less pronounced flavour than cod, so it benefits from a creamy, highly flavoured sauce. It is good for fish pies and soups and can be baked, braised, deep-fried or sautéed. It is suitable for any recipe for cod, haddock, hake or ling.

Pouting *(Trisopterus luscus)*

This sulky-sounding fish is a poor (and cheap) relation of the whiting and is often caught in the same nets. It is comparatively small (about 25cm/10in long), with light brown papery skin.
Other names It is also known as pout. In French it is *tacaud*, in Italian *merluzzo francese* and in Spanish *faneca*.
Buying Pouting goes off extremely quickly and must be eaten very fresh. Your nose will soon tell you if the fish is past its best. If possible, buy a whole fish and ask the fishmonger to fillet it. Then cook it as soon as you can, as the fillets will rapidly deteriorate.
Cooking As for whiting.

Whiting *(Merlangus merlangus)*

Similar in appearance to haddock, whiting are small fish (generally about 30–40cm/12–16in long). They have greenish-grey skin, a silvery belly and a black spot at the base of the pectoral fin. The head is pointed, with a protruding upper jaw and no barbel.
Habitat Whiting are found all over the Atlantic, from Iceland to northern Spain. They feed on crustaceans and small

Above: Pouting

fish such as sand-eels and herrings and are often found near rocky shores.
Other names Its old name was *merling*. The French call it *merlan*, the Italians *merlano* and the Spanish *merlán*.
Buying The fact that it is abundant all year and has soft, rather unexciting flesh means that whiting is cheap and tends to be undervalued. However, really fresh whiting is well worth buying. Whole fish should be scintillatingly shiny. Fillets should be pearly white and feel soft but definitely not flabby. Stale

Below: Whiting

whiting may have a woolly texture and taste unpleasant, so make sure that you buy only absolutely fresh fish. Whiting are small, so allow two fillets per serving. You may find whiting boned through the back, leaving the two fillets attached.
Cooking The whiting's meltingly tender flesh makes it an ideal basis for a soup, as it contributes a velvety texture. It is also excellent for quenelles and fish mousses. Whiting is a versatile fish that can be coated in breadcrumbs or batter and fried. it can also be pan-fried, grilled or gently poached in wine or court-bouillon and served with a lemony sauce or flavoured butter. Whatever cooking method you use, make sure the whiting is well seasoned.
Alternatives Plaice or sole can be used, and all the members of the cod family.

Whiting en colère

A once immensely popular dish was *merlan en colère* ("angry whiting"). Whole fish were baked with the skin on, then curled around so that their tails could be stuck through their eye sockets or into their mouths. Presumably the name came from the assumption that the fish was chasing its own tail in anger. Mercifully, this method of serving whiting has fallen out of favour.

THE GURNARD FAMILY

Gurnard are curious, almost prehistoric-looking fish with cylindrical bodies, high, armour-plated heads with wide mouths, and strange pectoral fins with the three lowest rays divided into "fingers". They use these to explore the sea bed. Another curiosity is the grunting noise they emit, caused by vibrating the swim bladder – for what purpose, no one has yet discovered.

Below: Gurnard

Gurnard weigh between 100g/3¾oz and 2kg/4½lb. There are several types, which are distinguished by their colour; all have lean white flesh with a firm texture but rather insipid taste. They are rich in iodine, phosphorus and protein.
Habitat Gurnard are found in the Atlantic and Mediterranean. They live on or near the sea bed, using their "fingers" to seek out the crabs, prawns and small fish that live in the sediment.
Other names Also known as sea robin and gurnet. The French name, *grondin*, echoes the grunting sound they make. In Italian, they are *capone* (meaning large head); in Spanish, *rubios*.

Grey gurnard (Eutrigla gurnardus)

These fish have brownish-grey backs and silvery bellies. They grow to a maximum length of 45cm/18in. The lateral line is scaly and should be removed before cooking.

Red gurnard (Aspitrigla cuculus)

The most attractive member of the gurnard family, this pinkish-red fish has bony extensions to the lateral line, which give it the appearance of vertical

stripes on its back. It has the finest flavour of all the gurnards and is sometimes substituted for red mullet.

Tub gurnard (Trigla lucerna)

This larger gurnard is orangey-brown with bright orange pectoral fins. It is an excellent swimmer and sometimes leaps right out of the water, high above the surface, which explains its alternative name of flying gurnard.
Buying Gurnard are bony fish with an unexceptional flavour, so they tend to be cheap. They are usually sold whole – ask the fishmonger to remove the spiny fins and the skin. Beware, especially in France, of buying red gurnard masquerading as red mullet (*rouget*). The latter is vastly superior.
Cooking Small gurnard are best used in soups and stocks. Larger fish can be braised or baked on a bed of vegetables with a little white wine. Take care when eating whole gurnard, as they are very bony. Fillets can be coated in breadcrumbs and fried, or steamed and served with a Mediterranean sauce.
Alternatives Red or grey mullet can be used in any gurnard recipe, and will generally give a better result

Above: Tub gurnard

Scorpion fish (Scorpaena scrofa, Scorpaena porcus)

Like gurnard, scorpion fish have huge heads and armour-plated cheeks. Their enormous scaly heads have loose folds of skin above and between the eyes. The dorsal fin is made up of large poisonous spines. The smaller brown scorpion fish has a finer flavour than its larger cousin.
Habitat Scorpion fish are found throughout the Mediterranean and off the coast of North Africa. They also live in Atlantic waters, ranging from the English Channel to Senegal.
Other names The French for scorpion fish is *rascasse* (*chapon* in the south of France). Italians call it *scorfano*; in Spanish it is *cabracho* or *rascacio*.
Buying Scorpion fish are usually sold whole. You should allow for a huge amount of wastage; a 2kg/4½lb fish will only serve four people.
Cooking Scorpion fish is best known as an essential ingredient in bouillabaisse. Whole fish can be baked or braised with fennel; scorpion fillets can be cooked *à l'antillaise*, braised with tomatoes, potatoes and red peppers.
Alternatives Monkfish, snapper, John Dory or gurnard can be used at a pinch.

Above: Scorpion fish

THE MULLET FAMILY

Over a hundred species of mullet are found in temperate and tropical seas. These belong to two main groups, grey and red, which are unrelated and very different in appearance and flavour.

Grey mullet (family Mugilidae)

Varieties of grey mullet are found all over the world. These beautiful silvery fish resemble sea bass, but have larger scales and small mouths, suited to their diet of seaweed and plankton. They are shoaling fish that live in the vicinity of the muddy sea bed, so they sometimes smell and taste rather muddy. A good grey mullet has lean, slightly soft, creamy white flesh with quite a pleasant flavour.

Habitat Grey mullet are found in coastal waters and estuaries all over the world.

Varieties The finest is the golden mullet (*Liza aurata*), which has a thin upper lip and gold spots on its head and the front

Above: Silver-skinned grey mullet are found all over the world

of the body. It is one of the smallest mullets, growing only to about 45cm/18in. In French, it is known as *mulet doré*. Thick-lipped mullet (*Crenimugil* or *Chelon labrosus*) has, as its name suggests, thick lips and a rounded body. This mullet is sometimes farmed. The thin-lipped mullet (*Liza ramada*) has a golden sheen, a thin upper lip and a pointed snout, which gives it its French name of *mulet porc*. The largest mullet is the common or striped grey mullet (*Mugil cephalus*), which can grow up to 70cm/28in. This fish has a brown body, silvery back and a large head. Its eyes are covered by a transparent membrane. In French it is called

mulet cabot. There is also a small Mediterranean mullet whose main claim to fame is its ability to leap out of the water to escape predators. This is the leaping grey mullet (*Liza saliens*).

Buying Except in France, you are unlikely to find any differentiation between the varieties of grey mullet at the fishmonger. If possible, choose fish that come from the high seas rather than estuaries, as the latter often have a muddy taste and can be flabby. Grey mullet are usually sold whole – ask the fishmonger to scale and skin them for you. Keep the roes, which are delicious. Larger fish may be sold filleted.

Cooking Grey mullet must be scaled before being cooked. Any muddiness can be eliminated by soaking the fish in several changes of acidulated water. Whole fish are very good stuffed with fennel and grilled. Slash the sides and add a splash of aniseed-flavoured alcohol before cooking the fish, and serve with a buttery sauce. Mullet roe is a delicacy and can be eaten fresh, fried in butter or used in a stuffing for a baked fish. When salted and dried, mullet roe is the authentic basis of taramasalata and *bottarga* or *boutargue*.

Red mullet (*Mullus surmuletus and Mullus barbatus*)

These are among the finest of all seafish. They are small (up to 40cm/16in long), with pinkish-red skins streaked with gold. Their Roman-nosed heads have two long barbels on the chin. They have lean, firm flesh. The flavour is robust and distinctive.

Below: Red mullet are considered one of the finest seafish.

Other varieties *Mullus surmeletus* is more correctly known as *surmullet*; it has rosy red skin and is larger than *Mullus barbatus*, which has three yellowish stripes along each side and grows to a length of 30cm/12in.

Goatfish Types of red mullet known as goatfish because of their long, beard-like barbels are found in the warm Pacific and Indian Oceans. They are smaller (up to 20cm/8in) and less colourful than cold-water mullet, and they have drier, less tasty flesh.

Habitat Red mullet are found in Atlantic and Mediterranean waters. They live on sandy or rocky areas of the sea bed, feeding on small sea creatures.

Other names Red mullet are usually cooked complete with their livers and sometimes all their guts. These impart a gamey flavour, giving the fish the nickname "woodcock of the sea". In America, all red mullet are known as "goatfish", regardless of size or place of origin. The French for mullet is *rouget*; depending on the variety, it is *rouget barbet*, *rouget de roche* or *rouget de vase* (*Mullus barbatus*). In Italian, red mullet is *triglia*; in Spanish, *salmonete de roca* (*Mullus surmuletus*) or *salmonete de fango* (*Mullus barbatus*).

Buying Red mullet has delicate flesh that is highly perishable, so it essential to buy extremely fresh fish. They should have very bright skin and eyes and feel very firm. The scales should be firmly attached, not flaking off the skin. Because they are small, red mullet are usually sold whole, but large fish are sometimes filleted. The flesh is quite rich, so a 200g/7oz fish will be ample for one person. Ask the fishmonger to scale and gut it for you, and keep the liver, which is a great delicacy.

Cooking The best ways to cook red mullet are grilling and pan-frying. Score the sides before grilling a whole fish to ensure even cooking. Red mullet marry superbly with Mediterranean flavours such as olive oil, saffron, tomatoes, olives, anchovies and orange. They can be cooked *en papillote* with flavourings such as fennel or basil, or made into mousses and soufflés. Very small, bony red mullet are often used in bouillabaisse.

THE WRASSE FAMILY

This large family of fish is notable for its varied and dazzling colours. Wrasse range from steely blue to green, orange and golden; in some species, the sexes have different colours. All wrasse have thick lips and an array of sharp teeth. They are small fish, seldom growing larger than 40cm/16in in length.

Habitat Wrasse are found in both Atlantic and Mediterranean waters. They live near rocky coasts, feeding on barnacles and small crustaceans.

Varieties The most common is the ballan wrasse (*Labrus berggylta*), which has greenish or brownish skin, with large scales tipped with gold. Male and female cuckoo wrasse (*Labrus mixtus*) have strikingly different coloration; the males are steely blue with almost black stripes, while the females are orangey-pink with three black spots under the dorsal fin. The name of the five-spotted wrasse (*Symphonus quinquemaculatus*) is self-explanatory, while the brown spotted wrasse is completely covered with spots. Rainbow wrasse (*Coris julis*) have spiny dorsal fins and a red or orange band along their body.

Right: Common wrasse

Below: Brown spotted wrasse

Other names In French, wrasse is variously known as *vielle*, *coquette* and *labre*. In Italian, it is *labridi*; in Spanish *merlo*, *tordo* or *gallano*.

Buying Wrasse are available in spring and summer. Look for scintillating skin and bright eyes. Ask the fishmonger to scale and clean the fish. Allow at least 400g/14oz per serving.

Cooking Most wrasse are fit only for making soup, but some larger varieties, such as ballan wrasse can be baked whole. Make a bed of sliced onions, garlic, smoked bacon and potatoes, bake at 200°C/400°F/Gas 6 until soft, then add the wrasse, moisten with white wine and bake for 10–15 minutes.

OILY FISH

Fish such as herrings, mackerel and sardines have always been popular because they are cheap and nutritious, but now they are considered the ultimate "good for you" food. In recent years they have received an excellent press, due to their healthy properties. Not only do they contain protein and vitamins A, B and D, but the Omega-3 fatty acids in their flesh are known to reduce the risk of clogged arteries, blood clots, strokes and even cancer. People who eat fish regularly tend to live longer – the Japanese, among the world's greatest fish eaters, have one of the lowest death rates from heart disease.

Oily fish are pelagic fish, which swim near the surface of the sea and live in shoals that can be quite enormous. The largest family of oil-rich fish are the *clupeiformes*: herrings and their relatives – sardines, anchovies, sprats and pilchards. Other oily fish are smooth-skinned mackerel and tuna.

Below: Herring

THE HERRING FAMILY

Herring *(Clupea harengus)*

There are numerous different varieties of herring, each confined to its own sea area – the North Sea, Baltic, White Sea (an inlet of the Barents Sea), the coast of Norway and many colder coastal areas. Herring are prodigiously fertile fish, which is just as well, since they have been overfished for centuries and are becoming more scarce.

Herring are slender silver fish with a central dorsal fin and large scales. They seldom grow to a length of more than 35cm/14in. Their oily flesh can be cured in many ways, including smoking, salting, drying and marinating in vinegar and spices.

Habitat Herring live in huge shoals in cold northerly waters, where they feed on plankton. They are migratory fish which come inshore to spawn. They sometimes change their habitual route for no apparent reason, so that there may be a glut in a particular area for several years, but no herring at all the next year.

Boning a whole herring

Herring must be scaled before cooking; the scales virtually fall off by themselves, so this is easy to do. Whether or not you leave the head on is a matter of choice.

1 First scale the herring, then slit the belly with a sharp knife and remove the innards.

2 Lay the fish on a chopping board, belly-side down. With the heel of your hand, press down firmly all along the backbone.

3 Turn the herring over and lift off the backbone. You will find that most of the small side bones will come away with it.

Varieties Herring are mostly known by the name of the region where they are located – North Sea, Norwegian, Baltic, for instance. Each variety has its own spawning season, which influences the eating qualities of the fish.

Buying Like all oily fish, herring must be absolutely fresh, or they will taste rancid. They are at their best before they spawn. Look for large, firm fish with slippery skins and rounded bellies containing hard or soft roes; hard roes are the female eggs, soft roes the male milt. Soft herring roes are considered a particular delicacy. By running your hands along the belly of the fish, you will be able to tell whether the roes are hard or soft.

Once they have spawned, herrings lose condition and weight and their flesh becomes rather dry. If the fishmonger cleans them for you, be sure to keep the roe. As herrings contain numerous soft bones, you might ask him to bone or fillet them for you.

They can be gutted either through the belly or through the gills, leaving the roe inside.

Above: Herring fillets

Cooking The oiliness of the flesh makes herrings particularly suitable for grilling and barbecuing. Score whole fish in several places on both sides to ensure even cooking. Herring benefit from being served with an acidic sauce such as gooseberry or mustard to counteract the richness.

Whole herrings are excellent baked with a stuffing of breadcrumbs, chopped onions and apples. They are also good wrapped in bacon and grilled, or grilled with a mustard sauce. Both whole herrings and fillets are delicious rolled in oatmeal and then pan-fried in bacon fat. Serve them with a squeeze of lemon juice.

Herring fillets can be made into fish balls, or cooked in a sweet-and-sour sauce made with tomato ketchup, wine vinegar, honey and Worcestershire sauce. They are also delicious soused in a vinegary marinade flavoured with herbs and spices.

Fillets are also traditionally made into rollmops or smoked to make kippers – these processes are explored fully in the chapters on Pickled and Smoked Fish.

Alternatives Sardines, sprats and mackerel can be cooked in the same way as herrings.

Herring roes

Soft roes have a creamy, melting texture. They can be tossed in seasoned flour, gently fried in butter and served as they are, or devilled with cayenne pepper and Worcestershire sauce and served on hot toast. They also make a delicious omelette filling. Poached in stock and mashed, they can be used as a spread, in a stuffing for whole baked herrings or added to a sauce or savoury tart filling. Hard roes have a grainy texture, which people tend either to love or loathe. They can be baked or braised under the fish to add extra flavour.

Above: Soft herring roes

Anchovies *(Engraulis encrasicolus)*

These small slender fish seldom grow to more than 16cm/6¼in; the average length is only 8–10cm/3¼–4in. They have steely blue backs and shimmering silver sides, and the upper jaw protrudes markedly. Most anchovies are sold filleted and preserved in salt or oil, but if you are lucky enough to find fresh fish, you are in for a treat.

Habitat Anchovies are pelagic fish and are found in tightly packed shoals throughout the Mediterranean, in the Black Sea (where, sadly, pollution has depleted stocks) and the Atlantic and Pacific Oceans.

Other names In French, anchovy is *anchois*, in Italian *acciuga* or *alice*, in Spanish *boquerón*.

Buying Ideally, fresh anchovies should be cooked and eaten straight from the sea. The best anchovies come from the Mediterranean and are at their peak in early summer. By the time they have been exported, however, they will have lost much of their delicate flavour. When buying fresh anchovies, look for scintillating skins and bright, slightly bulging eyes.

Preparing You are unlikely to find a fishmonger willing to clean anchovies for you, but they are easy to prepare at

Above: Anchovies

home. To gut, cut off the head and press gently along the body with your thumb to squeeze out the innards. To fillet, run your thumbnail or a stubby blunt knife along the length of the spine from head to tail on both sides and lift off the fillets.

Freezing Since fresh anchovies are hard to come by, it is worth freezing them when there are plentiful supplies. Remove the heads and clean the fish, then pack them head-to-tail in a shallow freezer box, separating the layers with

sheets of clear film or polythene. Cover the box with a lid and freeze. Defrost before using.

Cooking Whole anchovies can be grilled or fried like sardines, or coated lightly in egg and flour and deep-fried. They make an excellent *gratin* when seasoned with olive oil and garlic, then topped with breadcrumbs and baked. Fillets can be fried with garlic and parsley, or marinated for 24 hours in a mixture of olive oil, onion, garlic, bay leaves and crushed peppercorns. Anchovy essence and anchovy paste are useful ingredients.

Sardines and Pilchards *(Sardinia pilchardus)*

It is a common misconception that sardines and pilchards are different fish; in fact, a pilchard is merely a larger, more mature sardine. Even the largest pilchards grow only to 20cm/8in, while sardines may be only 13–15cm/ 5–6in long. They are slim fish, with blue-green backs and silvery bellies. They have thirty scales along the mid-line on either side. Their flesh is compact and has a delicious, oily flavour. Canned sardines and pilchards are very popular as store-cupboard items because they are so convenient and easy to prepare.

Left: Sardines

Habitat Sardines take their name from Sardinia, where they were once abundant. They are pelagic shoaling fish, and are found throughout the Mediterranean and Atlantic. Various related species are also found in other parts of the world.

Other names Sardines are easy to recognize on foreign menus: they are *sardine* in French, *sardina* in Italian and Spanish, and *pilchard* or *sardine* in German. Confusingly, the French use the word *pilchard* when speaking of canned herring.

Buying Sardines are at their best in spring and early summer. They do not travel well, so try to buy fish from local waters and avoid any damaged or stale-looking specimens. Small sardines have the best flavour, but larger fish are better for stuffing. Depending on the size, allow 3–5 sardines per serving.

Cooking Sardines should be scaled and gutted before being cooked. This is easy to do; just cut the head almost through from the backbone and twist, pulling it towards you. The innards will come away with the head. Whole sardines are

Below: Pilchards

Above: Sprats

superb simply grilled plain or barbecued, which crisps the skin. They can be coated in breadcrumbs, fried and served with tomato sauce, made into fritters or stuffed with capers, salted anchovies or Parmesan and baked. They make an excellent sauce for pasta and are also delicious marinated and served raw.

Alternatives Large anchovies or sprats can be used instead of small sardines.

Sprats *(Sprattus sprattus)*

These small silvery fish look very similar to sardines or immature herrings, but are slightly squatter. Once the sprat was an important fish, but they are seldom sold fresh these days, being mostly smoked or cured, or sold as fishmeal.

Habitat They are abundant in the Baltic, North Sea and the Atlantic, and, since they can tolerate low salinity, are also found in fjords and estuaries. In addition to being sold fresh, sprats are available smoked or canned in oil.

Other names Sprats are *sprat* in French, *papalina* in Italian and *espadin* in Spanish. Smoked sprats are called *brisling* in Norway.

Cooking Sprats can be cooked in the same way as anchovies and small sardines. They have very oily flesh and are delicious when fried in oatmeal or deep-fried in batter.

Raw sprats can be marinated in vinaigrette; they are often served as part of a Scandanavian smorgasbørd.

Above: Whitebait

shake them in a plastic bag containing flour seasoned with salt and cayenne pepper. Deep-fry until very crisp.

"Blue" fish

Although they are not related to each other, several species of particularly oily fish are known collectively as "blue" fish. All have very smooth, taut skin with virtually undetectable scales and firm, meaty flesh. Varieties of blue fish are found in almost all temperate and tropical seas.

Mackerel *(Scomber scombrus)*

These streamlined fish are easily identified, thanks to their beautiful greenish-blue skin. They have wavy bands of black and green on their backs, while the bellies are silvery. The smooth, pale beigey-pink flesh is meaty, with a distinctive full flavour.
Habitat Mackerel are pelagic shoaling fish, often found in huge numbers in the North Atlantic, North Sea and Mediterranean. They spend the winter near the bottom of the cold North Sea, not feeding at all.

Below: Mackerel

Whitebait

This name is given to tiny silver fish – only about 5cm/2in in length – that are caught in summer as they swim up estuaries. The name can refer to immature sprats or herrings, or to a mixture of both fish.
Other names Whitebait are *blanchaille* in French; this name is also used to describe tiny freshwater fish. The Italian name for them is *bianchetti*; the Spanish *aladroch*.
Buying Whitebait do not need to be cleaned. They are available fresh in spring and summer, and frozen all year round. Allow about 115g/4oz per person when serving them as a starter.
Cooking Whitebait are cooked whole, complete with heads. They are delicious deep-fried and served with brown bread and butter. Prepare them for cooking by dunking them in a bowl of milk, then

Below: Jack mackerel, which are not true mackerel, are common in New Zealand

Other names Larger mackerel are known as *maquereau* in French; small specimens are called *lisette*. In Italian, mackerel is called *sgombro* and in Spanish it is known as *caballa*.

Buying Mackerel are delicious when extremely fresh, but not worth eating when they are past their best. They are in their prime in late spring and early summer, just before spawning. Look for firm fish with iridescent skin and clear, bright eyes. Small mackerel are better than large fish.

Larger specimens are sometimes sold filleted, and either sold fresh or smoked. Mackerel is a popular canned fish, and may be canned in either oil or tomato sauce.

Cooking Whole mackerel can be grilled, barbecued, braised or poached in court-bouillon, white wine or cider. Make slashes on both sides of each fish before cooking them over direct heat. Like herrings, they need a sharp sauce to counteract the richness of the flesh; classic accompaniments are gooseberry, sorrel, horseradish or mustard sauce. Fillets can can be cooked in the same way as herring – either coated in oatmeal and fried, or braised with onions and white wine. Raw mackerel fillets can be marinated in sweet-and-sour vinaigrette to make a starter.

Below: Mackerel fillets can be cooked in the same way as herring – they are especially good lightly coated in oatmeal and pan-fried.

Bluefish
(Pomatomus saltatrix)
Found in the Mediterranean and American Atlantic waters, bluefish are highly aggressive and are often fished for sport. They have sheeny blue-green backs and masses of very sharp teeth. Bluefish are hugely popular in Turkey, where they are displayed in fish markets with their bright red gills turned inside out like elaborate rosettes to indicate their freshness. The flesh of bluefish is softer and more delicate than that of mackerel, but they can be cooked in the same way.

Right: Bluefish in a Turkish market with their bright red gills displayed.

Other varieties of mackerel
Chub mackerel *(Scomber japonicus colias)* are similar to Atlantic mackerel, but are also found in the Mediterranean and Black Sea. They have larger eyes and less bold markings on their backs. **Spanish mackerel** *(Scomber colias)* have spots below the lateral line. The rarer *Orcynopsis unicolor* is found near the coast of North Africa. It has silvery skin with spots of gold.

Horse mackerel *(Trachurus trachurus)* or **scad** and similar fish such as **jack mackerel** and **round robin** vaguely resemble herrings and are not, despite their name, true relatives of mackerel. They are perfectly edible, but their flesh is rather insipid and they tend to be bony. They can all be cooked in the same way as mackerel.

THE TUNA FAMILY

Tuna has been a popular food for centuries. The fish were highly prized by the Ancient Greeks, who mapped their migratory patterns in order to fish for them. The Phoenicians preserved tuna by salting and smoking them, and in the Middle Ages they were pickled. A shoal of immense tuna fish travelling through the high seas is a magnificent sight, although satellite tracking has robbed the experience of some of its excitement. These beautiful, torpedo-shaped fish can grow to an enormous size (up to 700kg/1540lb). They have immensely powerful muscles and firm, dark, meaty flesh. There are many varieties of tuna, but thanks to centuries of overfishing, only about half a dozen varieties are available commercially.

Habitat Tuna are related to mackerel and are found in warmer seas throughout the world, as far north as the Bay of Biscay.

Other names Tuna is also known as tunny fish. In French, it is *thon*, in Italian *tonno*, in Spanish *atun*. In Japan, where raw tuna is eaten as *sashimi*, it is called *maguro*.

Buying Tuna is usually sold as steaks. It is a very substantial fish, so allow only about 175g/6oz per serving. Depending on the variety, the flesh may range from pale beigey-pink to deep dark red. Do not buy steaks with heavy discolorations around the bone, or which are dull-looking and brownish all over. The flesh should be very firm and compact.

Below: Tuna steaks

Cooking Tuna becomes greyish and dry when overcooked, so it is essential to cook it only briefly over high heat, or to stew it extremely gently with moist ingredients like tomatoes and peppers. It has become fashionable to sear it fleetingly, leaving it almost raw in the middle; if this is not to your taste, cook the tuna for about 2 minutes on each side – no more.

The following cooking methods are suitable for most types of tuna. Steaks can be seared, grilled, baked or braised. They benefit from being marinated for about 30 minutes before cooking. Tuna marries well with Mediterranean vegetables such as tomatoes, peppers and onions, as well as olives. Most varieties can be eaten raw as *sashimi*, *sushi* or *tartare*, but they must be absolutely fresh. Thinly sliced raw tuna can be marinated in vinaigrette or Oriental marinades. Tuna fillets are delicious cut into very thin escalopes, dusted with flour and cooked like veal *scaloppine* in butter. Grilled fresh tuna makes a superb alternative to canned in a classic Salade Niçoise.

Albacore *(Thunnus alalunga)*

Also known as longfin, due to its long pectoral fins, this tuna is found in temperate and tropical seas, although only the smaller specimens venture into the North Sea. Albacore has pale, rosy flesh whose colour and texture resemble veal. Once known as "Carthusian veal", it could be eaten by monks when eating meat was not permitted. It is frequently used for canning.

Other names Albacore is also known as "white" tuna. In French it is *thon blanc* or *germon*; in Italian *alalunga* and in Spanish *atun blanco* or *albacora*.

Cooking Because its rosy-white flesh is so akin to veal, albacore is often cooked in similar ways – as escalopes or larded with anchovy fillets and pork back fat, and braised.

Above: Bigeye or blackfin tuna steaks

False albacore *(Euthynnus alletteratus)*

This comparatively small tuna (weighing about 15kg/33lb) is found only in warmer waters, generally off the coast of Africa. It is highly sought-after in Japan, where it is used for *sashimi*.

Bigeye *(Thunnus obesus)*

This fat relative of the bluefin is found in tropical waters. It has rosy flesh and is substituted for bluefin when that superior tuna is unavailable. It is sometimes known as blackfin tuna. Other languages continue the rather rude reference to its obesity; In French, it is *thon obèse*, in Italian, *tonno obeso* and in Spanish *patudo*.

Bluefin *(Thunnus thynnus)*

Considered by many to be the finest of all tuna, bluefin are also the largest, and can grow to an enormous size (up to 700kg/1,540lb), although the average weight is about 120kg/264lb. Bluefin have dark blue backs and silvery bellies. Their oily flesh is deep red and has a more robust flavour than albacore. Bluefin is the classic tuna for *sushi* and *sashimi*.

Habitat Bluefin are found in the Bay of Biscay, the Mediterranean and tropical seas. They are very strong swimmers and a dense shoal powering its way through the sea is an awesome sight.

Left: Bluefin tuna

Other names In Australia, the fish is known as Southern bluefin. Due to its bright red flesh, bluefin is *thon rouge* in French. In Italian it is merely *tonno*; in Spanish it is known as *atun*.

Buying Bluefin tuna is extremely expensive, largely because the Japanese will pay almost any price for it. It has an almost gamey flavour and is best when it has been kept for a week. Once the flesh has turned from bright red to light brown, however, it should be avoided at all costs – the tuna is past its prime.

Bonito (Sarda sarda) and Skipjack (Katsuwonus pelamis)

These fish fall somewhere between mackerel and tuna. There are two main types of bonito: Atlantic *(Sarda sarda)* and skipjack or oceanic. The Atlantic bonito is also found in the Mediterranean and Black Sea; skipjack is most commonly found in the Atlantic and Pacific Oceans.

Bonito are inferior to true tuna in quality and taste, with pale flesh which can sometimes be rather dry. Skipjack are usually used for canning. They are popular in Japan, where they are known as *katsuo* and are often made into dried flakes *(katsuobushi)*, which is a main ingredient of *dashi* (stock).

Other names
Skipjack have dark blue parallel lines along their bellies and are sometimes known as "striped tuna". This gives them the French name *bonite à ventre rayé* (striped belly). In Italian they are *bonita*; in Spanish, *listado*.

Frigate mackerel (Auxis rochei)

Despite its name, this fish is actually a tuna that is found in the Pacific and Indian Oceans. It grows to only about 50cm/20in and has red, coarse flesh. Some are small enough to cook whole.

Yellowfin (Thunnus albacores)

These large tuna are fished in tropical and equatorial waters. Weighing up to 250kg/550lb, they resemble albacore, but their fins are yellow. They have pale pinkish flesh and a good flavour.

Other names Confusingly, the French and Italians call yellowfin *albacore* and *tonno albacora* respectively. In Spanish, it is *rabil*.

Buying Since yellowfin tuna come from warm oceans, in Europe they are generally sold frozen as steaks. Make sure that they have not begun to thaw before you buy. Frozen yellowfin is available all year round.

Cooking Very fresh yellowfin can be eaten raw as *sashimi* or *sushi*, but is better cooked in any recipe that is suitable for tuna.

Above: Bluefin tuna steaks

Salade Niçoise
Tuna is the essential ingredient of this substantial Provençal salad, whose other components consist of whatever produce is fresh and available. Although the salad can be (and frequently is) made with drained canned tuna, it is infinitely nicer to use fresh seared or grilled fish. Arrange some coarsely shredded cos lettuce in a salad bowl and add the tuna, some quartered hard-boiled eggs, thickly-sliced cooked new potatoes, tomato wedges, crisply-cooked French beans, some pitted black olives and a few anchovy fillets. Just before serving, toss the salad in a little garlic-flavoured vinaigrette dressing.

FLAT FISH

All flat fish start life as pelagic larvae, with an eye on each side of their head like a round fish. At this stage, they swim upright near the surface of the sea. As they mature, the fish start to swim on one side only and one eye moves over the head on to the dark-skinned side of the body. Later, they gravitate to the sea bed and feed on whatever edible creatures pass by. Because they do not have to chase their food, their flesh is always delicate and white, without too much muscle fibre. They have a simple bone structure, so even people who are nervous of bones can cope with them. With the exception of flounder, flat fish are seldom found outside European waters. Dover sole, turbot and halibut possibly rank as the finest fish of all.

Brill (Scophthalmus rhombus)

Similar to turbot in appearance and taste, brill is regarded as the poor

Above: Brill

relation, although it has fine softish white flesh with a delicate flavour. Brill can grow to about 75cm/30in and can weigh up to 3kg/6½ lb, but are often smaller. The fish have slender bodies and there are small, smooth scales on the dark grey skin on the top. The underside is creamy or pinkish white.

Habitat Brill live on the bottom of the Atlantic, Baltic Sea and Mediterranean.

Buying Many people prefer turbot to brill; others think that brill is every bit as good as its plumper friend. Brill is considerably cheaper than turbot and available almost all year round, as whole fish or fillets. Brill lose condition after spawning and can contain a great deal of roe just before, so avoid

Left: Dab

buying them at that time. There is a high percentage of wastage in all flat fish, so you will need a 1.5kg/3–3½lb fish for four.

Cooking Brill can hold its own against robust red wine and is often cooked in a *matelote* (fish stew) or red wine sauce. Small fish (up to 2kg/4½lb) are best cooked whole; they can be baked, braised, poached, steamed, pan-fried or grilled. Whole poached brill is excellent garnished with prawns or other shellfish. Fillets of brill *à l'anglaise* are coated in egg and breadcrumbs and then pan-fried in butter.

Other names In French, brill is *barbue*, in Italian *rombo liscio*, "smooth turbot"; its Spanish name is *rémol*.

Alternatives Any halibut, sole or turbot recipe is suitable for brill.

Dab (Limanda limanda)

There are several related species of dab, none of which has much flavour. European and American dabs are small lozenge-shaped fish, which seldom grow to more than 35cm/14in. They have brownish, rough skin and a lateral line.

Habitat Dabs are found in shallow water on the sandy bottom of the Atlantic and off the coast of New Zealand.

Other names The so-called false dabs are more elongated than their European counterparts. In America, dabs are known as sand dabs. In French, they are *limande*, in Italian *limanda* and in Spanish *limanda nordica*.

Buying Dabs are only worth eating when they are very fresh. Near the seaside, you may find them still alive and flapping on the fishmonger's slab; if not, make sure they have glossy skins and a fresh smell. Dabs are usually sold whole, but larger fish may be filleted.

Cooking Dabs have rather soft, insipid flesh. Pan-fry them in butter or grill them. Fillets can be coated in egg and breadcrumbs and fried.

Above: Halibut

Below: Halibut Steaks

Halibut *(Hippoglossus hippoglossus)*

Halibut are the largest of the flat fish, sometimes growing up to 2m/6½ft and weighing well over 200kg/440lb, although they normally weigh between 3kg/6½lb and 15kg/33lb. Halibut have elegant, elongated greenish-brown bodies, a pointed head with the eyes on the right-hand side, and pearly white undersides. The flesh is delicious with a fine, meaty texture.

Habitat Halibut live in very cold, deep waters off the coasts of Scotland, Norway, Iceland and Newfoundland. They migrate to shallower waters to spawn. A warm water variety is found in the Pacific. These fish are voracious predators, which will eat almost any type of fish or crustacean, and will even devour birds' eggs that roll off cliffs.

Other names Beware of Greenland halibut *(Reinhardtius hippoglossoides)*, which is a vastly inferior fish. True halibut is called *flétan* in French and *halibut* in Italian and Spanish.

Buying: Whole young halibut, called chicken halibut, weigh 1.5–2kg/ 3¼–4½lb, and one will amply serve four. Larger fish are almost always sold as steaks or fillets. Go for steaks cut from the middle rather than from the thin tail end, and allow 175–200g/6–7oz per serving. Fresh raw halibut can be used for *ceviche*, *sashimi* and *sushi*.

Cooking Chicken halibut can be baked, braised, poached or cooked *à la bonne femme*, with shallots, mushrooms and white wine. The flesh of large halibut can be dry, so should be braised or baked with wine or stock.

Alternatives Brill can be substituted for halibut in any recipe. Turbot or John Dory can also be used.

Flounder *(Platichthys flesus)*

Another large family of fish, species of flounder are found in many parts of the world, from Europe to New Zealand. The mottled greyish-brown skin has orange spots and is rough. Flounders can grow to 50cm/20in, but they usually measure only 25–30cm/10–12in.

Below: Flounder

They sometimes hybridize with plaice, which they resemble, having a similar soft texture and undistinguished flavour.

Habitat Flounders live close to the shore and are sometimes found in estuaries. They spend their days on the sea bed, not feeding, but become active at night.

Other names Many types of flounder are found in America, where they are variously known as summer, winter and sand flounders. Other varieties have such descriptive names as arrowtooth, black, greenback and yellowbelly. In France, they are called *flet*, in Italy, *passera pianuzza*; in Spain, *platija*.

Buying Like dabs, flounders must be extremely fresh. Apply the same criteria.

Cooking As for dabs, brill or plaice.

Megrim (Lepidorhombus whiffiagonis)

Small yellowish-grey translucent fish with large eyes and mouths, megrim seldom grow to more than 50cm/20in in length. They have dryish, rather bland flesh and are not considered much worth eating.

Habitat Found mostly to the south of the English Channel.

Other names Megrim rejoices in the alternative names of whiff or sail-fluke. In France it is called *cardine franche*; in Italy *rombo giallo* (although you are unlikely to find it on a restaurant menu in either country). In Spain, where it is quite popular, it is called *gallo*.

Buying Megrim are either sold whole or as fillets. The flesh can be a little dry. They need to be extremely fresh, so make sure you smell them before you buy. Allow a 350g/12oz fish or at least two fillets per serving.

Cooking Whole fish can be coated in batter or breadcrumbs and deep-fried, or poached or baked. Their flesh can sometimes be rather dry, so use plenty of liquid. Fillets are best crumbed and deep-fried. Remove the coarse skin before frying or grilling.

Alternatives Lemon sole, plaice, dab or witch (Torbay sole).

Above: Megrim

Plaice (Pleuronectes platessa)

These distinctive-looking fish have smooth, dark greyish-brown skin with orange spots. The underside is pearly white. The eyes are on the right hand side; a ridge of bony knobs runs from behind them to the dorsal fin. Plaice can live for up to 50 years and weigh up to 7kg/15½lb, but the average weight is 400g–1kg/14oz–2¼lb. They have soft, rather bland white flesh, which can sometimes lack flavour.

Habitat Plaice are found in the Atlantic and other northerly waters, and in the Mediterranean. They are bottom-feeding fish which, like flounder, are most active at night.

Other names In France, plaice are *plie* or *carrelet*; in Italy, *passera* or *pianuzza*; in Spain, *solla*.

Buying Plaice must be very fresh, or the flesh tends to take on the texture of cotton wool. These fish are available all year, whole or as fillets, but are best

Above: Plaice

Left: Plaice fillets

avoided in the summer months, when the flesh is flaccid and tasteless. In fresh plaice, the orange spots on the dark skin will be bright and distinctive. Dark-skinned plaice fillets are cheaper than white-skinned, but there is no difference in flavour. There is a lot of wastage on plaice, so you should allow a whole 350–450g/12–16oz fish per serving, or 175g/6oz fillet.

Cooking Any sole or brill recipe is suitable for plaice. Deep-fried in batter, plaice is a classic fish and chip shop favourite. Whole fish or fillets can be coated in egg and breadcrumbs and pan-fried. Steamed or poached plaice is highly digestible and makes good invalid food. For plaice *à la florentine*, bake a whole fish or white-skinned fillets in stock and white wine, lay it on a bed of lightly-cooked spinach, cover with a cheese sauce and grill until bubbling and browned.

Alternatives Flounder, dab, sole and brill can all be substituted for plaice.

Sole/Dover sole *(Solea solea)*

Arguably the finest fish of all, Dover sole have a firm, delicate flesh with a superb flavour. Their oval bodies are well proportioned, with greyish or lightish brown skin, sometimes spotted with black. The eyes are on the right-hand side. The nasal openings on the underside are small and widely separated, which distinguishes these sole from lesser varieties. Dover sole can weigh up to 3kg/6½ lb, but the average weight is 200–600g/7oz–1lb 6oz.

The Ancient Romans adored sole and called them *solea Jovi* ("Jupiter's sandal"). The firm flesh was often preserved. During the reign of Louis XIV of France, sole was regarded as truly fit for a king, and the great chefs of the time created extravagant sole dishes. In the earlier part of the 20th century, it was the mainstay of English fish cookery.

Habitat Dover sole are found in the English Channel and the Atlantic and also in the Baltic, Mediterranean and North Seas. They come inshore to spawn in spring and summer. For the most part, they spend their days buried in the sand on the sea bed and hunt for food at night.

Other names Sand or partridge sole *(Pegusa lascaris)* are very similar in appearance to Dover sole and are sometimes sold as "Dovers", although they are smaller and inferior fish. Their distinguishing feature is a much larger nasal opening on the underside. Another species, known as "tongues", *(Dicologlossa cuneata)* are smaller still (only 7.5–10cm/3–4in in length). In France, these fish are sometimes sold as baby Dover sole, when they are known as *séteaux* (or *cétaux*) or *langues d'avocat* ("lawyers' tongues"). In French Dover sole is *sole*; in Italian, *sogliola*; in Spanish, *lenguado*.

Buying Sole are at their best three days after being caught, so if you are sure that you are buying fish straight from the sea, keep them for a couple of days before cooking. The skin should be sticky and the underside very white. Nowadays, whole sole are graded by weight; a

Above: Dover sole (top) and lemon sole

Below: Turbot

Other names In America, lemon sole are known as yellowtail flounder. In France, they are *limande-sole*, in Italy *sogliola limanda*; in Spain, *mendo limón*.
Buying Lemon sole are available all year round and are sold whole or as fillets. They must be very fresh and should have a tang of the sea.
Cooking Lemon sole are best cooked simply; use them in any dab, plaice or Dover sole recipe.

Turbot *(Psetta maxima)*

What turbot lacks in looks, it makes up for in texture and taste, and it is a clear contender for the fishy crown. Highly prized since ancient times, it was called *le roi de carême* ("the king of Lent") in the Middle Ages. All the great chefs of the time created sumptuous recipes for turbot, marrying the fish with langoustines, truffles, lobster sauce and beef marrow. Turbot have tiny heads and large, almost circular bodies with tough warty brown skin like a toad. Unusually, the white underside is sometimes pigmented with grey. They can grow to 1m/40in in length and can weigh as much as 12kg/26½lb. The flesh is creamy white, with a firm, dense texture and a superb sweet flavour.

225g/8oz fish will serve one person. If you want to serve two, buy a fish weighing at least 675–800g/ 1½–1¾lb (which will yield four decent-size fillets, but could prove costly). It is best to buy a whole fish; if you ask the fishmonger to fillet it for you, keep the bones and trimmings to make fish stock (and help to justify the cost).
Cooking There are umpteen recipes for sole, but a plain lightly-grilled fish served with a drizzle of melted butter and lemon juice is hard to beat. Skin both sides before cooking. Small sole can be coated in egg and breadcrumbs and pan-fried or deep-fried; larger specimens can be poached, steamed or cooked in butter *à la meunière*. Fillets can be fried, poached in wine or served with an elaborate sauce, or given an Oriental twist with soy sauce, lemon grass and ginger. They can be steamed and rolled up around a stuffing or used to line a mould which is then filled with shellfish mousse.

Alternatives
Nothing tastes quite like Dover sole, but lemon sole, plaice and other flat fish can be cooked in the same way.

Lemon sole *(Microstomus kitt)*

Despite the name, lemon sole is related to dab, plaice and flounder. These fish are oval in shape, with the widest part well towards the head. They have smooth reddish brown skin with irregular marbling and a straight lateral line, very small heads and bulging eyes. The flesh is soft and white, similar to that of plaice but slightly superior. It is a good alternative to the more expensive Dover sole.
Habitat Lemon sole are found in the North Sea and Atlantic Ocean and around the coast of New Zealand. They lead largely stationary lives on the stony or rocky sea bed and vary enormously in size depending on local conditions.

Turbot kettle
In the days of affordable luxury, a whole huge turbot might be steamed in a magnificent diamond-shaped copper turbot kettle with handles on the points and a grid for lifting out the cooked fish.
Nowadays you will only find one of these kettles in the kitchen of a stately home or a fine restaurant. Modern turbot kettles are made of stainless steel or aluminium.

Above: Chicken turbot

Habitat Turbot live on the sea bottom in the Atlantic, Mediterranean and Black Seas, and have been introduced to New Zealand coastal waters. They can be farmed successfully, and this has improved both the quality and the size of the fish.

Other names The name is the same – *turbot* – in French, *rombo chiodato* (studded with nails) in Italian; *rodaballo* in Spanish. Small young turbot, weighing up to 2kg/4½lb, are called chicken turbot.

Buying Turbot is extremely expensive; a really large wild fish can cost several hundred pounds (dollars). Farmed fish are cheaper, but can be fatty. Turbot should have creamy white flesh; do not buy fish with a blue tinge. It is available all year round, sold whole, as steaks and fillets. A chicken turbot weighing about 1.5kg/3–3½lb will feed four

people. There is a high percentage of wastage, so if your fishmonger fillets a whole turbot for you, ask for the bones and trimmings to make a superb stock.

Cooking It is neither practical nor economical to cook a whole turbot that weighs more than about 1.5kg/3–3½lb in a domestic kitchen. To cook a chicken turbot, grill it or poach in white wine and fish stock, using a large frying or roasting pan. Traditionally, turbot was poached in milk to

Below: Witch

keep the flesh pure white, then served with hollandaise sauce. Almost any cooking method is suitable for turbot, except perhaps deep-frying, which would be a waste; it is essential not to overcook it. Creamy sauces such as lobster, parsley and mushroom go well with plainly-cooked turbot. Chunks of poached turbot dressed with a piquant vinaigrette, make a superb salad.

Alternatives Nothing quite equals turbot, but brill, halibut, John Dory and fillets of sole make good substitutes.

Witch *(Glyptocephalus cynoglossus)*

This member of the sole family has an elongated body like a sole, with a straight lateral line on the rough, grey-brown skin. The flesh tastes rather insipid, and resembles megrim.

Other names Also known as Torbay sole, witch flounder and pole flounder. In French, it is *plie grise*, in Italian *passera cinoglossa*; in Spanish *mendo*.

Buying Witch are available all year round, usually only near the coast where they are caught – mostly off the south-west coast of England. They are only worth eating when very fresh.

Cooking Because these fish taste rather dull, it is important to season them well before cooking. Witch are best grilled, but any sole recipe is suitable.

MIGRATORY FISH

Certain species of fish undertake an astonishing annual mass migration from one area to another to spawn or feed. They follow a specific route, although how they know which route to take remains a mystery. Each year salmon and sea trout migrate from the sea to spawn in the fresh water of the river; having spawned, they return to the sea, and so the pattern continues. Eels, on the other hand, travel from rivers and lakes to spawn in salt sea water, entailing a journey of thousands of miles. The whole process is truly one of nature's miracles.

EELS (Anguillidae)

There are more than twenty members of the eel family. All are slim snake-like fish with smooth slippery skin and spineless fins. Most have microscopic scales, but these are not visible to the naked eye. The *Anguillidae* family are freshwater fish, but other species, such as conger, moray and snake eels, are marine fish. Eels have fatty white flesh with a rich flavour and firm texture.

Eels have been a popular food since Roman times, and were highly prized in the Middle Ages. Their mysterious life cycle gave rise to all sorts of improbable myths; one popular belief was that they were loose horsehairs which came to life when they touched the water. The less fanciful but equally amazing truth was only discovered by a Danish scientist at the end of the 19th century.
Habitat Freshwater eels are born in the Sargasso Sea. Each female lays up to 20 million eggs and both she and her male partner die immediately after the eggs have been laid and fertilized. The eggs hatch into minuscule larvae, which are carried on the ocean currents to the coasts of Europe and America, then back to the rivers where their ancestors matured. This journey takes a year for American eels and between two and three years for European eels. No one has yet fathomed how the babies know which direction to take, since they have never seen "home". When the baby elvers enter the estuaries in huge

Above: Young eels

flotillas, they are tiny transparent creatures not more than 8cm/3¼in long. As they mature, their skin colour changes to yellow, then to green and finally to silver. At this stage, the eels begin the long journey back to the Sargasso Sea, where they spawn and immediately die.
Varieties Tiny elvers are known as glass eels (*civelles* or *piballes* in French). Adult European eels (*Anguilla anguilla*) and American eels (*Anguilla rostrata*) are *anguille* in French, *anguilla* in Italian and *anguila* in Spanish. The Japanese eel (*Anguilla japonica*) and Australian eel (*Anguilla australis*) are both known as the shortfinned eel, while *Anguilla dieffenbachii* is the longfinned eel.
Buying You may find tiny elvers for sale in the spring – these are a great delicacy and are extremely expensive. One kilo consists of up to two thousand tiny elvers.

Adult eels are at their plumpest and best in autumn when they have turned silver with almost black backs. Females weigh three times as much as males, so a female silver eel is highly prized.

Farmed eels are available all year round. Eels should be bought alive, as they go off very quickly once dead. Ask the fishmonger to skin them for you and to chop them into 5cm/2in lengths.

Skinning an eel

You will probably prefer to ask your fishmonger to kill and skin your eel, but if this is not possible, this is how to do it yourself. Grip the eel in a cloth and bang its head sharply on a hard surface to kill it. Put a string noose around the base of the head and hang it firmly on a sturdy hook or door handle. Slit the skin all round the head just below the noose. Pull away the top of the skin, turn it back to make a "cuff", then grip with a cloth or two pairs of pliers and pull the skin down firmly towards the tail. Cut off the head and tail. Alternatively, kill the eel and chop it into sections, leaving the skin on. Grill the pieces, skin-up, turning frequently until the skin has puffed up on all sides. When cool enough to handle, peel off the skin.

Cooking Tiny elvers can be tossed in seasoned flour and deep-fried; soak them first in acidulated water to remove the mud. Eel is a versatile fish that can be fried and served with parsley sauce. It is good poached or braised in red wine. If you grill it, marinate it first, then wrap it in streaky bacon to keep it moist. Eel is excellent in soups and casseroles, such as *matelote*, and the rich flesh marries well with robust Oriental flavours. Two classic English eel recipes are jellied eels and eel pie with mashed potatoes and green "liquor". Eels are also delicious smoked.

Conger eel (*Conger conger*)

These marine eels can grow to an enormous size – sometimes up to 3m/9ft 9in, although the average length is 60–150cm/2–5ft. They are ferocious carnivores with long, thick scaleless bodies and very bony firm white flesh, which is quite good to eat.
Habitat Conger eels are found in temperate and tropical seas, living in rocky crevices and wrecks. Many live in deep water, but some prefer to lurk in shallow inshore waters, causing panic among unfortunate swimmers who inadvertently disturb a large specimen.
Other names In French conger eel is *congre*, in Italian *grongo*, and in Spanish *congrio*.

Below: Conger eel steaks

Buying Conger has the merit of being cheap. It is available from early spring to autumn and is usually sold cut into chunks or steaks. Ask for a middle cut from near the head end; the tail end is extremely bony. If you are offered a whole conger, ask the fishmonger to fillet it and keep the head and bones for soup or stock.
Cooking Conger is best used for soups or hearty casseroles. Its dense flesh makes it good for terrines. Thick middle cuts can be roasted, poached or braised and served with a *salsa verde*.

Above: Fierce-looking conger eel, which is a ferocious carnivore.

Moray eel (*Muraena helena*)

These eels are even more fearsome than the conger eel. They grow to only about 2m/6ft 6in, but are extremely vicious and will not hesitate to bite. Moray eels have long, flattened bodies and thick, greenish leathery skin with a pattern of light spots and no scales. The white flesh is rather tasteless and very bony.
Habitat Most species of moray eel are found in tropical and sub-tropical waters, but some occur in the Atlantic and Mediterranean. These eels typically anchor the tail end of their bodies in rock crevices and corals and wait with their mouths agape for catching prey that comes too close.
Buying Morays are mostly fished for sport and are seldom found in fishmongers. When they are available, they are sold in chunks.
Cooking Morays are really fit only for soup, and are often used in the traditional *bouillabaisse*. They can be cooked gently in cider, then the flesh removed from the bone and used in fish pies or fish cakes. The tail end is full of sharp bones. Avoid it, unless you are making stock.

Right: Atlantic salmon

THE SALMON FAMILY

Known as the "king of fish", salmon is probably the most important of all fish, prized by sportsmen and gastronomes alike. Various species are found throughout the world, but the finest by far is the Atlantic salmon. All salmon spawn in fresh water. Some species spend their lives in landlocked waters, but after two years, most salmon migrate upstream to the sea to feed before returning to spawn in the rivers where they were born. This arduous trek makes them sleek and muscular. Once they return to fresh water, they stop feeding, only starting again when they go back to the sea.

Salmon have suffered from over-fishing and environmental disturbance, and wild fish have become rare and expensive. Once, it was possible to land salmon weighing 20kg/44lb or more, but such magnificent fish have now disappeared. Fortunately, salmon can be farmed successfully, although early salmon farms produced fish with flabby, bland flesh, often riddled with sea lice, which attacked and further decimated the wild stocks. Lessons have been learned, and it is now possible to buy healthy, well-flavoured farmed salmon.

Atlantic salmon *(Salmo salar)*

These magnificent fish have silvery-blue backs, silver sides and white bellies. In comparison to their large, powerful bodies, their heads are quite small. The heads and backs are marked with tiny black crosses. Salmon's fine fatty flesh is deep pink and firm with a superb, rich flavour.

Habitat Atlantic salmon are found in all the cold northern waters of Europe and America. They are spawned in rivers, then undertake the exhausting journey back to the sea, returning to the river to spawn in their turn. When young salmon, which are 10–20cm/4–8in long, first migrate to the sea, they are called smolts. After a year or two of voracious feeding, they reach a weight of

Below: Salmon steaks

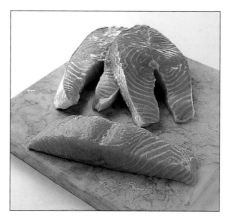

1–2kg/2¼–4½lb and make their first spawning run; these young fish are called grilse. The males develop elongated hooked jaws; this is just to help them fight the strong currents, since they do not feed during the spawning run. Some fish may spawn only once or twice in their lifetimes; others up to four times.

Salmon were a popular food in the Middle Ages, when they were braised with spices, potted or salted, or made into pies and pâtés. Once they became rarer, they were regarded as a luxury and chefs vied to marry them with extravagant ingredients such as lobster, crayfish and cream. Only recently has salmon once again become affordable.

Other names The deep, cold lakes of Canada and North America are home to landlocked salmon; these are variously known as ouananiche, lake salmon and sebago. In French, salmon are *saumon*, in Italian *salmone*; in Spanish *salmón*.

Buying Salmon are sold whole, as steaks, cutlets, fillets and large middle and tail cuts. The best (and most expensive) salmon are wild fish. Ethical fishmongers will tell you which are wild and which farmed and charge accordingly. Wild salmon are sleeker, with firmer, lustrous skin and deep pink flesh. They are available from spring to late summer. Late-spawning fish which return to the sea in autumn are known as kelts; because they have not eaten for many months, kelts are thin and in poor condition and are not worth buying. Grilse – young salmon with an average weight of 1.4kg/3lb – are cheaper than large wild fish and will

Above and left: Parrot fish come in a huge variety of colours.

Parrot fish *(Scarus* spp*)*

Perfectly adapted to living in proximity to coral reefs, parrot fish have hard, parrot-like beaks (evolved from fused teeth) with which they nibble the coral. There are almost a hundred species of parrot fish. All have compact, brightly coloured bodies and large scales. They come in an incredible variety of vibrant hues – green, blue, red and multi-coloured. The largest is the rainbow parrot fish, which can grow up to 1m/3½ft, but most are only 30cm/12in long. Like many types of exotic fish, parrot fish look much better than they taste.

Habitat Parrot fish are found in tropical and sub-tropical seas. They live in large numbers around coral reefs, crushing the coral to reach the soft sea creatures inside, or scraping algae from surrounding rocks.

Other names In French, they are *perroquet;* in Italian *pesce pappagallo;* in Spanish *vieja.*

Buying Many supermarkets now stock parrot fish. Make sure that the colours are clear and bright; avoid fish that look faded. The average fish from the fish market or fishmonger's slab will feed one person; a larger 800g–1kg/1¾–2¼lb fish will serve two. Larger fish are sometimes sold filleted, or can be filleted on request.

Cooking Parrot fish can be rather bland, so spice them up with tropical flavours, such as coconut milk, garlic, chilli and lemon grass. Whole fish can be baked or braised; they look pretty and taste good when served with a spicy salsa.

Alternatives Red snapper, bream and John Dory can all be used instead of parrot fish.

Pomfret *(Stromateus* spp*)*

These small silvery fish look rather like coins if seen as though through the eyes of Salvador Dali. Their almost circular bodies have very pointed dorsal and anal fins and curved forked tails, not unlike those of flat fish. Scales are almost absent and the white flesh is fairly soft, with a mild flavour. Together with their close relation, the American butterfish, pomfret make good eating.

Above: Pomfret

Habitat A variety of pomfret is found in the Mediterranean, but the best-flavoured fish come from the Indian and Pacific oceans. Butterfish are found off the north-west coast of America.

Buying Pomfret are available most of the year, either fresh or frozen. Small fish weighing about 400g/14oz are sold whole and will feed one person. Fillets from small fish are rather thin, so it is best to choose a larger fish if possible and ask the fishmonger to fillet it.

Other names Pomfret from the north-west Atlantic are known as butterfish, and in America also go by the names of dollar fish, and pumpkinseed fish, due to their shape, which in Europe is likened to that of the chestnut. In France, they are called *castagnole du Pacifique*; in Italy *pesce castagna* and in Spain *castagneta*.

Buying Pomfret are available most of the year. A small whole fish weighing about 400g/14oz will feed one person. Fillets from small pomfret are rather thin, so if possible, buy a larger fish and ask the fishmonger to fillet it for you.

Cooking Whole pomfret can be grilled, fried, baked, poached or steamed. This fish goes well with spices and Oriental flavours such as coconut, lemon grass and tamarind. Beloved of Indian chefs, pomfret makes excellent curries and is often cooked in a tandoor as tikka masala. Because the fillets are thin and the flesh is soft, pomfret fillets should be cooked only briefly.

Alternatives Trout can be used instead of pomfret, as can any flat fish.

Pompano *(Alectis ciliaris)* **and Jack** *(Seriola)*

This large family of fish comprises more than two hundred species. All are oily fish, similar to mackerel, but with a stronger flavour. The dark flesh becomes lighter on cooking. Jacks vary enormously in size and shape, but all have forked tails and virtually scaleless iridescent skin. Among the most common jacks and pompanos are the small leatherjacket, the larger yellowtail , the amberjack and crevalle jack. The best of all for culinary purposes is the Florida pompano, which has white, meaty flesh, while the oddest-looking is the lookdown, a small glum-looking fish with a flat, thin body and a high domed forehead.

Habitat Pompano and jacks are found in warm seas all over the world. They travel in schools, either around coral reefs or, like Florida pompano, close to the shore.

Other names In Australia and New Zealand, yellowtail jack are known as kingfish. In French, jack is *carangue*; in Italian *carango*; in Spanish *caballa*. Pompano is *palomine* in French; *leccia stella* in Italian and *palometa blanca* in Spanish.

Buying Pompano and jack are available all year round. They are usually sold whole, but may be filleted. Outside Florida, you are likely to find only farmed pompano, but this is of excellent quality.

Cooking Jack can be cooked in the same way as mackerel. The robust flesh lends itself to spicy Oriental flavours such as chilli, ginger and coriander. Pompano and jack can be stuffed with breadcrumbs or crab meat and baked, barbecued or grilled. They can be cooked *en papillote*, steamed or poached in court-bouillon flavoured with Oriental ingredients such as soy sauce or Thai fish sauce and fresh ginger. The Japanese use the fillets raw as *sashimi*.

Below: Yellowtail jack or kingfish

Below: Yellowtail jack steaks

Above: Red and emperor snappers

Snapper *(Lutjanidae)*

More than 250 species of snapper are found in warm seas throughout the world. The best-known and finest to eat is the American red snapper (*Lutjanus campechanus*), which is bright red all over, including the eyes and fins. The silk snapper is similar, but has a yellow tail. Other species include the pink snapper, or *opakapaka*, mutton snapper, which is usually olive green with vertical bars (but can change colour), the yellowtail snapper and the African and Indo-Pacific. All have domed heads with large mouths and big eyes set high on the head. Most snappers weigh between 1.5 and 2.5kg/3¼ and 5½lb, although mutton snappers can weigh up to 10kg/22lb, while yellowtails average only 250g/9oz. Snappers have firm, slightly flaky well-flavoured white flesh.

Habitat Red snapper come from deep waters around Florida and Central and South America. Other varieties are found in warm waters from the Atlantic to the Caribbean and Indo-Pacific.

Other names Snapper from the Indian Ocean and Arabian Sea are known as job or jobfish. In French, *vivaneau*; in Italian, *lutianido*; in Spanish, *pargo*.

Buying Snapper are available all year round. Many fish sold as red snapper are a different, inferior species; true American red snapper have red eyes. A whole fish weighing about 1kg/2¼lb will feed two people, while a 2kg/4½lb fish makes a good meal for four people.

Cooking Snapper is a versatile fish that can be baked, grilled, poached, steamed and pan-fried. It lends itself to exotic and Caribbean flavours, such as chilli, mango and coconut.

Alternatives Grey mullet, bream, John Dory and sea bass can be substituted.

Tilapia *(Tilapia)*

Members of the enormous *Cichlids* family, tilapia have only one nostril on either side of their heads. The female is considerably smaller than the male, and scientists have now successfully bred tilapia which produce offspring that are almost exclusively male. Tilapia are freshwater fish, but can also live in salt water and are found in tropical seas. There are many varieties, with colours ranging from grey to bright red. Their flesh is white and moist, with a pleasant, sweet flavour.

Habitat Tilapia are found in warm tropical waters, both fresh and salt. They are farmed all over the world.

Other names In Egypt and Israel, tilapia are sometimes marketed as St. Peter's fish (not to be confused with John Dory).

Buying Tilapia are available all year round. Small fish are sold whole, but larger fish are filleted. A small whole fish (about 350g/12oz) will serve one person; a 675g/1½lb fish serves two.

Cooking Whole tilapia can be stuffed and baked, grilled or barbecued. The bland flesh benefits from Chinese flavourings and spices. Fillets can be coated in egg and breadcrumbs or batter and deep-fried.

Alternatives Carp, bream and zander can be used instead of tilapia.

Above: Tilapia

CARTILAGINOUS FISH

This curious group of fish, called *chondrichthyes*, have no bones. Their skeletons are made entirely of cartilage. Many of these very ancient fish exist only as fossils, but about 500 species are still living, including edible fish such as shark, dogfish, ray and skate. Cartilaginous fish are thought to have evolved from freshwater fish which adapted to life in the sea. Unlike other fish, they have no swim bladders to control buoyancy, but in compensation have developed very large livers, whose high oil content helps the fish to float. This oil is often extracted and used for medicinal purposes.

Almost all cartilaginous fish have long snouts and mouths set well back on the underside of the head. They have several rows of teeth, arranged one behind the other. As one row wears away, they start to use the next. They have stiff fleshy fins and no scales, but their bodies are covered with backward-facing denticles, which give them a rough texture. Once these fish die, the urea they contain turns into ammonia, imparting an unpleasant smell and taste, so it is essential that they are eaten very fresh.

THE SHARK FAMILY

The shark family is a large one, ranging in size from the small dogfish to the huge basking shark, which can weigh up to 4000kg/8800lb, and whose liver alone weighs 500–700kg/1100–1540lb. Edible sharks include porbeagle, blue shark, mako, tope and dogfish. They are an unattractive bunch, with a bad reputation, but some of them make excellent eating. Shark flesh is firm and slightly sweet, with a meaty texture.
Buying Shark is sold as steaks, loin or fillets. The flesh has a faint smell of ammonia, which disappears during cooking if the shark is fresh. However, after a week or so, it becomes very pungent and nothing will get rid of it.
Cooking Shark meat is a match for robust and aromatic flavours and is excellent in curries. Steaks can be grilled, pan-fried or barbecued. They

can be dry, so marinate them in olive oil and lemon juice, or lard them with pork back fat before cooking.

Steaks can also be braised or baked au gratin in a mornay sauce and glazed under the grill. Shark makes a good addition to a fish soup or casserole and can be served cold in salads, dressed with a lemony mayonnaise. It is also ideal for home-smoking.
Alternatives Any meaty fish can be used instead of shark in recipes; try monkfish, swordfish and tuna.

Blue shark *(Prionace glauca)*

This migratory shark has exceedingly sharp teeth and is regarded as a man-eater. It has a sleek indigo-blue back, shading to bright blue on the sides and a snow white belly. It seldom grows to more than 4m/13ft in length. The very white flesh is not especially good, but the fins are used to make the Oriental favourite, shark's fin soup.
Other names In French, blue shark is *peau bleu*, in Italian *verdesca*; in Spanish *tintorera*.

Above: Shark loin can be bought as a piece or cut into steaks. The meat can be dry, so is best marinated.

Dogfish *(Scyliorhinus caniculus)*

Three species of these small members of the shark family are commonly eaten; the lesser spotted dogfish, the spur-dog or spiny dogfish *(Squalus acanthius)* and the larger, more portly nursehound *(Scylorhinus stellaris)*. The first has grey-brown skin with numerous brown spots, the second has grey skin, while the nursehound's skin is reddish. The thick rough skin is almost always removed before sale to disguise the shark-like appearance of these fish. Lesser spotted dogfish grow to about 80cm/32in, spur-dogs to 1.2m/4ft and nursehounds to 1.5m/4ft 9in; the fish you find in the market are usually half that size. The flesh is white or pinkish with a firm texture and a good flavour. It is, of course, boneless.
Habitat Different varieties of dogfish are found in cool temperate waters all around the world.

Shark à la Créole
Shark is a very popular fish in the Caribbean and the southern states of America. This recipe reflects the mixture of the two cultures.

For 4 people you will need 4 shark steaks. First, make a marinade with the juice of 2 limes, 2 crushed garlic cloves, 2 seeded and chopped red chillies, salt and ground black pepper. Dilute the marinade with 15ml/1 tbsp water and pour into a non-metallic dish. Add the shark steaks, turn them over in the marinade so that they are coated, then cover and leave to marinate for several hours in a cool place or in the fridge.

When ready to cook, slice 2 red onions, 4 shallots and 4 tomatoes. Remove the seeds from 2 red or green fresh chillies and chop the chillies finely. Heat 30ml/2 tbsp oil in a shallow saucepan, add the vegetables and chillies and brown. Drain the shark steaks and lay them on top of the vegetables. Cover and cook gently for about 20 minutes, until tender. Squeeze over the juice of a lime and garnish with chopped parsley. Serve with creole rice and black-eyed beans.

Above: The lesser spotted dogfish, which is generally sold skinned but not filleted, is more commonly known as huss or even rock salmon.

Filleting dogfish
The central cartilage in dogfish is very easy to remove, and there are no small bones. It is usually sold as a whole skinned fish. To fillet it, use a sharp knife with a long blade to cut down through the flesh on either side of the cartilage, using the full length of the blade and keeping it as close to the cartilage as possible. The fillets will fall away.

Other names Dogfish are variously known as huss, flake, rigg and even rock salmon, although this last is a complete misnomer. Spur-dogs are also known as spinebacks or spiky dogs. In French, they are *petite* or *grande roussette*, depending on their size, or, misleadingly, *saumonette* (little salmon). In Italian they are *gattopardo* (leopard); in Spanish *pata-roxa*.
Buying Dogfish are sold skinned, often as fillets. They are cheap and available all year round. They must be very fresh, so sniff before you buy to make sure they do not smell of ammonia.
Cooking Dogfish has good firm flesh and can be cooked in the same ways as monkfish and skate. It is excellent in casseroles and chunky soups and is the perfect fish for fish and chips. This fish can also be grilled or barbecued with a good coating of olive oil, or cooked and flaked and used in salads. Dogfish is delicious smoked.

Mako shark *(Isurus oxyrinchus)*

Part of the family of mackerel sharks, mako are swift surface swimmers with streamlined blue-grey bodies and bright white bellies, which grow to 2–3m/6½–9¾ft. They are found in subtropical and temperate–warm seas. Prized by game fishermen, they have a habit of raiding and damaging fishing nets and lines. Mako sharks have firm white flesh. They are usually sold as loins or fillets, but the flesh tends to be flavourless, so it will benefit from a robust marinade.

Other names In French, *taupe bleu*, in Italian *squallo mako* or *ossirina*; in Spanish *marrajo*.

Porbeagle *(Lamna nasus)*

These stocky, dark mole-grey sharks are closely related to the great white shark. They are surface swimmers, found in cold and temperate seas, but little is known about their growth or longevity. Porbeagles are widely regarded as the finest of all the sharks for eating, with firm, meaty pink flesh which is sometimes likened to veal. It is usually sold as loin or fillets.

Other names In French, porbeagle is known as *taupe* or *veau de mer*; in Italian it is *smeriglio*; in Spanish *cailón*.

Cooking Porbeagle so closely resembles veal that it can be sliced into thin escalopes, dipped in egg and breadcrumbs and then pan-fried like *scallopine alla milanese*. It can also be used in any other shark recipe.

Tope *(Galeorhinus galeus)*

These small grey sharks have pointed upward-tilting noses and serrated triangular teeth. Although edible, they do not taste particularly good and are best cut into chunks and used in mixed fish soups and casseroles.

Other names In French it is *milandre*, in Italian *cagnesca*; in Spanish *cazón*.

Above: Porbeagle, which is sometimes sold in fishmongers and markets by its French name, taupe.

Below: Tope

Ray and Skate *(Raja)*

Although they are different members of the same family, it is virtually impossible to distinguish between ray and skate on the fishmonger's slab, since only the "wings" are sold, never the whole fish. These fish have large, kite-shaped bodies with long thin tails and enlarged flattened pectoral fins (the wings). The skin is greyish-brown and smooth, knobbly or even thorny, depending on the species. Ray and skate have short snouts and large mouths on the underside with sharp slashing teeth. They can be

Below: Skate wing

differentiated by the shape of the snout; in skate, this is pointed. The largest rays can grow to 2.5m/8ft and weigh up to 100kg/220lb.

The thornback ray (*Raja clavata*) is considered to have the best flavour, but gastronomically speaking, there is little to distinguish between the edible skates and rays. They have moist, meaty pinkish flesh with a fine texture and good flavour. Normally, only the wings are eaten, but the cheeks are regarded as a delicacy, as are the small medallions from the tail known as "skate knobs". The liver also makes good eating.

Habitat Rays and skates are found in cold and temperate waters. They are lazy bottom-living fish that hide on the sea bed waiting for their prey to pass by. They have evolved a way of breathing without opening their mouths. Most rays lay eggs, each enclosed in a four-horned black sac known as a "mermaid's purse".

Other names Among the edible rays and skates are the common skate (*raie* in French, *razza* in Italian; *raya* in Spanish), thornback ray or roker, rough skate and butterfly skate.

Buying Skate is available most of the year, but is best in autumn and winter. Smaller wings are sold whole; if you want a larger piece, ask for a middle cut. The wings are covered with a clear slime, which regenerates itself even after death. To test for freshness, gently rub off the slime and make sure that it reappears. Even fresh skate smells faintly of ammonia. This is normal, and the smell will disappear during cooking.

Cooking Before cooking skate, wash it well in cold water to eliminate the ammoniac smell. If the skin is still on, leave it and scrape it off after cooking. The classic skate dish is *raie au beurre noir* (with black butter). Poach the wings in water acidulated with a little vinegar or *court-bouillon* for about 10 minutes, then drain and sprinkle with capers. Brown some butter (do not let it burn and blacken) and pour it over the fish. Skate can also be grilled, deep-fried in batter or curried, and makes a delicious salad. Its gelatinous quality makes it good for soups and fish terrines and mousses.

Alternatives Fillets of brill, sole, John Dory or turbot can be used instead.

Skinning cooked skate

1 Lay the fish on a board. With a blunt knife, scrape off the skin from the thicker part towards the edge.

2 Discard the skin. Scrape the flesh off the cartilage in the same way.

Deep Sea and Game Fish

Deep in the world's oceans live several varieties of fish that never come close to the shore. Many have odd shapes and vibrant colours, which consumers seldom see, since the fish are filleted on board the boats that travel far out to sea to trawl the fish. Most edible deep-sea fish are found around the coasts of New Zealand, South Africa and South America. The Caribbean is home to huge game fish, such as marlin, and keen fishermen will pay vast sums for a day's sport. Little is known about the life cycles of these monsters of the deep, but it is certain that, as stocks of the more common inshore fish decline, we shall see more and more deep-sea fish appearing in the supermarkets.

Antarctic sea bass *(Dissostichus eleginoides)*

Not a true sea bass, this fish is also known as toothfish, icefish and Chilean sea bass. It has only recently been fished commercially and little is known about it. The white flesh has a good texture and a pleasant flavour, but it does not compare to true sea bass.
Habitat Antarctic sea bass inhabits the southern oceans from Antarctica to the Falklands and Chile.
Buying Available all year round as fillets. Prod the flesh to make sure that it is

Below: Hoki fillets are very long and thin. The flesh is pinkish white, and has a flaky texture that is similar to hake when cooked.

firm. When buying Antarctic sea bass, make sure that you are not paying for real sea bass, which is much a more expensive fish.
Cooking Cook Antarctic sea bass in the same way as cod or any round white fish. A well-flavoured sauce will enhance the rather bland flavour.

Grenadier/Rattail *(family Macrouridae)*

There are about fifty species of these curious-looking shoaling fish. They may be the most abundant of all fish, although since they live at depths of between 200m/656ft and 6000m/19,700ft, it is hard to be sure. Grenadiers have large pointed heads which contain sensors to help them navigate in the dark ocean depths, and bodies which taper into filament-like tails (hence their alias). Their swim bladders vibrate to produce a grunting sound. Despite their odd appearance, grenadiers are good to eat. The white flesh has a delicate, fairly moist texture.
Habitat Grenadiers are distributed throughout the world. They live at great depths, feeding on luminous creatures that they can detect even in the dark.
Buying Grenadier fillets are available all year round. You may find fresh fish, but in the northen hemisphere it is more usual to find the fish frozen.
Cooking Fillets can be deep- or pan-fried or brushed with oil and grilled. They benefit from a creamy sauce and are good baked *au gratin*.
Alternatives Cod, hake, hoki or any other fairly firm white fish can be used instead of grenadiers.

Hoki *(Macruronus novaezelandiae)*

Although hoki resemble grenadiers in appearance, they are actually related to hake and have the same white flesh and flaky texture. They have blue-green backs with silvery sides and bellies, and their tadpole-like bodies taper to a point. The average length of a hoki is 60cm–1m/24–39in.
Habitat Hoki occur in large numbers around the coasts of Southern Australia and New Zealand; a similar species is found around South America. They live at depths of 500–800m/1640–2626ft.
Other names In Australia, hoki are inaccurately called blue grenadier. In New Zealand, they are sometimes called whiptail or blue hake.
Buying Hoki is available all year round, as fillets, loins and other cuts. It is frequently used to make fish fingers or ocean sticks.
Cooking The delicate white flesh is suitable for most cooking methods, particularly frying. It can sometimes taste insipid, so is best served with a robust tomato-based sauce or a creamy sauce. Hoki can be cubed for kebabs and is an excellent fish for smoking.
Alternatives Hake, monkfish and huss can be substituted for hoki.

Marlin *(family Istiophoridae)*

More usually fished for sport than for commerce, marlin are magnificent-looking billfish, renowned for their speed and endurance. The name billfish comes from their greatly elongated upper jaw, which forms a bill or spear. They have beautiful slender bodies with smooth iridescent skin and a high dorsal fin, which they fold down when speeding through the water.

There are several species of marlin, the best-known being blue, black (the largest marlin), white (the smallest) and striped. All can attain enormous weights of up to 300kg/660lb but the average size is 160–200kg/352–440lb. The deep pink flesh is high in fat and has a fairly firm texture with a disappointingly undistinguished flavour.
Habitat Marlin are found in warm seas throughout the world. Unusually for predators, they have no teeth, but use

their bill to stun schooling fish, and then to spear them.

Other names In French, marlin are *makaire*, in Italian *pesce lancia*, in Spanish *aguja*.

Buying Marlin are available in summer usually as loins and steaks. Try to buy cuts from smaller fish if possible. In the United States, marlin is almost always sold smoked rather than fresh.

Cooking Cook as swordfish, or cut into cubes and marinate to make ceviche.

Alternatives Swordfish, shark, and tuna can be used instead of marlin.

Sailfish *(Istiophorus* spp*)*

The sailfish resembles marlin, but looks even more spectacular. It has a beautiful streamlined body with a golden back spotted with blue, and a high, wavy blue dorsal fin which it unfurls like a sail to travel through the water at up to 96kph/60mph. Sailfish are tremendous fighters and will perform amazing aerial acrobatics when hooked.

Habitat As for marlin.

Other names Sailfish are *voilier* in French, *pesce vela* in Italian and *pez vela* in Spanish.

Buying Available in summer as loins and steaks. Buy cuts from smaller fish.

Cooking As for marlin.

Below: Marlin steaks

Orange roughy *(Hoplosthetus atlanticus)*

These ugly, but very delicious fish have orange bodies and fins and massive heads with conspicuous bony ridges and cavities. Although they are not large (the average weight is about 1.5kg/ 3–3½lb), they are always cleaned and filleted at sea. The pearly white flesh is similar in texture to that of cod, but has a sweet shellfish flavour.

Habitat For many years, orange roughy were believed to inhabit only Icelandic waters. In the 1970s, however, large numbers were found on the opposite side of the world in the deep waters around New Zealand and most of the world's stocks now come from there.

Other names In Australia roughy is sometimes known as sea perch. In French it is *hopostète orange*, in Italian *pesce specchio* (mirror fish); and in Spanish *reloj*.

Buying Orange roughy is available all year round, usually as fillets. If you are

Above: Orange roughy fillets

Above: Redfish

lucky enough to find fresh fish, you are in for a treat; most is frozen at sea.

Cooking Orange roughy holds together well when cooked, and its crab-like flavour marries well with other seafood. It can be used for soups and stews, and is good poached, pan-fried, roasted or steamed. It can also be dipped in batter or egg and breadcrumbs and fried.

Alternatives Cod, haddock or any firm white fish can be substituted.

Redfish/Ocean perch *(Sebastes marinus)*

These beautifully-coloured red fish were once the most important deep-sea fish, with vast catches being landed every year in northern fishing ports. As new varieties of fish have become widely available, however, their popularity has declined. Redfish can grow to about 5kg/11lb. The flesh is white and moist, with a sweet flavour.

Habitat Redfish inhabit the cold, deep waters of the Atlantic and Arctic Oceans. Related species *(Helicolenus spp)* are found in the Pacific.

Other names Redfish are known as ocean perch or Norway haddock. In French, they are *rascasse* (not to be confused with their relative, the scorpion fish); in Italian, *scorfano* (ditto); in Spanish, *gallineta nórdica*.

Buying Redfish are available all year round, sold whole or as steaks and fillets. A whole fish weighing 400–600g/ 14oz–1lb 6oz will feed one person; a 1–1.5kg/2¼–3½lb fish will feed two.

Cooking Redfish is suited to all cooking methods. It marries well with Mediterranean flavours and spices, and is very good baked in a creamy sauce.

Alternatives Hake or cod can be used instead of redfish.

Blackened Redfish

A favourite recipe from New Orleans is blackened redfish, a spicy Creole dish. Fillets of redfish are thickly coated on both sides with a mixture of dried herbs and spices – crushed peppercorns and coriander seeds, cayenne pepper, paprika, dried thyme and oregano – then seared on both sides in a very hot frying pan or griddle until the spice crust is blackened and charred and the fish is cooked. The contrast between the aromatic, crunchy crust and the tender white fish is delicious. However, this fierce cooking method produces plenty of smoke, so remember to open the kitchen window.

Above: Swordfish

Stuffed Swordfish Rolls

Swordfish steaks can be pounded lightly between two sheets of clear film and used to roll round a stuffing. Choose 1cm/½in thick steaks and pound them lightly using a meat mallet or rolling pin until they are only 5mm/¼in thick.

Make a stuffing using finely grated Parmesan cheese, breadcrumbs and chopped fresh herbs bound together with an egg. Roll the swordfish steaks around the stuffing and secure with wooden cocktail sticks.

Place the swordfish rolls in a shallow, heavy-based pan and pour over about 300ml/½ pint/1¼ cups well-flavoured tomato sauce. Bring gently to the boil, then reduce the heat and simmer gently for 30 minutes, turning once. Remove the swordfish rolls from the sauce and discard the cocktail sticks, then return to the sauce and serve hot.

Below: Swordfish steaks

Swordfish *(family Xiphiidae)*

Famous as both a culinary and game fish, swordfish differs from other billfish in having neither scales nor teeth. In all other respects, it is as dramatic and graceful to look at as it powers through the water with only the curve of its dorsal fin visible above the surface. Its long "sword" represents up to one-third of its total length and appears to be a powerful weapon, but no one is certain whether it is actually used to kill its prey, or merely to stun small fish. Swordfish can grow to an enormous size, sometimes weighing up to 600kg/1320lb. Their excellent white, meaty flesh is very low in fat and tends to dryness, so it needs careful cooking.

Habitat Swordfish are migratory fish which are widely distributed in warm, deep waters around the world. They occasionally migrate into northern European seas, but are more commonly found in the Mediterranean.

Frozen fish is also available, but is best avoided. Because swordfish is so meaty and substantial, 150–165g/5–5½oz will provide an ample portion for one person. Try to buy fairly thick steaks, as thinner ones are more apt to dry out during cooking.

Cooking It is essential not to let swordfish dry out during cooking, so baste it frequently with olive oil when grilling or barbecuing and serve with a drizzle of extra virgin olive oil or some herb butter. Swordfish makes excellent kebabs and can withstand a robust or spicy sauce. It is delicious marinated in a mixture of olive oil and lemon juice that has been flavoured with garlic and fresh herbs, then seared in a very hot ridged pan or chargrilled. Swordfish can also be braised with Mediterranean vegetables such as peppers, tomatoes and aubergines. Grilled or barbecued swordfish are particularly good served with a spicy, fresh tomato salsa made using chopped fresh coriander.

Other names In French, swordfish is *espadon*; in Italian it is *pesce spada*; in Spanish, *pez espada*.

Buying Fresh swordfish is available all year round, usually sold as steaks.

Alternatives Shark and tuna can be used instead of swordfish.

MISCELLANEOUS FISH

Right: Garfish

A few fish do not slot neatly into any obvious category. The only connection between the fish described in this chapter is that they are all exceptionally good to eat. They are a strange-looking collection, from the hideously ugly monkfish to the slimline but no more beauteous John Dory and the needle-like garfish with its unappealing phosphorescent green bones. Monkfish and John Dory are seldom sold whole, so there is an enormous amount of wastage, which sadly makes these gastronomically excellent fish extremely expensive to buy.

Garfish/Needlefish *(family Belonidae)*

There are more than fifty species of needlefish. Most inhabit tropical seas, but some, like the garfish, are found in cooler waters, and one species is found only in fresh water. Many people find the needle-like appearance of the garfish off-putting, despite (or perhaps because of) their vibrant silver and blue-green colouring and their long spear-like beaks.

Needlefish can grow to 2m/6½ft, but are more commonly up to 80cm/32in in length. Their bones are a phosphorescent green even when cooked (this coloration is completely harmless), and even their flesh has a greenish tinge, although this whitens on cooking. Despite these physical disadvantages, garfish are good to eat, with firm flesh from which the backbone can easily be removed, since you can hardly miss it.
Habitat Garfish inhabit the Atlantic Ocean and Mediterranean Sea, sometimes straying into fresh water. Other needlefish are found in the

tropics, the Black Sea and the Pacific Ocean, while the Atlantic is also home to the saury, another sub-species. When they are frightened or being chased by predators, needlefish sometimes leap out of the water and launch themselves through the air like dangerous missiles. It has been known for fishermen to be severely injured by their needle-sharp beaks.
Other names The French for garfish is *aiguille* or *orphie*, the Italian is *aguglia*, and the Spanish is *aguja*. Saury is also known as skipper, because of its habit of skipping over the water to escape from predators. Saury and needlefish are *balaou* in French; *costardello* in Italian and *paparda* in Spanish.
Buying Garfish are sold whole. If you do not want to serve it that way, ask the fishmonger to clean the fish and cut it into 5cm/2in chunks.
Cooking To cook a whole garfish, wash it thoroughly inside and out, rub the cavity with lemon juice, then curl the fish round and stick the pointed beak into the tail end so that it forms a ring. Brush with a marinade of olive oil, lemon juice, garlic and chopped parsley and grill or barbecue for about 15 minutes, basting frequently.

Chunks of garfish or saury can be coated in seasoned flour and pan-fried in butter and oil, or stewed with onions and tomatoes. They are gelatinous fish, so make excellent soups and stews or fish couscous.

John Dory *(family Zeidae)*

These fish were sacred to Zeus, hence the Latin name of *Zeus faber*. The olive-brown bodies of these fish are so slim that they look almost like upright flat fish. Dories have extremely ugly faces and spiny dorsal fins from which long filaments trail. Their most distinguishing feature is a large black spot ringed with yellow right in the middle of their bodies; this is said to be the thumbprint of St Peter. The story goes that the saint lifted a John Dory in the Sea of Galilee, leaving his thumb and finger prints on either side, and found in its mouth a gold coin, which he used to pay the unpopular tax collectors. This delightful fable is highly unlikely, since John Dory are not found in the Sea of Galilee, which is a freshwater lake. John Dory is also known as "St Peter's fish". Despite its unattractive appearance, John Dory is one of the most delicious of all fish, with firm, succulent white flesh which is on a par with turbot and Dover sole.
Habitat Dories are found in the Atlantic; those from American coastal waters are known as American dories *(Zenopsis ocellata)*, while fish from the eastern Atlantic, from Britain and Norway to Africa, and from the Mediterranean are European dories *(Zeus faber)*. Another species, from the southern hemisphere *(Zeus japonica)*, inhabits the Indo-Pacific oceans.
Other names The name John Dory is said to come from the French *jaune doré* (golden yellow), which describes

the golden sheen of very fresh dories. Another theory is that it comes from the Italian *janitore* (janitor). However, most countries celebrate the St Peter legend in describing the fish. The French call it *St Pierre*; the Italians *San Pietro*; the Spanish *pez de San Pedro*.

Buying Thanks to its large head, almost two-thirds of a dory's weight is wastage, which makes it a very expensive fish. Small dories weighing 1–2kg/2¼–4½lb are sold whole; a 1kg/2¼lb fish will feed two people. For fillets,

buy the largest fish you can afford, otherwise the fillets will be too thin. Allow 150–200g/5–7oz per serving.

Cooking Whole fish can be grilled, braised, baked, steamed or poached; boiled dory served with mayonnaise is a popular Venetian and Catalan dish. Its succulent flesh goes well with Mediterranean flavours such as tomatoes, fennel, red peppers, olives and saffron. Fillets can be cooked in the same way as sole, brill and turbot. They are superb served with a red wine, white wine or creamy sauce. Small fillets can be used in substantial fish soups such as bouillabaisse and *cacciucco*, or used in combination with other fish in a mixed grill or *panaché*.

Alternatives Brill, sole, halibut and turbot can be used instead of John Dory.

Bouillabaisse

One of the world's great classic dishes is the Provençal fish soup, bouillabaisse. More of a stew than a soup, this dish was originally cooked on the beach by fishermen, using those fish that had little market value, such as spiny scorpion fish. This fish is regarded as the most important ingredient in bouillabaisse. The soup can also contain monkfish, weaver fish, John Dory and other Mediterranean fish, plus small crabs and other shellfish, all cooked with tomatoes, potatoes and onions and flavoured with garlic, olive oil and saffron. Sometimes, the cooking liquid is served on its own as soup, accompanied by garlicky croûtons, with the fish served as a separate course. Nowadays, bouillabaisse is no longer an ad hoc fishermen's stew, but a hugely expensive treat served in the smartest restaurants.

Left: John Dory

Monkfish/Anglerfish (Lophius piscatorius)

This extraordinarily ugly fish has an enormous head equipped with a "rod and lure" to catch its food; hence its alternative name of anglerfish. It has a huge mouth fringed with lethally sharp teeth and a dangling "rod" (actually the first spine of the dorsal fin) on its nose. Its comparatively small body has brown, scaleless skin. On the fishmonger's slab, the only part of a monkfish you are likely to see is the tail, since the head is almost always removed because of its extreme ugliness, disproportionate weight and the fact that only the cheeks are worth eating. The tail is quite another matter; it is one of the finest of all fish, with a superb firm texture and a delicious sweetness, rather like lobster meat. In fact, some unscrupulous caterers have been known to pass off monkfish as lobster or scampi. The only bone the tail contains is the backbone, which makes it especially easy to prepare and pleasant to eat. Monkfish liver, if you can find it, is considered to be a great delicacy.

Habitat Monkfish are found in the Atlantic and Mediterranean. They lurk on the sea bottom dangling their "fishing rods" to lure passing fish. They are extremely predacious and will sometimes swim up to the surface to prey on small birds.

Varieties The best monkfish are Lophius piscatorius and the similar L. budegassa, which is highly prized in Spain.

American monkfish or goosefish (L. americanus) is considered inferior, while New Zealand monkfish (Kathetostoma giganteum) is truly a poor relation.

Other names Monkfish is also known as monk or angler. In French, it is lotte or baudroie, crapaud or diable de mer ("sea toad" or "devil"). In Italian, it is coda di rospo or rana pescatrice ("fishing frog"); in Spanish, rape.

Buying Monkfish is available all year, but is best in spring and summer before spawning. It is sold as whole tails, fillets or medallions. Generally speaking, the larger the tail,

Below: Monkfish

the better the quality; avoid thin, scraggy tails. For tails with the bone in, allow about 200g/7oz per person. A 1.5kg/3¼lb tail will serve four to six people. Ask the fishmonger to skin the tail and remove the membrane.

Cooking One of the best ways to cook a whole monkfish tail is to treat it like a leg of lamb; tie it up with string, stud with slivers of garlic and thyme or rosemary leaves, anoint with olive oil

and roast in a hot oven. This dish is known as gigot de mer. Monkfish can also be grilled, made into kebabs, pan-fried, poached and served cold with garlicky mayonnaise, or braised with Mediterranean vegetables or white wine, saffron and cream. It goes well with other seafood such as salmon, red mullet and shellfish, and is classically used in bouillabaisse and other hearty fish soups. Thin escalopes are delicious marinated in olive oil and lemon juice, then coated with flour and sautéed in butter.

Alternatives Nothing has quite the same nice firm texture as monkfish, but conger eel, John Dory, shark or cod can all be used instead.

Below: Monkfish cheeks, round nuggets of monkfish flesh, are sometimes available from specialist fishmongers.

Preparing monkfish tails

The tails are the best part of the monkfish. Because of their high water content, fillets should be cooked with very little liquid. They are easy to prepare.

1 Grasp the thick end of the tail firmly with one hand and peel off the skin with the other, working from the thick to the thin end.

2 Carefully pull off the thin, dark or pinkish membrane.

3 Fillet the tail by cutting through the flesh on either side of the backbone with a sharp knife (there are no small bones). The bone can be used to make stock.

Above: Monkfish tail can be filleted and then roasted like a leg of lamb in a hot oven with olive oil, herbs and garlic.

Opah (*Lampris regius*)

Variously called moonfish, sunfish or mariposa, this beautiful, slim, oval fish has a steel blue back shading into a rose pink belly, with silver spots all over its body. It has glorious red fins, jaws and tail, and, unusually, is the only member of its family. It is toothless and scaleless, and can grow to an enormous size. Some specimens weigh over 200kg/440lb and measure more than 2m/6½ft, though the average weight of those caught is about 20kg/44lb. The flesh is salmon pink, with a flavour similar to tuna.

Habitat Opah are found in warm waters throughout the world, but so far only solitary specimens have been caught, and little is known about them.

Other names In French, opah is *poisson lune*, in Italian, *lampride* or *pesce rè*; in Spanish, *luna real*.

Buying Should you be lucky enough to find opah on the fishmonger's slab, ask for it to be cut into steaks or escalopes.

Cooking Treat opah in the same way as salmon or tuna, taking great care not to overcook, and serve with a creamy sauce or mayonnaise.

Alternatives Tuna, shark or salmon.

FRESHWATER FISH

Nothing can beat the taste of a freshwater fish, caught, cleaned and cooked within a couple of hours of being pulled from the lake or river, especially if you have caught it yourself. The flesh of freshwater fish is fragile, so generally speaking, they are only really good to eat when they are absolutely fresh. Sadly, many of the world's rivers and lakes are so polluted that supplies of good, untainted fish are low, so many of the freshwater fish we buy are farmed. A major problem with all freshwater fish is that they often contain numerous small, very fine bones, which many people find off-putting. Apart from trout and zander, you will find few of the fish in this chapter on the fishmonger's slab; most are eaten by the anglers who catch them for sport. If you are lucky enough to be given a freshly caught fish, you will relish the experience.

Barbel (Barbus)

These "bearded" fish (the Latin name means "beard") live in fast-flowing rivers. They have brown backs, yellowish sides and white bellies. Barbel have rather tasteless flesh and are extremely bony, so they are not regarded as prime river fish. They are popular in the Loire and Burgundy regions of France, where they are typically poached or braised with a red wine sauce.

Cooking Barbel need strong flavours to enhance their intrinsic blandness. Small young fish can be grilled and served

Above: Carp rouge

with a well-seasoned butter; larger fish (weighing up to 1.75kg/4–4½lb) are best used in a stew, such as *matelote*.

Bream (Abramis brama)

The appearance of bream, with their flat oval greenish-brown bodies covered with gold scales, is more attractive than their taste. The bony flesh is soft and bland, and can sometimes taste muddy, since bream live in the silt near the bottom of pools and slow-flowing rivers. Despite this, bream was an extremely popular fish in the Middle Ages. It was caught in fishponds around the country and used in numerous recipes.

Cooking Bream is best used in braised dishes and stews. It should be soaked in acidulated water for several hours before being cooked to eliminate the taste of silt.

Carp (Cyprinus carpio)

Carp are members of the minnow family, which contains more than 1500 different species. They are among the hardiest of all fish and can live for hundreds of years. Although they can grow to over 35kg/77lb, most of the carp caught weigh only about 2kg/4½lb; anything larger than this and the keen angler is in seventh heaven. There are three main varieties of carp; the very scaly common carp; the scaleless leather carp, and the mirror carp,

Above: Bream

Right: Carp

Carp roe
This roe has a delicate texture and flavour and is much sought after in France, where it is poached and served in pastry cases or ramekins, or made into fritters, omelettes and soufflés. A classic dish is *tourte de laitances* (soft roe or milt), which combines puréed carp and pike with soft carp roes; the mixture is then baked in a puff pastry tart.

which has only a few large irregularly spaced scales that can easily be removed with a fingernail. All carp are handsome fish with compact, meaty flesh that varies in taste according to how the fish is cooked.

Originally natives of Asia, carp were highly prized by Chinese emperors as ornamental pets and as food; they frequently featured on festive banquets. Travellers along the Silk Routes brought them to Europe, where they proliferated in unpolluted fresh water and became a staple food of Eastern European Jews who lived far from the sea, but could cultivate carp in ponds. The tongues were regarded as a delicacy. Carp are still immensely popular in Chinese cuisine; the lips are considered the finest part and they command high prices in restaurants.
Habitat In their natural state, carp like living in muddy and polluted waters, which they seem to prefer to clean streams and lakes. Nowadays, they are extensively farmed

in clean ponds. In the wild, they are considered the most difficult of all freshwater fish to catch; despite being toothless, they are powerful fighters, and can demolish fishing tackle.
Other names In French, carp is *carpe*, in Italian and Spanish, *carpa*.
Buying Most commercially available carp are farmed and weigh 1–2kg/2¼–4½lb. A 2kg/4½lb fish will amply serve four. Look for a plump fish, preferably containing roe or milt, which are considered a delicacy. You may find live carp for sale; if so, ask the fishmonger to prepare the fish, gutting it and removing the bitter gall bladder from the base of the throat. If you buy a common carp, ask the supplier to scale it for you.
Preparing If you have to scale carp yourself, pour boiling water over the fish to loosen the scales before scraping them off.
Cooking Carp is a very versatile fish, which can be delicious if prepared with interesting flavourings. It can be stuffed with fish mousse or forcemeat and baked, and is also excellent braised,

opened out and grilled or deep-fried, or poached in a sweet-and-sour sauce. A traditional German or Polish Christmas Eve dish is carp cooked in beer or white wine. It marries well with Oriental flavours such as ginger, soy sauce and rice wine, and makes a good addition to fish stews and soups that have been well flavoured with plenty of tomatoes and garlic.

Carp can be cooked *au bleu*, as described in the chapter on Buying and Preparing Fish, or stewed with red wine and mushrooms to make a *meurette*. A classic dish is *carpe à la Juive*, a sweet-and-sour cold dish made with whole or thickly-sliced carp braised with onions, garlic, vinegar, raisins and almonds. When cooked, the whole fish (or the sliced reformed into the original shape), is left to go cold in the sauce, which solidifies into a flavoursome jelly.
Alternatives Catfish, perch and zander can be substituted for carp.

Catfish *(Ictalurus* spp*)*
These fish take their name from the long whiskery barbels which help them to locate their prey in the muddy waters where they live. There are dozens of species, ranging from tiny fish to gigantic specimens weighing several hundredweight. Catfish are extremely hardy and can live out of

Above:
Catfish

water for a considerable time. These fish are found all over the world, but the best fish for eating are the American species known as bullheads, which have firm, meaty, rather fatty white flesh and very few bones.

Habitat Catfish are bottom-living fish which feed on live and dead prey. They inhabit muddy waters throughout the world and are successfully farmed in America and Canada.

Other names In French, catfish is *silure*; in Italian *pesce gatto*; in Spanish *siluro*.

Buying Catfish is sold skinned and usually filleted. Its chunky flesh is filling, so 175g/6oz is ample for one person. Sniff the fish before you buy to make sure that it smells fresh and sweet. Avoid fillets from very large fish, which can be rather coarse.

Cooking The classic southern American cooking method for catfish is to coat it in cornmeal, deep-fry it and serve with tartare sauce. It can also be grilled or pan-fried in butter, baked, or cooked like eel, whose flesh it resembles. The tough skin must be removed before cooking. Catfish makes a good addition to fish soups and stews with hearty flavourings such as garlic and tomatoes, or Caribbean spices.

Alternatives Any trout or perch recipe is also suitable for catfish.

Char *(Salvelinus alpinus)*

These trout-like fish are members of the salmon family. They have attractive silvery-green sides dotted with pale spots, and rose-pink bellies. The white flesh is firm and succulent, with a delicate flavour. Sadly, these fish, which once inhabited cold lake waters in large numbers, are becoming increasingly rare in the wild. They can, however, be farmed successfully. The most common varieties are Arctic char, char, brook trout and lake trout. All can be distinguished from trout by their smaller scales and rounder bodies.

Habitat Arctic char are found in cold-water lakes in North America, Canada, Britain and Iceland. Other species inhabit the lakes of northern France and the Swiss Alps. Brook and lake trout (which are actually char) live in the

Potted Char

When char proliferated in the Lake District in England in the 18th and 19th centuries, potted char became a popular delicacy. It was often sold in white china pots that were decorated with painted fish.

1 To make potted char, flake some leftover cooked fish, removing all skin and bones.

2 Weigh the boned fish. Melt an equal quantity of butter in a saucepan. Flavour the butter with nutmeg or mace and salt and pepper. Pour the butter over the flaked fish.

3 Put the prepared fish into ramekins. Cover with clear film and chill until the mixture is firm.

4 Seal with a thin layer of clarified butter and cover again; it will keep in the fridge for a week. Salmon, trout, whitefish and grayling can be prepared in the same way.

lakes of North America; Dolly Varden is found from Western North America to the Asian coast.

Other names Char is *omble chevalier* in French, *salmerino* in Italian, and *salvelino* in Spanish.

Buying You may be lucky enough to find wild char in summer and early autumn. Farmed Arctic char from Iceland and America are available all year round. Small fish are sold whole; larger char may be cut into steaks.

Cooking Char can be cooked in the same ways as trout and salmon trout. It can be poached, baked, braised, fried, grilled or barbecued.

Grayling *(Thymallus arcticus)*

A relative of trout, grayling is an attractive silvery fish with a small mouth and a long, high dorsal fin spotted with gold. These small fish (rarely weighing more than 1.2kg/2½lb) have firm white flesh with a delicate trout-like flavour; they are said to smell of thyme when first caught, but their scent and flavour is fleeting, so they should be eaten within hours of being caught.

Habitat Grayling are found in lakes from Europe to North America and the northern coasts of Asia, but as these become more polluted, their numbers are declining.

Other names In France, grayling is called *ombre*; in Italy *temolo*; in Spain *salvelino* or *timalo*.

Cooking Grayling must be scaled before cooking. Pour boiling water over the fish and scrape off the scales with a blunt knife. These fish are excellent brushed with melted butter and grilled or pan-fried, preferably on the shore where they were caught. To enhance the faint aroma of thyme, put a few fresh thyme leaves inside the fish. Grayling can also be baked and potted like char.

Gudgeon *(Gobio gobio)*

Small fish with large heads and thick lips, gudgeon have delicious, delicate flesh. They live at the bottom of lakes and rivers all over Europe and freshly caught and crisply fried, gudgeon were once a common sight in cafés on riverbanks in France.

Other names Gudgeon are *goujon* in French, a name that has come to have a much wider application. Nowadays, deep-fried strips of any white fish are known as *goujons*.

Cooking Gudgeon must be gutted and wiped clean before cooking. Coat them in flour or very light batter and deep-fry until very crisp and golden. Sprinkle with salt and serve with lemon wedges.

Roach *(Rutilis rutilis)*

These members of the minnow family have greenish-grey skin and golden eyes. They can weigh as much as 1.75kg/4–4½lb. Their white flesh is firm and has quite a good delicate flavour. Their greenish roe (which turns red on cooking) is excellent to eat. Roach are not the easiest fish to eat, because they contain so many bones. Use tweezers to remove as many bones as possible before cooking.

Above: Roach

Habitat Roach inhabit sluggish waters in Europe and North America. Unusually for members of the minnow family, they are also sometimes found in brackish coastal waters.

Other names In French, roach is *gardon*, in Italian *triotto*, in Spanish *bermejuela*.

Cooking Small roach can be fried with other tiny fish to make a friture. If you can cope with the bones, larger fish can be grilled or pan-fried, or baked in white wine.

Pike-Perch/Zander *(Stizostedion lucioperca)*

Zander (sometimes spelt sander) look like a cross between perch and pike, but have a much more delicate and appealing flavour than the latter. They have greenish-grey backs with dark bands, and hard, spiny dorsal fins and gills. Zander can grow quite large, sometimes weighing up to about 5kg/11lb, and fillets from fish this size are delicious and meaty. American pike-perch are known as walleye. Zander can be farmed successfully, and are cooked in the same way as perch.

Perch *(Perca fluviatilis)*

These beautiful fish have greenish-gold skins and coral fins. Their humped backs have a spiky dorsal fin, which makes them difficult to handle. Perch are highly prized for their firm, delicate white flesh and are considered to be one of the finest freshwater fish. They grow slowly and can reach a weight of 3kg/6½lb, but the average weight is only about 500g/1¼lb.

Above: Zander

Habitat Perch are found in sluggish streams, ponds and lakes throughout Europe and North America, and as far north as Siberia.

Other names The American yellow perch is very similar to the common perch and is often simply called "perch". In French, perch is *perche*; in Italian *pesce persico* ("Persian fish"); in Spanish, *perca*.

Cooking Unless perch are scaled the moment they are caught, this is a near impossible task. The only solution is to plunge the fish into boiling acidulated water for a few moments, then peel off the entire skin. Small perch can be pan-fried or deep-fried in oil. Fillets can be pan-fried and served with a buttery sauce such as hollandaise, a herby béarnaise or *beurre blanc*. Larger fish can be baked, poached or grilled, or stuffed with seasoned breadcrumbs and braised in wine.

Pike *(Esox lucius)*

Described by Isaac Walton in *The Compleat Angler* as the tyrants of fresh water, pike are indeed fearsome creatures, with their elongated upturned noses and jaws equipped with hundreds of sharp teeth. Pike can grow to an enormous size, sometimes up to 1.5m/ 5ft. The larger the fish, the better the sport for anglers, but fish this size are not good to eat, as the flesh is dry and tough; the best size for eating is 1–2kg/ 2¼–4½lb. Pike have soft white flesh that is full of lethally sharp bones. Despite this, they are highly regarded in France. During the spawning season, pike roes can become toxic, so they should never be eaten.

In the Middle Ages, pike were highly prized in France and were cultivated in the fish ponds of the Louvre for the delectation of the king. Monks also farmed the fish to enjoy on meatless

Above: Pike are large, fearsome-looking freshwater fish.

days. The voracious appetites of these fish earned them the nickname *grands loups d'eau* ("great water wolves").

Habitat Pike lurk in the streams and ponds of Eastern Europe, Britain and France. They are solitary, aggressive predators who like nothing better than to eat a duckling or water rat. Their close relations, muskellunge and pickerel, are found in the United States and Canada. Fish from fast-flowing streams taste better than those that are fished from ponds.

Other names The large American pike, muskellunge (a corruption of the French for "long mask", *masque allongé*) is also known as musky. In France, pike is called *brochet* (pickerel is *brocheton*); in Italy, *luccio (luccio giovane)*; in Spanish *lucio (lucio joven)*.

Pike Quenelles

The most famous recipe involving pike is *quenelles de brochet,* featherlight oval fish dumplings poached in water or fish stock. To make enough for four people, you need 450g/1lb skinned pike fillets, 4 egg whites, 475ml/16fl oz/2 cups chilled double cream, salt, white pepper and nutmeg.

1 Purée the fish until smooth, adding the egg whites one at a time until completely amalgamated. Chill.

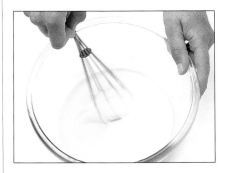

2 Whip the cream until stiff, then fold it into the fish mousse. Season and chill for at least an hour.

3 To cook, bring a pan of water or fish stock to a bare simmer. Shape the fish mousse into ovals using two tablespoons dipped in hot water and drop them into the trembling (not boiling) liquid, a few at a time.

4 Poach for about 10 minutes, until the quenelles are cooked through, but still creamy in the centre. Lift the cooked quenelles out of the water with a perforated spoon and drain on kitchen paper.

5 The quenelles are delicious served with a creamy sauce. Alternatively, cover them with a rich béchamel and bake *au gratin.*

Buying Pike are at their best in autumn and early winter. The best fish to buy are small whole fish weighing 1.2–1.7kg/2½–4½lb, which will feed four to six people. Large pike are sold cut into steaks; these can be tough.

Cooking Scale pike before cooking. Pour over a little boiling water – not too much, as the natural slime on the fish keeps it tender. Whole fish can be stuffed and baked or braised. Small pike are good cooked *au bleu,* or poached in a *court-bouillon* and served with *beurre blanc.* Pike is also traditionally cooked *à la Juive,* like carp. Sorrel, horseradish and similar sharp-flavoured ingredients make excellent accompaniments. Fillets and steaks are best marinated for several hours before cooking to offset any dryness. They can then be pan-fried, braised or baked with white wine and served with a creamy shellfish sauce. They can be made into mousses, terrines and fish cakes.

Shad *(Alosa)*

The largest member of the herring family, shad is a migratory fish which spawns in fresh water. It resembles a fat silvery-green herring and can weigh up to 5kg/11lb. The three main species of shad are the allis, thwaite and American. They resemble fat silvery-green herrings. Although the white flesh has a fine, rich flavour, it is full of fine bones, which make eating the fish rather difficult. The best part of the shad is the large-grained roe, which has the wonderfully crunchy texture of caviar and is said by some to have aphrodisiac qualities.

Habitat Allis and thwaite shad are caught in the Loire and Garonne rivers in France during the spawning season. American shad is found all along the US coast from Canada to Florida. In the 19th century, American shad were introduced to the Pacific and are now fished from Alaska to southern California. Pollution and overfishing for the highly-prized roe have decimated the numbers of shad in this region.

Other names In French, shad is *alose,* in Italian *alosa,* in Spanish *sábalo.*

Buying Shad are at their best in spring when they are full of roe. They are usually sold whole. A 1.5kg/3–3½lb fish will amply serve four. Ask the fishmonger to clean and scale the fish and persuade him, if you can, to bone it for you. Make sure you keep the roe, which is also good to eat.

Cooking Once the fish is cooked, make a series of incisions about 10cm/4in apart along its length and pull out as many bones as possible with your fingers. Whole shad can be stuffed with fish mousse (whiting is traditionally used), spinach or sorrel and baked, or poached and served on a bed of sorrel with *beurre blanc.* Fillets and steaks are good grilled, deep-fried or pan-fried and served with tomato sauce; check for small bones before serving. Shad roes are delicious briefly poached, then creamed with butter, cooked finely chopped shallots, cream, egg yolks and lemon juice. Serve them on toast as a rich starter or savoury, or use them to garnish a cooked shad.

Sturgeon (family Acipenseridae)

You have only to see a sturgeon to know that it is a "living fossil", part of a family of fish which were abundant in prehistoric times. The bodies of these long thin fish are armour-plated with several rows of bony scales which extend along their length. They have long, shovel-shaped snouts, with four whiskery barbels which are used for detecting food. Sturgeons are noted for their longevity, sometimes living more than 150 years, growing to a length of 9m/29½ft and weighing up to 1400kg/ 3080lb. There are about two dozen species of sturgeon, among them European, Beluga, Sevruga, Oscietra and the sterlet, which is found in Russian rivers. They have firm white flesh with a rich texture. Sturgeon can, however, be dry and somewhat indigestible. The fish is often sold smoked, but its real glory is its roe (caviar), the ultimate luxury food (see Dried and Salted Fish). In Russia, the bone marrow (vésiga) of the fish is dried and used in the classic recipe, coulibiac.

Habitat Sturgeon are migratory fish which live in the sea but swim into rivers to spawn. Once plentiful in European and American rivers, they are now found mainly in the rivers that feed the Black and Caspian Seas. Recently,

Below: Sturgeon steaks

Above: Brown and rainbow trout

they have been successfully farmed in France and California.

Other names In French, sturgeon is called *esturgeon*, in Italian it is *storione*, and in Spanish, *esturión*.

Buying Wild sturgeon is at its best in spring and early summer. Farmed fish is available all year round. It is sold as steaks or large cuts.

Cooking Sturgeon needs careful cooking to make it palatable, and should be marinated or barded with canned anchovy fillets to keep it moist. Its texture is similar to veal and it is often cooked in the same ways, as breaded escalopes or braised steaks. It can be poached in white wine (or, for a touch of luxury, champagne), or baked in a creamy sauce with onions. In Russia, sturgeon is traditionally poached with vegetables and served hot with tomato sauce, or cold with a piquant garnish of

mushrooms, langoustines, horseradish, lemon, gherkins and olives. It can also be home-smoked very successfully.

Tench (Tinca tinca)

This fat-bodied relative of the minnow has a coppery-green body covered with small scales and a thick coating of slime. Tench are hardy, fighting fish, which make great sport for anglers. They live in sluggish streams and have a tendency to taste muddy, but they make a good addition to a fish stew. They can also be baked or fried, and should be served with a robustly flavoured sauce to enliven the rather bland flesh. They must be scaled and thoroughly cleaned before cooking; scalding them with boiling water helps to remove the scales.

Trout *(family Salmonidae)*

The best-known of all freshwater fish, trout are popular with gourmets and fishermen alike. The two main species are brown trout *(salmo trutta)* and rainbow trout *(salmo gairdneri)*. Rainbow trout are probably the more familiar since they are extensively farmed and are available everywhere. They have silvery-green bodies with dark spots and a pinkish band along the sides. Wild fish have moist white flesh with a sweet flavour; farmed rainbow trout are often fed on a special diet to give the flesh a pink tinge, which is considered to be more appealing.

Brown trout come from cold mountain streams and lakes. They have coppery-brown skin dotted with red or orange and brown spots. Their flesh is a delicate pink and their flavour exquisite, but sadly they are seldom found in shops; to enjoy a fresh brown trout, you should befriend an angler.

Golden trout and coral trout are both farmed hybrid trout, with beautiful, vibrantly coloured skin. Their pinkish flesh is more like that of rainbow trout and tastes very similar.

Habitat Rainbow trout are native to America, but have been introduced to many other parts of the world. Brown trout are natives of Europe; they too have been introduced to America. Golden trout are not found naturally in the wild, but are increasingly farmed for their attractive coloration.

Other names In French, trout is *truite*, in Italian *trota*; in Spanish *trucha*.

Buying Trout are available all year round, usually farmed. Unlike many other fish, they are quite robust and freeze well, so frozen trout are perfectly acceptable. For fresh trout, look for a good coating of slime, bright clear eyes and red gills. Trout are almost always sold whole with the head on. They are very inexpensive, and you should allow one fish per person, unless they are very large.

Cooking Trout are arguably the most versatile of all fish and can be cooked in myriad ways. They are easy to eat, as the flesh falls away from the bone once cooked. The best way to cook a freshly-caught trout is *à la meunière*; dust it with flour, fry in clarified butter until golden brown, and season with lemon juice and parsley. Live trout can be cooked *au bleu*. Other cooking methods include poaching in *court-bouillon*, baking, braising, frying, grilling and barbecuing. Trout marry well with many flavours, such as bacon, onions, garlic, mushrooms and truffles. In Normandy, they are often

Left: Coral trout

baked *en papillote* with apples, cider and cream. They are also excellent for home-smoking and make delicious mousses and terrines. A classic, if clichéd, recipe is trout with almonds (hazelnuts make good alternatives). If you find roes in your trout, these can be puréed, mixed with seasoned breadcrumbs and used as a stuffing for the fish.

Alternatives Almost any freshwater fish can be used instead of trout.

Whitefish *(family Salmonidae)*

Members of the salmon family, whitefish are silvery white in colour. They resemble trout, but have larger scales and smaller mouths. White fish live in cold, clear lochs and lakes in northern Europe and America. In Britain they are sometimes called vendace or powan. They have a pleasant texture and flavour, somewhere between trout and grayling, but not as fine as either.

Left: Golden trout are spectacular in appearance, with iridescent golden skin.

DRIED AND SALTED FISH

Since prehistoric times, the dehydrating effects of sun and wind have been used as a means of preserving fish almost indefinitely. Even today, in remote communities, long ropes strung with split and salted fish hung out to dry like washing are a common sight. Any fish can be dried in this way; before the days of frozen fish, fishermen would salt and dry whatever they had caught in their nets – cod, haddock, herring, mackerel and even freshwater fish such as eel, pike, salmon and sturgeon.

Dried/Salt cod and Stockfish

The most common commercially available dried fish is cod and its relatives (haddock, ling and pollack). When dried, these look – and feel – like old shoe leather, but once reconstituted in water, the flesh softens and tastes delicious when cooked. Depending on its country of origin, dried cod is known as *baccalà* (Italy), *bacalhau* (Portugal) and stockfish (Scandinavia, northern Europe, the Caribbean and Africa). Stock fish differs from other types of dried cod in that it is not salted before being dried. Whatever the type, dried cod must be soaked for many hours in fresh, cold water – sometimes for up to a couple of weeks – before it becomes palatable. Stockfish needs to be beaten with a rolling pin to tenderize it, and you may find you need a saw to cut it.

Above: Bombay duck

The world is divided between those who believe that the result is worth all this effort and those who detest salt cod in all its forms. The Portuguese boast that they have a different recipe for every day of the year. The Scandinavians and the northern Italians love salt cod, too, while the French pound it into a rich creamy mousse, *brandade de morue*, with lashings of olive oil and garlic.

Buying Depending on where you buy it, dried and salt cod may be split down the backbone or sold whole. Make sure you buy the best quality fish, or no

Below: Salt cod

amount of soaking will restore its original texture. Thick middle cuts are better than end cuts. Salt cod will keep for months if stored in a dry place.

Preparing Salt cod needs less soaking than stockfish, but it still needs to be left to soften in a bowl of cold water for at least 24 hours. The best way to reconstitute it is to leave the tap trickling into the bowl; if this is not practical, change the water every 8–12 hours. Taste the fish before cooking to check that it is not excessively salty; if it is, continue to soak it.

Cooking Dried and salt cod can be poached or baked. Never cook it in boiling water, as it tends to toughen. It is a classic ingredient of Provençal *allioli*, a salad consisting of vegetables and hard-boiled eggs served with garlic mayonnaise. Olive oil complements it well. In Spain and Portugal, salt cod is often cooked with tomatoes, peppers, olives, onions and garlic. It marries well with potatoes and split peas, in a stew or on top of a mound of creamy mash or pease pudding. It makes wonderful fish cakes, fritters and mousses.

Bombay duck

Quite why this dried form of a small transparent fish from the Indian sub-continent should be called Bombay duck, no one knows for sure; it is

Shark's fin

Dried shark's fin is highly prized in China, where it is served at banquets, either braised or as the central ingredient in an extremely expensive soup. The fins from the many species of sharks that inhabit the Indo-Pacific oceans are sun-dried and preserved in lime. In its dried state, shark's fin looks like a very bushy beard, but after long soaking it reconstitutes into a gelatinous, viscous mass with a texture resembling calf's foot jelly. It is highly nutritious and is eaten as a tonic.

SALTED FISH ROE

The best-known and most expensive salted fish roe is caviar, the eggs of the sturgeon. Other salted roes include grey mullet, cod, lumpfish and salmon. In Sweden, bleak roe is compressed into a form of caviar paste called *løjrom* or *kaviar*, which has a pretty orangey-pink colour. It tastes rather sweet, and is definitely an acquired taste.

Caviar

Made from sturgeon roe lightly cured with salt and borax, caviar is the most expensive luxury food in the world. It has a unique texture, the tiny eggs bursting on the roof of the mouth to release a salty liquid with an elusive, incomparable flavour. The three main types of caviar take their names from the species of sturgeon from which the eggs come. The rarest and most expensive is beluga, which comes from the largest fish; one beluga can contain over 50kg/110lb of roe. The dark grey eggs are quite large

Above: Mojama

Mojama

Popular in Spain, Sicily and other countries with an Arabic influence, *mojama*, *mosciame* or *missama* is made from fillets of tuna that are salted, then dried in the sun for about three weeks. It is eaten as a nibble with a glass of chilled fino sherry, or served on slices of baguette that have been rubbed generously with garlic and drizzled with olive oil.

Above: Shark's fin

possibly a corruption of the Bombay name for the fish, *bommaloe macchli*. As soon as the fish is caught, it is filleted and hung on cane frames to dry. Bombay duck looks and tastes vaguely like pork scratchings. It is served as an appetizer or used as a garnish for curries and rice dishes. Uncooked Bombay duck has an unpleasantly pungent smell which fades a little when it is grilled, but is intensified when it is deep-fried. When grilling Bombay duck, keep the heat low. It is ready when it is crisp and curls at the edges. When cold, serve with drinks or crumble over curries or rice.

Below, clockwise from bottom left: sevruga, oscietra and beluga caviar

and well separated. Oscietra is golden brown, with smaller grains and an oily texture, which many prefer to beluga. sevruga is the cheapest caviar. It comes from the smallest and most prolific fish and has small pale greenish-grey grains with a markedly salty flavour. Arguably the best caviar of all comes from Iran; the finest is marketed as "Imperial caviar" and each tin contains only the eggs from a single fish. The best caviar is "harvested" from fish that are just about to spawn; the eggs are very pale and full of flavour.

Each type of caviar is graded. The finest, malassol, is slightly salted. Second grade caviar is saltier and may be made from a mixture of roes. Inferior quality sevruga roe is pressed into a solid mass (pressed caviar), which squashes the eggs. It has a strong, salty taste and can be oily. It is fine for cooking, however, and has the advantage of being cheaper. The best caviar is always fresh; pasteurization will ensure that it keeps longer, but the quality will be compromised.

Despite its high price, caviar is so sought-after that the world's population of sturgeon is endangered almost to the point of extinction, due to over-fishing, poaching and pollution. Sturgeon were once common in European rivers, but are now found almost exclusively in the Caspian Sea. Recently, however, the fish have been farmed successfully in France, so there may be some hope for the future of caviar.

Buying Never buy caviar that seems suspiciously cheap; it may not have been cured properly, or may have been made with damaged eggs. There is a huge illicit trade in second-rate caviar, which can taste unacceptably oily or salty. At worst, it might even poison you. You get what you pay for, so buy the best you can afford from a reputable dealer. Caviar should be kept in the fridge at 0–3°C/32–37°F; any warmer and it will become too oily. Once you have opened a can or jar of caviar, eat the contents within a week.

Above: Black and red lumpfish roe

Serving Caviar should be served chilled, preferably on a bed of crushed ice. Never serve or eat it with a silver spoon, as this will react with the caviar and give it a metallic taste. A proper caviar spoon is made of bone, but a plastic spoon would do at a pinch. Traditionally, caviar is served with *blinis* and soured cream. Chopped hard-boiled egg and onions make it go further. It is also delicious served with

toast and unsalted butter. Some people believe that a squeeze of lemon enhances the flavour; others that it spoils the taste. Allow about 25g/1oz caviar per person as a first course. Or use a few grains to garnish seafood or egg dishes.

Above: Grey mullet roe or bottarga

Right: Trout caviar

Far right: Salmon caviar, which is also known as keta.

Lumpfish roe

Sometimes known as "mock" or Danish caviar, this is the roe of the arctic lumpfish, which is as unpleasant as its name. The tiny eggs are dyed black or orange-red and look pretty as a garnish for canapés. They can be eaten with soured cream and blinis, but bear no resemblance to real caviar. Lumpfish roe is sold in glass jars.

Grey mullet roe/Bottarga/Tarama

Dried grey mullet roe is regarded as a great delicacy and is very nutritious. The orange roe is salted, then dried and pressed. It is usually packed in a sausage shape inside a thin skin, which should be removed before the roe is used. Wrapped in clear film, it will keep for several months. Grey mullet roe is the traditional ingredient of taramasalata, although smoked cod's roe is often used instead. In Mediterranean countries it is also known as bottarga or *poutargue.*

Salmon caviar/Keta

This is made from vibrant orange-pink salmon roe. The eggs are much larger than sturgeon caviar and have a pleasant, mild flavour and an excellent texture. They make a very attractive garnish for fish pâtés and mousses, or can be eaten like caviar with soured cream and blinis. A good squeeze of lemon enhances the flavour. The name *keta* comes from the Russian for chum salmon. Salmon caviar is sold in jars. Trout caviar is also available.

PICKLED FISH

Pickling in vinegar or brine is another effective way of preserving fish. It is particularly well suited to oily fish such as herrings and eels.

Baltic/Bismarck herring

The herrings are split like kippers and marinated in white wine vinegar and spices. The fillets are layered with onion rings and carrot rounds for 24 hours. These are delicious with soured cream.

Maatjes herring

Fat young female herrings (the name means "maiden" or "virgin" in Dutch) are lightly cured in salt, sugar, spices and saltpetre, which turns the flesh

Below: Maatjes herring

Above: Baltic or bismarck herring

brownish-pink. In Holland and Belgium they are eaten with chopped raw onion. The Scandinavian equivalent is *matjes*. These have a stronger flavour and are generally eaten with soured cream and chopped hard-boiled egg.

Pickled herring

Herring fillets are marinated in vinegar and spices, then coated in a soured cream sauce.

Soused herring and Bratheringe

These marinated herrings are simple to prepare at home. In the German version, *bratheringe*, herring fillets are lightly floured and fried until golden, then steeped in a boiled marinade of vinegar, pickling spice and herbs. Soused herring are not fried before being marinated.

Below: Pickled herring

Rollmop Herrings

Like *ceviche*, rollmops are not cooked by heat, but by the action of vinegar. For four servings, halve 8 herring fillets lengthways and soak them for several hours in heavily-salted water. Make a marinade by mixing about 600ml/ 1 pint/2½ cups vinegar with 2 bay leaves, 2.5ml/½ tsp coarsely crushed white peppercorns, 15ml/ 1 tbsp pickling spice and 1 sliced sweet onion in a saucepan. Bring to the boil, then leave until cold. Drain and dry the herring fillets. Slice a second sweet onion finely. Roll each herring fillet around a little sliced onion and some of the peppercorns and spices. Secure with a toothpick and pack tightly into a preserving jar. Pour over the marinade and leave for at least five days before eating.

Below: Rollmop herrings

Rollmops

These consist of herring fillets rolled up, skin side out, around whole peppercorns and pickling spice, and secured with wooden cocktail sticks. The rolls are marinated in white wine vinegar with onion slices and, sometimes, gherkins. Serve rollmops with rye bread and butter, or a cucumber salad dressed with a soured cream and dill sauce.

Gravad lax/Gravlax

A wonderfully succulent Swedish speciality, *gravad lax* has achieved great popularity. It is fresh raw salmon fillet cured with dill, sugar, salt and coarse peppercorns. *Gravad lax* is widely available, often packed with a sachet of dill-flavoured mustard sauce, which makes the perfect accompaniment.

Jellied eels

Market stalls in Britain selling this traditional Cockney dish are becoming increasingly rare, but jellied eels are available frozen and in cans. Jellied eels are made by boiling pieces of eel in a

Below: Gravad lax

Below: Jellied eels

marinade of white wine vinegar and herbs, then leaving them in the liquid with masses of chopped parsley until the mixture sets to a light jelly. Serve with thick slices of bread and butter.

Home-cured Gravad Lax

Although almost every supermarket sells ready-cured *gravad lax*, it is very easy to prepare at home. For eight people, you will need 1–1.2kg/2¼–2½lb absolutely fresh middle-cut salmon, boned and cut lengthways into two fillets. For the curing mix, mix together 30ml/ 2 tbsp coarse sea salt, 30ml/2 tbsp caster sugar, 15–30ml/1–2 tbsp coarsely crushed peppercorns (black or white) and a good handful of fresh dill, chopped. Lay one salmon fillet skin-side down in a non-metallic dish. Cover with a generous layer of the curing mix. Lay the second fillet on top, skin-side up, and sprinkle on the remaining curing mix. Cover with clear film. Place a wooden board slightly larger than the fish on top of the salmon and weight down with heavy cans or weights. Leave in the fridge for at least 72 hours, turning the salmon every 12 hours and basting it with the juices that have oozed out. To serve, slice the *gravad lax* on the diagonal, a little thicker than you would for smoked salmon. Serve with a sweet mustard and dill sauce.

CANNED FISH

This is a very useful store-cupboard ingredient. While it never has the subtle texture and flavour of fresh fish, canned fish can be excellent in its own right and is invaluable for salads and sandwiches.

Anchovies

Fillets of this fish are canned in oil (olive oil is best) in small oblong cans or bottled in jars. The salty fillets are a staple ingredient of *salade niçoise* and *tapenade* (olive and anchovy paste), and are used as a topping for pizzas and *crostini*. They can be mashed into butter as a topping for grilled fish, or chopped and mixed into tomato sauces. Anchovies enhance the flavour of many non-fish dishes (roast lamb, for example) without making them taste fishy. Once opened, anchovies perish quickly, so try to use the whole can or jar at once. Any leftovers should be submerged in oil and kept for only a day or two. As an alternative to canned anchovies, try salted anchovies, which are packed in barrels with masses of salt and cured for several months. Rinse well before using.

Pilchards

These fish are large, older sardines. They lack the subtle flavour of their younger siblings, so are usually canned in tomato sauce.

Salmon

Canned salmon is quite different in flavour and texture from fresh fish, but is useful to have in the store cupboard. It is richer in calcium than fresh salmon, because

the bones are softened during the canning process and can easily be eaten. Canned salmon was once the mainstay of sandwiches, salads, fish cakes and fish pies, but it has been overshadowed by inexpensive farmed fresh salmon. Canned salmon is available in several grades, from the cheapest pink chum salmon to the best-quality wild red Alaskan fish, which has a better flavour and texture. Canned salmon is good for making mousses, soufflés and fish cakes.

Sardines

These were the first fish to be canned; in 1834, a canning factory opened in Brittany to process the sardines that abounded on the Breton coast. For years, tiny Breton sardines were the best, but these fish have all but disappeared and most sardines canned in France now come from North Africa. Large numbers of sardines are also canned in Spain and Portugal. The finest sardines are fried in olive oil before canning, a time-consuming process that makes them expensive. Most sardines are beheaded and gutted before being packed raw, complete with backbones, in groundnut or olive oil. Inferior or damaged fish are packed in tomato or mustard sauce. Sardines in

Above: Canned tuna

Above: Canned anchovies

Left: Sardines in olive oil, which were the first fish to be canned.

olive oil are the best; the more expensive varieties are left to mature for at least a year before being sold to soften the bones and mature the flavour. The best way to enjoy canned sardines is to serve them whole on hot toast. They can also be mashed with lemon juice and cayenne pepper to make a pâté, stuffed into hard-boiled eggs or made into sandwiches.

Tuna

In recent years, canned tuna has received a bad press because dolphins were often caught in the tuna nets and slaughtered unnecessarily. Nowadays, tuna canners have become more ecologically aware and most tuna is line-caught. The best canned tuna is the pale albacore, which is usually canned in one solid piece. Cheaper varieties such as skipjack and yellowfin are often sold as chunks or flaky broken pieces. Tuna comes packed in olive oil (the best), vegetable oil or brine, which is healthier and lighter.

Canned tuna is a versatile ingredient that can be served with pasta, used in sandwiches and salads, made into a pâté or fish loaf. It is used in the classic Italian dish *vitello tonnato,* which comprises loin of veal coated in a thick tuna-flavoured mayonnaise.

SMOKED FISH

Another ancient and traditional way of preserving fish is smoking. Today it is used less for preserving and more for imparting a unique flavour. There are two methods of smoking fish, cold and hot smoking, which give very different results. For both methods, the fish must first be salted in dry salt or brine. They are then smoked over different types of wood, which impart its distinctive flavour to the fish. Every smokery produces fish with a different texture and taste; it is a matter of individual choice which appeals to you.

COLD-SMOKED FISH

A high degree of skill is required when cold smoking to get the flavour and texture just right. The process is done at a temperature of about 30–35°C/86–95°F, which cures but does not cook the fish. Some cold-smoked fish such as smoked salmon, halibut and trout are eaten raw; others such as kippers and haddock are usually cooked, although they can be marinated and eaten just as they are.

Smoked salmon

The best-loved of all smoked fish, smoked salmon is made by brining the fish, then dry curing it in sugar with flavourings such as molasses or whisky, and smoking it over wood chips (usually oak). Different wood chips give different flavours; some Scottish and Irish salmon is smoked over a fire made from old whisky barrels, which impart the flavour of the spirit. Depending on the strength of the cure, the type of wood used and the smoking time, smoked

Below: Smoked halibut

Above: Smoked salmon

salmon can vary in colour from very pale pink to deep brownish-red. The best smoked salmon has a fairly mild flavour and a moist, succulent texture.

Buying Smoked salmon is usually sold ready-sliced, with the slices separated by sheets of transparent paper. Whole sides are sliced and the slices are reassembled to restore the original shape of the fillet. Avoid buying sliced fish that is not layered with paper, as the slices stick together. The thinner the salmon is sliced the better; thickly-sliced fish can be coarse. Whole sides are sometimes sold unsliced; these are cheaper, but you need an extremely sharp flexible knife and a degree of skill to slice the fish yourself. The most expensive smoked salmon is made from wild fish, but good-quality farmed fish give excellent results, and it can be difficult to distinguish between the two.

Freshly-sliced smoked salmon is best, but vacuum packs are better value and perfectly acceptable when purchased from a reliable supplier. Frozen smoked salmon is also available and can be used at a pinch. Smoked salmon trimmings are much cheaper than slices and are perfect for mousses, pâtés and omelettes. In Jewish delicatessens, you will find *lox*, a heavily-cured salmon with a deep reddish-gold colour.

Serving Top-quality smoked salmon should be eaten just as it is, served with thinly sliced brown bread and butter. Cheaper salmon can be served in traditional Jewish style, with cream cheese as a topping for bagels (add some thin rings of raw onion, if you like), or in sandwiches. Smoked salmon makes a delicious salad. Scraps can be stirred into omelettes, quiches or flans, mixed into pasta, puréed to make mousses, or mashed into hard-boiled egg yolks and piled back into the whites. If you are slicing smoked salmon yourself, slice thinly across the grain, working from head to tail. You will need a very sharp, flexible knife with a long blade.

Cold-smoked trout

A cheaper alternative to smoked salmon is cold-smoked trout, which looks like salmon, but has a more delicate flavour. It can be eaten in the same way as smoked salmon, with thinly sliced brown bread and butter.

Smoked halibut

Sold thinly sliced like smoked salmon, smoked halibut has translucent white flesh and a very delicate flavour. It makes an excellent addition to a plate of assorted smoked fish, or can be used like smoked haddock. The flavour can be enhanced with a mild, creamy horseradish sauce.

Above: Finnan haddock

Above: Smoked haddock fillets

Smoked Sturgeon

This smoked fish has pale pinkish flesh with a rich flavour and a succulent texture. Like smoked salmon, it should be thinly sliced across the grain. As it is a luxury fish, it should be treated like the very best smoked salmon and served in the same way. Eat it with thinly-sliced brown bread and butter.

Below: Smoked sturgeon

Smoked haddock

There are various forms of smoked haddock, from fluorescent dyed yellow fillets to pale naturally cured fillets and finnan haddock or "haddie", which are split and look like pale golden kippers. It is now known that the artificial dyes used to colour smoked haddock can be carcinogenic; dyed fillets are also often artificially flavoured with chemicals which simulate the effect of smoking, so avoid these and enjoy natural pale beige fillets in preference.

Finnan haddock or "haddie"

These distinctively pale, whole split haddock (with the bone left in) are named after the Scottish village of Findon where the special smoking process originated. The process gives the fish a beautiful pale corn colour and a subtle smoked flavour. Finnan haddock can be used in any smoked haddock recipe, but must be boned and skinned after cooking. They are delicious served topped with a poached egg.

Glasgow pales

Similar to finnan haddock, Glasgow pales are lightly brined and smoked, resulting in a very delicate flavour.

Buying If possible, avoid buying dyed smoked haddock whose only dubious merit is that it adds colour to fish pies and similar dishes. Undyed smoked fillets are fine for such dishes, but for plain grilled or poached haddock, you cannot beat finnan haddock.

Cooking Smoked haddock is succulent and delicious. It is usually eaten hot, but fillets can be thinly sliced and marinated (a splash of whisky works wonders) and eaten raw as a starter. Smoked haddock can be grilled like kippers or poached in milk or water. Serve it with butter or topped with a poached egg, or *à la florentine* on a bed of creamed spinach. A classic Scottish dish is ham 'n' haddie: in which finnan haddock is fried in ham fat and topped with slices of fried ham.

Smoked haddock is used in another Scottish dish, cullen skink, a substantial chowder. It makes excellent mousse or pâté, and also features in kedgeree and omelette Arnold Bennett, a sumptuous omelette oozing with cheese, cream and smoked haddock.

Smoked Herrings

Kippers

These are made by briefly brining split herrings, then hanging them up in pairs and smoking them over oak fires for 4–18 hours. Dye is often added to the brine, resulting in deep reddish-brown kippers, but the best (notably Manx and Loch Fyne kippers) are undyed. Kippers can be unpopular because they have so many bones, but these are easy to deal with once you know how.

Buying Look for the plumpest kippers you can find; lean kippers can be dry. As a rule of thumb, the darker the fish, the poorer the quality. Always buy undyed kippers if possible. Frozen boil-in-the bag kipper fillets are convenient,

Left: Kippers

boneless and odour-free, but they have a flabby texture and insipid taste, and are really hardly worth eating.

Cooking Many people are nervous about cooking kippers because of the smell. To avoid any unpleasant odour, put them head-down into a tall jug, pour over boiling water and leave to stand for 10 minutes, by which time the kippers will be cooked. If you serve kippers often, it is better to keep a jug especially for cooking them. Kippers can also be microwaved and are good grilled (skin-side up) or shallow fried in butter. They make a delicious breakfast dish topped with a poached egg. Poached kippers make excellent mousse and pâté. Raw kippers can be marinated and served as a starter.

Bloaters

Herrings that are left ungutted before being briefly salted, then smoked for 12 hours are called bloaters. The guts impart a slightly gamey flavour and the enzymes they contain cause the herring

Below: Bloaters

Boning cooked kippers

1 Lay the kipper on a plate, skin-side up. Run a knife point around the edge to lift up the skin.

2 Run the knife point down the backbone and eat the flesh that lies on top of the fine bones.

to become bloated during smoking. Because they are not gutted, bloaters do not keep as well as other smoked herring and should be eaten within a few days. Always gut them before serving. Despite their unattractive name, they are quite pleasing to look at, with silvery skin and moist flesh.

Other varieties *Harengs saurs* are a speciality of Boulogne; they are even more bloated than English bloaters. The most bloated of all are the Swedish *surströmming*. Like *harengs saurs,* they are traditionally eaten with potatoes.

Cooking Bloaters can be eaten as they are in salads and sandwiches. They can also be mashed into a paste with lemon juice and cayenne pepper or grilled and served with butter. To skin bloaters, pour over boiling water and leave for 2 minutes, then peel off the skin.

Above: Smoked eel fillets

HOT-SMOKED FISH

Fish that are cured or hot-smoked at a temperature of 80–85°C/176–185°F, which simultaneously cooks and cures them, need no further cooking. Trout, mackerel, eel and herrings can all be hot-smoked. Recently it has become fashionable to hot-smoke salmon, producing a very different flavour and texture from that of salmon that has been cold-smoked.

Arbroath smokies

These hot-smoked haddock have been beheaded and gutted but left whole. They have deep golden skin and soft pale gold flesh with a more delicate

Below: Smoked eel

flavour than cold-smoked haddock. In their native Scotland, they are a favourite breakfast or supper dish. Smokies are sold whole, so ask the fishmonger to split them open for you. Grill gently and serve with plenty of butter. When mashed with butter and lemon juice, Arbroath smokies make a delicious pâté.

Below: Arbroath smokies are always sold in pairs, tied with string.

Smoked eel

This fish has a very rich, dense texture and can only be eaten in small quantities. The skin, which is easily removed, is black and shiny and the flesh has a pinkish tinge. The eel can be served on its own as an hors d'oeuvre, with horseradish or mustard sauce to cut the richness, or made into a salad or pâté. It is particularly delicious served on a bed of celeriac *rémoulade* (grated celeriac in a mustard-flavoured mayonnaise). Smoked eel also makes a good addition to a platter of mixed smoked fish.

When buying smoked eel, check that the skin is shiny and has not dried out. For an ample serving for one, you will need about 90g/3½oz.

Brisling, Sild and Sprats

Not to everyone's taste, these small, hot-smoked herring with rich oily flesh are usually skinned and filleted and served cold as a starter with brown bread and butter. They can also be brushed with melted butter and lightly grilled, then served hot with toast.

Below: Hot-smoked sprats

Above: Smoked trout fillets

birch with the addition of a little peat for a smokier flavour. Smoked trout is usually sold as skinned fillets, but you may occasionally find them whole, with the head on. Skin them like smoked mackerel. Smoked trout is delicious served on its own with dill or horseradish sauce. It can be made into mousses or pâté and is also good in salads, omelettes and flans. Allow one fillet per person as a starter; two as a main course.

Buckling

These are large, fat ungutted herrings with a rich flavour. They are best eaten cold with bread and butter, but can be mashed into a paste or grilled and served with scrambled eggs.

Smoked mackerel

This has a rich flavour and a succulent velvety-smooth texture. The fillets are sold loose or pre-packed. They are sometimes coated in a thick layer of crushed peppercorns. Smoked mackerel can be eaten cold in a salad, or with horseradish sauce and lemon. It makes an excellent pâté and can be flaked and added to an omelette or quiche. Try it instead of smoked haddock in a kedgeree. Allow one fillet

Above: Buckling

per person. To skin smoked mackerel, lay the fish on a board, skin-side up. Starting at the tail end, peel back the skin towards the head. Pull away any fins together with their bones.

Smoked trout

Among the finest of all hot-smoked fish, trout should be plump and moist, with a beautiful golden-pink colour. The flesh has a delicate flavour and is less rich than smoked herring or mackerel. The best smoked trout is first brined, then gutted and smoked over

Below: Smoked sea trout

Above: Smoked mackerel fillets

Below: Smoked mackerel

FISH SAUCES AND PASTES

For centuries, man has produced fish sauces made by fermenting whole fish or various parts, including the entrails, into a savoury, salty liquid to flavour and enhance fish dishes. The Romans' favourite condiment was *garum*, a pungent, evil-smelling sauce obtained by soaking pieces of oily fish and their guts in brine flavoured with herbs. Similar sauces exist today, notably in the Far East. The area around Nice also boasts *pissalat*, a sauce made from fermented anchovies. Don't be confused by the term "sauce"; these are flavourings or condiments, not to be served on their own.

Anchovy essence

Salted anchovies are processed into a thick, rich pinkish-brown sauce with an intensely salty flavour. A few drops will enhance the flavour of almost any savoury dish, but anchovy essence must be used sparingly, or it will overpower the other ingredients.

Nam pla/Thai fish sauce

Almost unheard of in the West a few years ago, *nam pla* is now an essential ingredient in every adventurous cook's store cupboard. It is a staple ingredient in all Far Eastern cooking; in Vietnam, it is called *nuoc cham*. The pungent, salty brown liquid is

Right, from left: Nam pla, Worcestershire sauce and anchovy essence

produced by packing small fish such as anchovies in brine in barrels and leaving them to ferment in the hot sun for several months. Curiously, the resulting sauce does not taste of fish; it is more like a very intense soy sauce. It can be added to any savoury dishes, or mixed with flavourings such as garlic, lime juice and chilli to make a dipping sauce, or can be used to add flavour to salad dressings. The colour of *nam pla* should be a clear amber; if it is dark brown it will taste too fishy.

Above: Shrimp paste

Shrimp paste

A speciality of Malaysia and Indonesia, shrimp paste is made from salted, fermented shrimps. This powerful smelling paste, called *blachan*, *terasi* or *belacan*, is sold in blocks and is mixed with other ingredients to make a flavouring for stir-fries, soups and other savoury dishes.

Worcestershire sauce

Anyone who has tasted this spicy sauce may be surprised to learn that it contains anchovies. Originally produced in India, the precise ingredients of Worcestershire sauce remain a closely-guarded secret, but they include malt and spirit vinegar, molasses, tamarind, garlic, onions and spices as well as anchovies.

Worcestershire sauce gives a lift to any savoury dish and can be used sparingly to enliven a marinade for fish or meat. It is also essential for making a Bloody Mary cocktail. The "original and genuine" Worcestershire sauce made by Lea and Perrins is superior to all its imitators.

CRUSTACEANS

All crustaceans belong to the enormous family of decapods, ten-limbed creatures that are believed to be descendants of invertebrates that lived on the earth over 200 million and possibly up to 390 million years ago. One can only marvel at the imagination of the first person who thought of eating a crustacean. These curious-looking creatures with their hard carapaces and spidery limbs hardly look like the most attractive of foods, but the sweet flesh concealed within the shell is delicious.

CRABS AND LOBSTERS

CRABS

There are dozens of varieties of crab, ranging from hefty common crabs that will make a meal for several people, to tiny shore crabs that are good only for making soup. They are great wanderers, travelling hundreds of miles in a year from feeding to spawning grounds. As a result, crabs are often caught in baited pots sited on the sea bed far from the shore. As their bodies grow, crabs outgrow their shells and shed them while they grow a new carapace. At first the new shells are soft. These "soft-shell" crabs are a delicacy and can be eaten shell and all. Female crabs are known as hens. They have sweeter flesh than the males, but are smaller and their claws contain less flesh.

Below: Blue crabs

Above: Common or brown crab

Right: Soft-shell crabs

Other names In French, crab is *crabe*, *tourteau* (common edible crab) or *araignée* (spider crab). In Italian, *granchio* or *granseola*; in Spanish: *cangrejo* or *centolla*.

Blue crab *(Callinectes sapidus)*

These crabs have steely-grey bodies and bright, electric blue legs and claws. They are found in American waters and are prized for their white meat.

Soft-shell crabs are blue crabs that have shed their hard carapaces, leaving them deliciously tender, with sweet creamy flesh. They are extremely delicate and do not keep or travel well, so they are generally sold frozen, although you may find fresh soft-shell crabs in the United States in the summer months.

Common edible or Brown crab *(Cancer pagarus)*

The bodies of these large brownish-red crabs can measure well over 20cm/8in. They have big, powerful claws that can deliver an extremely nasty nip, but they contain plenty of tasty meat. Common edible crabs are found on Atlantic coasts and parts of the Mediterranean.
Cooking These are the perfect crabs for boiling to serve cold with mayonnaise. The claws contain plenty of firm meat. After cooking, this can be removed from

Below: Spider crab

the shell in one piece, marinated in a dressing containing Worcestershire sauce and Tabasco and served as a cocktail snack. The claw meat is also delicious deep-fried. The liver and roe of these crabs are also delicious.

Dungeness/California crab (*Cancer magister*)

These trapezium-shaped crabs are found all along the Pacific coast, from Mexico to Alaska. They are very similar to common edible crabs and can be cooked in exactly the same way.

King crab (*Paralithodes camtschiatica*)

Looking like gigantic spiny spiders, king crabs are hideous to behold, but very good to eat. Their very size is awe-inspiring; a mature male king crab can weigh up to 12kg/26½lb and measure 1m/39in across. Their triangular bodies are bright red, with a pale creamy underside. Every part tastes good, from the body meat to that from the narrow claws and long, dangly legs.

Buying Only male king crabs are sold; they are much larger and meatier than the females. Cooked legs are available frozen, and king crab meat is frequently canned. Unlike most crab meat, canned king crab is of excellent quaity and highly prized. The best comes from Alaska, Japan and Russia, where it is sold as Kamchatka crab.

Snow crab (*Chionoetes* spp*)*

Also known as queen crabs, these crabs from the north Pacific have roundish pinkish-brown bodies and exceptionally long legs. The delicious, sweet flesh is difficult to remove from the body, but the claw meat is more accessible. Snow crab meat is usually sold frozen or canned.

Spider crab (*Maia squinado*)

These alarming-looking crabs have spiny shells and long slender legs, which give them the appearance of enormous reddish-pink spiders; hence their alternative name of "sea spider". Those found along the Atlantic coasts measure about 20cm/8in across, but the giant species, found in the waters around Japan, measures up to 40cm/16in, with a claw span of almost 3m/9¾ft – a truly terrifying sight for arachnophobes.

Stone crab (*family Lithodidae*)

Similar in appearance to king crabs, stone crabs live at great depths. They have a superb flavour, but are usually sold frozen or canned rather than fresh.

Below: King crab claws

Above: Swimming crabs

Swimming crab *(family Portunidae)*

The main distinguishing feature of swimming crabs is their extra pair of legs, shaped rather like paddles. Among the many species of swimming crabs are mud or mangrove, shore and velvet crabs. Shore crabs are eaten in Italy in their soft-shelled state; they also make delicious soup. Mud crabs, with their excellent claw meat, are popular in Australia and South-east Asia.

Cooking Crab can be cooked in a multitude of ways. The sweet, succulent meat is rich and filling, so it needs a light touch when cooking; refreshing flavours suit it better than creamy sauces. Picking it out of the shell is hard work, but the result is well worth the effort. Recipes for crab meat include devilled crab (where the meat is removed from the shell and cooked with mustard, horseradish, spices and breadcrumbs); crab mornay, in which the meat is combined with a Gruyère cheese sauce enriched with sherry and mushrooms, and potted crab. The flesh marries well with clean Oriental flavours such as lime juice, coriander and chilli; combined with these, it makes the perfect summer salad. Crab meat is

perfect for fish cakes such as Maryland or Thai crab cakes. It also makes excellent soup; a classic Scottish dish is *partan bree*, a creamy crab soup made with fish stock, milk and rice.

In the shell, crab can be boiled and served with mayonnaise, steamed with aromatics or baked with ginger and spring onions.

Soft-shell crabs are usually lightly coated in flour and deep-fried. A Venetian speciality is *molecchie fritte*; the crabs are soaked in beaten egg before being fried. In China, soft-shell crabs are served with a spicy garnish of chilli or ginger. Soft-shell crabs can also be sautéed in butter and sprinkled with toasted almonds, or brushed with melted butter and lemon juice, then tossed lightly in flour before grilling.

Crawfish *(Palinurus vulgaris)*

Crawfish are similar to lobsters, except that they have spiny shells and no claws. They are variously known as spiny lobsters, rock lobsters, langouste and crayfish (but must not be confused with freshwater crayfish). Crawfish are found on the rocky sea bed in many parts of the world. The colour of their shells varies according to where they come from: Atlantic crawfish are dark

reddish-brown; those from the Florida coast are brown with pale spots; warm-water varieties can be pink or bluish-green. All turn pink or red when cooked. Crawfish have dense, very white flesh, similar to that of lobster, but with a milder flavour. Those from the Atlantic are the finest and sweetest. Crawfish from warmer waters can tend to be a little coarse.

Other names In France, crawfish are called *langouste*; in Italy they are *aragosta*; in Spain *langosta*.

Buying Crawfish are generally sold cooked. Females have the better flavour, so look for the egg sac underneath the thorax. Because there is no claw meat, allow one 450g/1lb crawfish per person. Florida crawfish are often sold frozen as "lobster" tails.

Cooking Cook as lobster. Crawfish benefit from spicy seasonings and are excellent in Oriental recipes.

Crayfish *(Astacus astacus)* **and yabby** *(Cherax)*

Crayfish are miniature freshwater lobsters, which grow to a maximum length of 10cm/4in. The exception is a species found in Tasmania, which can weigh up to 6kg/13lb. Crayfish have a superb flavour and, whatever their colour when alive, turn a glorious deep scarlet when cooked. Over three hundred species are found in well-oxygenated streams throughout Europe, America and Australia, although most of the European species have been wiped out, largely through pollution and disease. Crayfish can be farmed successfully; unfortunately, the most prolific variety are the voracious American signal crayfish; these are prone to a killer disease, which they pass on to wild native crayfish, resulting in near-extinction.

Other names The most commonly available crayfish are the European, the red-claw, the American signal, the red Louisiana swamp, the greenish Turkish crayfish, the Australian yabby and the large marron, which is a deep purplish-grey colour. In France, crayfish are called *écrevisse*; in Italy, *gambero di fiume*; in Spain, *cangrejo de rio*.

Buying Fresh crayfish should be bought alive. There is a lot of wastage, so allow 8–12 crayfish per serving. Keep the shells to make stock, soup or sauces. Frozen crayfish are also available. These are fine for made-up dishes, but are not worth eating on their own.

Cooking Crayfish feature in many luxurious dishes, including bisque (a rich creamy soup), sauces and mousses. They are superb poached in a court-bouillon for about 5 minutes and served cold with mayonnaise or hot with lemony melted butter. Only the tail and claw meat is eaten; the head is often used as a garnish. The cleaned heads and shells can be used to make a shellfish stock or soup.

Below: Crayfish are tiny freshwater lobsters; there are hundreds of species.

Langoustines/Dublin Bay prawns/Scampi
(Nephrops norvegicus)

Smaller relatives of lobsters, langoustines have smooth-shelled narrow bodies with long thin, knobbly claws. They are salmon pink in colour. The largest can measure up to 23cm/ 9in, but the average length is about 12cm/4½in. Langoustines were originally found in Norway, hence their Latin name, and they are still sometimes known as Norway lobsters. Nowadays, they are caught all along the Atlantic coast, in the Adriatic and western Mediterranean. The colder the water in which langoustines live, the better the flavour.

Other names The French know them as *langoustine*; the Italians call them *scampo*, while in Spain they are called *cigala* or *langostina*.

Shelling cooked crayfish

1 Hold the crayfish between your finger and thumb and gently twist off the tail.

2 Hold the tail shell between your thumb and index finger, twist and pull off the flat end; the thread-like intestinal tract will come away. Peel the tail.

3 Hold the head and thorax in one hand. Use the other index finger to prise off the whole underside, including the gills and innards, and discard these.

4 Finally, gently twist off the claws from the head.

Left: These freshwater crustaceans, called cherabin in Australia and black Tiger or African prawns elsewhere, are sometimes confused with crayfish and scampi, because, unlike all other prawns, they have a pair of extremely long, thin claws.

delicate and delicious. They must be cooked very briefly. Roast in oil and garlic in a hot oven for 3–5 minutes; split them and grill or barbecue for about 2 minutes on each side; or poach in a court-bouillon and serve hot with melted butter. Remember that most langoustines on sale are already cooked, so subject them to as little heat as possible. Whole langoustines are delicious served cold with mayonnaise. They make a wonderful addition to a *plateau de fruits de mer*. Langoustine tails can be baked *au gratin* in a creamy sauce with mushrooms and Gruyère cheese, or served Scottish-style in a whisky-flavoured sauce. They can also be deep-fried and served with lemon wedges, but take care not to overcook them.

Buying Langoustines deteriorate very rapidly once caught, so are often cooked and frozen at sea. Live langoustines are therefore something of a rarity in British fish markets, although you will often find them in Europe. If you are lucky enough to find live langoustines, and can be certain of cooking them soon after purchase, they will be an excellent buy. It is important to check that they are still moving; if they have died, they will have an unpleasant woolly texture. Unlike other crustaceans, langoustines do not change colour when cooked, so make sure you know what you are buying. Langoustines are graded by size; larger specimens are better value, as they contain more meat. They are also available frozen, often as scampi tails. If they have been shelled, allow about 115g/4oz per person; you will need twice this quantity if the langoustines are in the shell.
Cooking Most people must have encountered tasteless, badly cooked scampi at some time in their lives. When langoustines are properly cooked, however, their flavour is

Above: Langoustines, which are also known as Dublin Bay prawns and scampi

Left: Canadian lobsters are air-freighted live to Europe.

If you buy a live lobster, make sure that the pincers are secured with a stout rubber band.

Other names In French, lobster is called *homard*; in Italian, it is *astice* and in Spanish, *bogavante*.

Canadian/American lobster *(Homarus americanus)*

The hardiest species of lobster, these are found in large numbers in the waters around Canada and the North American Atlantic. They resemble the European lobster, but are greener in colour and the claws are slightly rounder and fleshier. Although they make excellent eating, their flavour does not quite match up to that of the European lobster. The best-known American lobster is the Maine lobster. Canadian and Maine lobsters are air-freighted live to Europe to meet the demand for these crustaceans. Even taking into account the freight costs, they are considerably cheaper than their European counterparts.

Below: Maine lobster resembles the European lobster, but is less expensive.

LOBSTER

These are the ultimate luxury seafood. Their uniquely firm, sweet flesh has a delicious flavour and many people regard them as the finest crustaceans of all. The best lobsters live in cold waters, scavenging for food on the rocky sea bed. Like crabs, they "moult" every couple of years, casting off their outgrown shells. Their colour varies according to their habitat, from steely blue to greenish-brown to reddish-purple; all turn brick red when cooked. Lobsters grow very slowly, only reaching maturity at six years old, by which time they are about 18cm/7in long. If you are lucky enough to find a 1kg/2¼lb lobster, it will be about ten years old. This explains why lobsters are in such short supply.

Lobsters must be bought live or freshly boiled. The powerful pincers, which the creature uses for catching and crushing its prey, can be dangerous.

European lobster *(Homarus gammarus)*

These lobsters, which come from England, Scotland, Ireland, Norway and Brittany, are regarded as having the finest flavour of all. They have distinctive blue-black colouring, and are sometimes speckled with bright blue. European lobsters are becoming increasingly rare and expensive. If they are caught in reasonable numbers during the summer months, they are often held in vivariums, massive holding tanks built into the sea.

Unfortunately, lobsters do not eat in captivity, so although the vivariums ensure that they are available

Right: Squat lobster is a warm-water variety from Australia and is seldom sold in Europe.

Below: The European lobster, which is becoming rare – and very expensive – is considered the best lobster of all.

throughout the year, the quality deteriorates as the season progresses; by early spring, they tend to be thin and undernourished.

Slipper/Squat lobster *(Scyllarus arctus)*

There are over fifty species of these warm-water lobsters. They have wide, flattened bodies and spindly clawed legs. The best known squat lobsters are the Australian "bugs", and the best known of these are the Balmain and Moreton Bay bugs. The comparatively small tails contain deliciously sweet flesh. Squat lobsters are seldom sold in Europe, but can occasionally be found in France, where they are known as *cigales* (grasshoppers). Italians call them *cicala di mare* and in Spain they are called *cigarra*.

Cooking lobster

All types of lobster are best cooked very simply to allow the delicate flavour to speak for itself. They can be boiled in salted water or court-bouillon and served hot with melted butter or cold with mayonnaise, plainly grilled or fried in the shell with oil and butter. A plain boiled lobster can be the crowning glory of a *plateau de fruits de mer.*

Classical French cookery has a plethora of rich lobster recipes that reflect the luxurious quality of these crustaceans. These dishes, which are usually served with rice to offset the richness, include Lobster Cardinale, with mushrooms and truffles in a velvety sauce; Lobster Newburg, with a cognac and sherry-flavoured cream sauce; Lobster Bretonne, with prawns and mushrooms in a white wine sauce, and the world-famous Lobster Thermidor, with its unctuous brandy and mustard-flavoured sauce. More modern recipes combine lobster with Oriental flavours such as ginger and star anise, but these spices should be used in moderation.

Lobster is superb with fresh pasta. Use it as a filling for ravioli or toss it into tagliolini with lemon juice and butter. Cold boiled lobster can be diced and made into a lobster cocktail or added to a salad. When cooking lobster, keep the shells to use in a shellfish stock or soup.

Preparing a cooked lobster

You'll need a large, heavy knife or cleaver and a lobster pick to remove the meat from the legs.

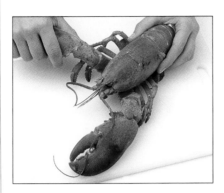

1 Hold the body of the lobster firmly in one hand and twist off the claws one at a time.

2 Hold the lobster the right way up on a chopping board. Insert a large sharp knife at right angles to the seam between the body and head and press down firmly to split the body and tail lengthways.

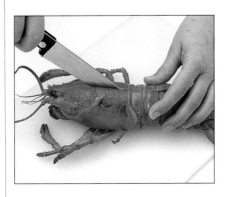

3 Turn the lobster round to face the other way and cut firmly through the head. Separate the lobster into two halves and discard the stomach sac.

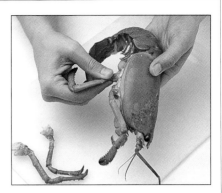

4 Twist off the legs and then flatten them lightly with the back of the knife. Use a lobster pick to remove the flesh.

5 To remove the meat from the claws, first break up the claws into sections. Hold the larger section of the claw, curved side down, in one hand and sharply pull off the smaller pincer. Twist off the lower section of the claw at the joint.

6 Gently crack the claw shell with a mallet or the end of a rolling pin and remove the flesh.

7 The lobster can be grilled in the shell with butter, or the flesh can be diced and used in sauces.

PRAWNS AND SHRIMPS

Prawns are the world's most popular crustaceans and are eaten in huge quantities around the globe. Thousands of species of prawns and shrimps are found in all the world's oceans and also in fresh water. Technically, there is no difference between shrimps and prawns; the names are merely an indication of size. In the fish trade, any prawns measuring less than about 5cm/2in are known as shrimps. Most prawns have narrow, tapering bodies, curled over at the tail, and long antennae. As is the case with other crustaceans, prawns that come from colder waters have a better flavour than those that come from warm waters.

COLD-WATER PRAWNS

Common prawn/Pink shrimp *(Palaemon serratus)*

These translucent, brownish prawns can grow up to 10cm/4in in length. They are found in deep waters in the Atlantic Ocean and Mediterranean Sea, but related species are found throughout the world. The French and Italians consider these prawns the best of all; they have an exceptionally good flavour

Below: Mediterranean prawns

Above: Pink shrimps

and turn a glorious red when cooked. As a result, they command enormously high prices.

Other names Common prawns are also known as sword shrimp or Algerian shrimp. In France, they are called *crevette rose* or *bouquet*; in Italy, they are *gamberello*; in Spain, *camarón* or *quisquilla*.

Deep-sea prawn *(Pandalus borealis)*

Sometimes sold as large shrimps, these cold-water prawns live at great depths in the North Sea. They are hermaphrodite. All begin life as males, but become female halfway through their lifespan. Deep-sea prawns have translucent pink bodies, which turn pale salmon-pink on cooking. They have a delicate, juicy flavour and are almost always sold cooked.

Other names In France, these prawns are *crevette*; Italians know them as *gambero*; while in Spain they are *camarón*.

Peeling and deveining prawns

1 Hold the prawn in the middle and pull off the head and legs. Peel off the shell, leaving on the end of the tail if you prefer.

2 To devein, use a small sharp knife to make a shallow incision down the centre of the curved back of the prawn. Use the knife tip to remove the black vein (intestinal tract) and discard it.

Mediterranean prawn *(Aristeus antennatus)*

These large prawns can measure up to 10cm/4in. The colour varies – the heads can be anything from blood-red to deep coral – but once cooked, they turn a brilliant red. The flesh is delicious and very succulent. Mediterranean prawns are sold cooked and should be served as they are, with mayonnaise and French bread. Allow 3–4 each as a starter.

Other names Also known as blue or red shrimp, Mediterranean prawns are called *crevette rouge* in France; they are called *gambero rosso* in Italy and *carabinero* in Spain.

Common/Brown shrimp *(Crangon crangon)*

These small shrimps have translucent grey bodies and measure only about 5cm/2in. They live in soft sand in shallow waters, emerging at night in darker camouflage to hunt for their prey. When cooked, they turn brownish-grey. Their small size makes them difficult to peel, but they can be eaten whole and their flavour is incomparable, with a wonderful tang of the sea. They are used to make potted shrimps.

Other names The French call these shrimps *crevette grise* or *boucaud*; the Italians know them as *gamberetto grigio*; the Spanish call them *quisquilla*.

Left: Brown shrimps

Below: Tiger prawns

Butterflied prawns

Prawns look very attractive when they are butterflied.

1 The easiest way of doing this is to deepen the incision made to remove the vein, cutting almost but not quite through to the belly.

2 The prawn is then opened out flat. If the prawns are large, make the incision through the belly to give a more pronounced shape.

WARM-WATER PRAWNS

Gulf shrimp *(Hymenopenaeus robustus)*

Warm-water prawns from the Gulf of Mexico, these are usually bright red, but may sometimes be greyish-pink in colour. Gulf shrimps can grow very large, up to 40g/1½oz in weight, and have very succulent flesh.

Kuruma/Japanese prawn *(Penaeus japonicus)*

These large prawns can grow to a length of 23cm/9in. They have yellowish tails flecked with black. Kuruma are found throughout the Indo-Pacific region and in the Red Sea; some have migrated through the Suez Canal to the eastern Mediterranean.

Tiger/King prawn *(Penaeus monodon)*

These huge prawns are found throughout the Indo-Pacific. They can grow up to 33cm/13in in length and are ideal for barbecuing. In their raw state,

Below: Gulf shrimps

they are a translucent greenish-grey. Although their flavour is not as good as that of cold-water prawns, tiger prawns have succulent, firm flesh. In Europe, they are seldom sold fresh, but they freeze well and are available peeled or in the shell. Peeled tiger prawns usually have the end of the tail left on so that they can be eaten with the fingers.

Cooking The cardinal rule with any prawns or shrimps is not to overcook them. Ready-cooked prawns should preferably be eaten without further cooking. Serve them simply, with lemon and brown bread and butter, or in a prawn cocktail or salad. If you must cook them, use them in a dish such as pasta where they need only be heated through. They add extra flavour and texture to other fish dishes, such as fish pies, terrines and flans, and combine well with other shellfish. Small prawns or shrimps make an excellent filling for omelettes, vol-au-vents or tartlets.

Raw prawns can be boiled briefly in salt water or court-bouillon and are delicious grilled, barbecued or deep-fried in batter. Combined with squid and other fish, deep-fried prawns are an essential ingredient of an Italian *fritto misto*. Warm-water prawns can be used for stir-fries, curries or kebabs.

GASTROPODS

Also known as univalves, gastropods are single-shelled creatures belonging to the snail family. Most marine gastropods have the familiar snail shape, with a single spiral shell, but some look more like bivalves and others have no shell at all. All gastropods have a single, large foot which they extend and contract to crawl along at a "snail's pace". Edible gastropods vary in size from tiny winkles to conches measuring up to 30cm/12in. All can be delicious if properly cooked.

Abalone/Ormer/Sea ear

You could be forgiven for thinking that abalone *(Haliotis tuberculata)* were bivalves, since their ear-shaped shells give them the appearance of large mussels. Like all gastropods, they have a large, muscled foot that they use to cling to rocks and cliffs. This immensely strong foot can withstand strains up to four thousand times the weight of the abalone, which makes it very difficult to prise them from the rocks, and helps to explain why they are so expensive. Another reason for their cost is that they feed exclusively on seaweed; as their habitat becomes polluted, they die, so they are becoming increasingly rare. In some countries abalone have become a protected species. They are highly prized not only for their flesh, but also for their beautiful shells. These are lined with iridescent mother-of-pearl. There are over a hundred species of abalone living in warm waters throughout the world. Most can grow to about 20cm/8in in length, but the shell of the red abalone *(Haliotis rufescens)*, found in the American Pacific, grows up to 30cm/12in. Their firm flesh, which must be tenderized before it can be eaten, has a subtle flavour of iodine.

Other names In the Channel Islands, one of the few places in Europe where abalone are still found, they are known as ormers. In South Africa, they are known as *perlemoen* or Venus' ear. The French call them *ormeau* or *oreilles de St Pierre*; the Italians, *orecchia marina*; the Spanish, *oreja de mar.*

Buying In Europe, there is a closed season for abalone, and they are limited to only a few days in early spring. You are more likely to find fresh abalone in America, Australia and the Far East. These are often sold sliced and tenderized ready for cooking. Abalone is also available canned, frozen and dried.

Preparing and Cooking Before cooking, the intestinal sac and dark membrane and skirt must be removed. To remove the white flesh, run a sharp knife between it and the shell. Abalone flesh

Below: Abalone are large shellfish, which can grow to 30cm/12in in length.

Above: Limpets

must be beaten vigorously with a wooden mallet to tenderize it. In Japan, it is then sliced thinly and eaten raw as sashimi. If it is cooked, the technique is the same as that for squid – it must either be cooked very briefly, or given long, slow cooking. Thin slices can be sautéed quickly in hot butter, or cut into strips and deep-fried in batter or egg and breadcrumbs. In China, abalone is braised with dried mushrooms; in France, it is stewed slowly with dry white wine and shallots. In the Channel Islands, ormers are traditionally casseroled with bacon and potatoes. Abalone makes an excellent chowder.

Conch *(Strombus gigas)*

Pronounced "konk", conch is a large relative of the whelk. It has a distinctive spiral shell. As with all such gastropods, the opening is protected by a hard operculum, or "trap door" which must be removed for access to the flesh inside. Conch are native to Florida, the Pacific coast and the Caribbean. The shells are sought after as ornaments and musical instruments. The pinkish flesh is tasty and chewy, and must be beaten to tenderize it before eating.

Buying In their native countries, conches are available all year round. The best are young specimens, known as "thin-lipped" conches; older conches are described as "thick-lipped". They are generally sold out of the shell.

Cooking After tenderizing, conch meat can be marinated and eaten raw, or cooked in a chowder. Some conches can cause stomach upsets; the risk of this occurring can be reduced if the conch is boiled in two changes of water.

Above: Whelks

Cooking and picking winkles and whelks

1 Bring a large pan of well-salted water to the boil. Drop in the winkles or whelks and simmer for about 5 minutes for winkles; 10 minutes for whelks. Drain.

2 If the operculum is still covering the opening of the shell, remove it with a cocktail stick or pin. Insert the cocktail stick or pin into the shell and pull out the flesh.

Limpets *(Patella vulgata)*

These gastropods have conical shells. They are found throughout the world, clinging tightly to rocks. When the tide goes out, they nestle into holes in the sand, emerging at night to crawl in a 1m/39in circle around their hole in search of food. Limpets have quite a good flavour, but the small amount of flesh they contain can be very tough. It takes a great deal of effort to prise them off the rocks, so only the larger varieties, which yield more flesh, are eaten. Limpets are not available commercially so you will have to harvest them yourself.

Cooking Wash the limpets and boil them in sea water or heavily-salted water for 5–7 minutes, or cook the flesh in seafood dishes or soups.

Whelks *(Buccinum undatum)*

Smaller relatives of the conch, whelks have pretty spiral shells measuring up to 10cm/4in. They have rubbery, pinkish flesh with a good flavour, largely because they are scavengers and will bore through the shell of other shellfish to eat their flesh.

Other names There are many varieties of whelk, including the common, the dog, the spiral and the knobbled or giant American whelk, which can grow to 20cm/8in in length. In French, they are variously known as *bulot*, *buccin* and *escargot de mer* (sea snail); in Italian, *buccina*; in Spanish, as *bocina* or *caracola*.

Buying Whelks should be bought alive; check that the operculum is tightly closed. They are sometimes sold ready-boiled and removed from the shell, but these can be rather dry. You will also find whelks pickled in vinegar, or ready-cooked and bottled in brine.

Cooking The best way to cook whelks is to boil them in sea water or heavily salted water for about 5 minutes. Use a toothpick to prise the flesh out of the shell. The flesh of large whelks can be sautéed after boiling, or deep-fried in batter. It can be used instead of clams in a chowder, or added to cooked shellfish dishes or salads.

Winkles/Periwinkles *(Littorina littorea)*

These tiny marine snails have thick greenish-brown or black shells, each with a pointed end. Most grow no larger than 4cm/1½in and contain a morsel of chewy flesh.

Other names In France, they are *bigourneau* or *littorine*; in Italy, *chiocciola di mare*; in Spain, *bigaro*.

Buying Fresh winkles should be bought alive; check that the operculum is tightly closed. They are also available cooked and bottled in vinegar.

Cooking Like whelks, winkles need only brief cooking. Serve as an appetizer with vinegar or mayonnaise, or as part of a shellfish platter.

Left: Winkles

MOLLUSCS

The mollusc family is divided into bivalves such as mussels and oysters, which have a hinged external shell, and gastropods such as whelks and winkles, which have a single external shell. Cephalopods (squid, cuttlefish and octopus) are yet another group; unlike gastropods and bivalves, they have internal shells.

BIVALVES

CLAMS

There are hundreds of species of clam, ranging from the aptly-named giant clam which can grow to a length of 1.3m/4¼ft, to tiny pebble-like Venus and littleneck clams measuring barely 5cm/2in. Americans are passionate about clams and eat them in all sizes and forms. Their enthusiasm has spread to Europe, where clams are now extensively farmed. Large species, such as the fully mature American quahog (pronounced co-hog), have very thick warty shells; small varieties have smooth shells marked with fine circular striations. Clams have a fine, sweet flavour and firm texture, and are delicious cooked or raw.

Below: Palourde or carpetshell clams have tender flesh that can be eaten raw.

Cherrystone/Littleneck clam *(Mercenaria mercenaria)*

These small clams have an attractive brown and white patterned shell. They are actually *quahogs*, the popular name deriving from their size. The smallest are the baby littlenecks, with 4–5cm/1½–2in shells. The slightly larger cherrystones (about 7.5cm/3in), named after Cherrystone Creek in Virginia, are about five years old. Both are often served raw on the half shell; cooked,

Above: Venus clams

they make wonderful pasta sauces. Larger *quahogs*, which are unsuitable for eating raw, are known as steamer clams. They have quite a strong flavour and are often used for making clam chowder or pasta sauces.
Other names The French call them *palourde*; the Italians, *vongola dura*; the Spanish, *almeja* or *clame*.

Geoduck clam *(Panopea generosa)*

These enormous clams are the largest of all American Pacific shellfish and can weigh up to 4kg/8¾lb. Half this weight is made up of two long siphons, which can be extended to more than 1.3m/4¼ft to take in and expel water. Unlike the soft-shell clam, the geoduck cannot retract these siphons into the shell, and they are often sold separately. Geoducks can bury themselves up to 1.2m/4ft deep in sand and it takes two people to prise them out. The siphons and flesh are sliced before cooking.

Palourde/Carpetshell clam *(Venerupis decussata)*

These small (4–7.5cm/1½–3in) clams have attractive grooved brown shells with a yellow lattice pattern. The flesh is exceptionally tender, so they can be eaten raw, but are also good grilled.

Other names In French they are *palourde*; in Italian, *vongola verace*; in Spanish, *almeja fina*.

Praire/Warty Venus clam (*Venus verrucosa*)

The unattractively named warty Venus is a smallish clam measuring 2.5–7.5cm/ 1–3in. The thick shell has concentric stripes, some of which end in warty protuberances. These clams are widely distributed on sandy coasts, from Africa to Europe. They are often eaten raw on the half shell, but are also excellent cooked. The Italians dignify them with the name of "sea truffles".

Below: Cherrystone clams

Other names
Sometimes known as baby clams, the word *praire* comes from the French, who also call these molluscs *coque rayé*. In Italy they are *verrucosa* or *tartufo di mare*; in Spain *almeja vieja*.

Razorshell/Razor clam (*Solen marginatus*)

Resembling an old-fashioned cut-throat razor, these clams have tubular shells that are striped gold and brown. Their flesh looks slightly obscene but tastes delicious. Razorshells are often served raw, but can be cooked like any other clam. They can often be found on sandy beaches at low tide, but as they can burrow into the sand at great speed to conceal themselves, you will need to act fast if you want to catch them.
Other names Razorshells are sometimes known as jack-knife clams. The French call them *couteau*; the Italians, *cannolicchio* or *cappa lunga*; their Spanish name is *navaja* or *longuerión*.

Soft-shell/Long-neck clam *(family Myidae)*

The shells of these wide oval clams gape slightly at the posterior end, giving them their nickname of "gapers". They burrow deep into sand and silt, so have a long tube that acts as a siphon for taking in and expelling water. This siphon can be eaten raw, or made into chowder or creamed dishes. Soft-shell clams are often used in clambakes.
Other names In French they are *mye*; in Italian, *vongola molle*; in Spanish, *almeja de rio*.
Cooking Small clams and razorshells can be eaten raw, steamed or cooked in soups and sauces. Larger clams can be stuffed and baked or grilled like mussels, cut into strips and deep-fried in batter or breadcrumbs, or stewed with white wine or onions and tomatoes. Steamed clams can be added to salads or sauces or used as a garnish. Never throw away the juices which clams contain; these are extremely nutritious and delicious, and can be used for drinks such as *clamata*, shellfish stock or soup.

Below: Razor clams are often served raw.

Clambakes
A favourite American pastime is the clambake, a beach picnic in which soft-shell or hard-shell clams are steamed over seaweed laid on hot rocks. A pit is dug in the sand, rocks are placed inside and heated, then draped with wet seaweed. The clams are steamed over the seaweed, along with sweetcorn, sweet potatoes and, sometimes, lobsters or soft-shell crabs. The process of digging the pit and cooking the clams takes at least 4 hours, so a clambake can provide a whole day's entertainment.

Cockles

Although traditionally thought of as a typically British food, varieties of cockle (*Cardium edule*) are found all over the world. Their two equal heart-shaped shells are 2.5–4cm/1–1½in long and have 26 defined ribs. Inside lies a morsel of delicate flesh and its coral.
Other names In America, cockles are sometimes known as heart clams. In France, they are *coque*; in Italy, *cuore*; in Spain, *berberecho*.
Buying Fresh cockles are sold by volume; 1 pint weighs about 450g/1lb. Those with paler flesh are said to taste better than those with dark flesh.

Above: Cockles

The colour of the shell is an indication of the colour of the flesh, so choose cockles with pale shells. Shelled cockles are available frozen and bottled in brine or vinegar.

Cooking Cockles are full of sand, so must be soaked in salted cold water for several hours before eating. They can be eaten raw or boiled and served with vinegar and brown bread and butter. They are excellent steamed, stewed with tomatoes and onions or made into soup. Cockles can be added to risotto, pasta and other seafood dishes or served cold as an hors d'oeuvre or salad.

Below: Large New Zealand greenshell or green-lipped mussels.

Right: Ever-popular, black-shelled mussels

Dog cockle
(Glycymeridae)

With their large, flat striated shells, dog cockles resemble scallops. There are four known species of these tropical and warm-water bivalves – the true dog cockle, the bittersweet cockle, the violet bittersweet and the giant bittersweet. All are perfectly good to eat, but have a coarser texture and flavour than true cockles. They can be cooked in the same way as cockles and mussels.
Other names In French they are *amande*; in Italian, *pié d'asino* (ass's foot); in Spanish, *almendra de mar.*

Mussels *(Mytilus edulis)*

Once regarded as the poor relation of the shellfish family, mussels are now very popular, but still comparatively cheap. These succulent bivalves, with their elongated blue-black shells, have been eaten since earliest times. Unlike most other bivalves, they do not use a muscly foot to anchor themselves to rocks and poles, but with a byssus or "beard", a wiry substance produced by a gland at the base of the foot. Clumps

of mussels grow wild on sea shores throughout the world and are great fun to harvest. It is essential that the waters they come from are unpolluted. Their sweet, tender flesh is nutritious and versatile. Nowadays, most commercial mussels are farmed.

There are many varieties of mussel. The best and most succulent are the blue or European mussels from cold British waters, which can grow to a length of 10cm/4in, although the average size is nearer 5cm/2in. They are large, with sweet-flavoured flesh which in the female is a beautiful orange; males have paler, cream-coloured flesh. The largest of all are the New Zealand greenshell or green-lipped mussels *(Perna canaliculus),* which have a distinctive green lip around the internal border of the shell. These can grow to over 23cm/9in and are very meaty and substantial. They are ideal for stuffing, but their flavour is not as good as that of blue mussels.
Other names In French it is *moule*; in Italian, *cozza*; in Spanish, *mejillón.*
Buying Most mussels are farmed and are usually cleaned. They are available all year round and are cheap, so buy more than you think you will need to allow for wastage; 1kg/2¼lb will provide a generous meal for two people. Shelled mussels are available frozen, smoked and bottled in brine or vinegar.

Cooking Mussels are enormously versatile. They can be eaten raw or steamed very simply as in *moules marinières*. They are also good steamed with Mediterranean or Oriental flavours. Large mussels can be stuffed and baked or grilled with flavoured butter, bacon or pesto. They can be wrapped in bacon, threaded on to skewers and grilled; cooked in cream, wine or cider; deep-fried; or used in omelettes, soufflés, hot or cold soups, curries, pasta sauces, rice dishes such as paella, or seafood salads. The national dish of Belgium is *moules frites*, crisply fried mussels with chips, served with a glass of beer. For an unusual and piquant hors d'oeuvre, serve cold steamed mussels *à la ravigote*, with a vinaigrette flavoured with chopped hard-boiled egg, fresh herbs and gherkins.

OYSTERS

One of life's great luxuries, oysters evoke passionate feelings – people tend either to love or loathe them. Their unique, salty, iodised flavour and slippery texture may not appeal to everyone, but their reputation as an

Below: Native oysters are the finest and most expensive of all oysters.

aphrodisiac (Casanova was said to eat at least fifty every day) has contributed to their popularity, and they are highly prized all over the world. It was not always so; for centuries, oysters were regarded as food for the poor. Apprentices revolted at having to eat them every day of the week. As they became scarce, however, their popularity increased.

Over 100 different varieties of oyster live in the temperate and warm waters of the world. All have thick, irregular, greyish shells, one flat, the other hollow. The highly nutritious flesh is pinkish-grey with a darker mantle and a slippery texture. Their reproductive life is highly unusual. Some are hermaphrodite; others change sex from male to female in alternate years.

Oysters have been eaten for millions of years. They were enjoyed by the Celts and Ancient Greeks, but it was the Romans who first discovered the secret of oyster cultivation. By the 19th century, European oyster beds had been so comprehensively over-fished and stocks were so low that Napoleon III ordered that shipments of oysters be brought from abroad. It is as well that he did; in 1868, a ship carrying quantities of Portuguese oysters was

forced to take shelter from a storm in the Gironde estuary. Fearing that his cargo of oysters was going bad, the captain flung them overboard. They bred prolifically, rapidly replenishing the native stocks, and managed to survive a catastrophic epidemic in 1921, which wiped out the native oysters. In 1967, however, they too were totally decimated by the deadly bonamia virus. Oyster cultivation on a massive scale was the only answer; nowadays, oysters are commercially produced throughout the industrialized world.

Oyster cultivation
Centuries of over-fishing and disease have decimated the world's natural stocks of oysters, a sad state of affairs which has been somewhat alleviated by oyster farming. Oysters have been farmed since Roman times, but cultivation has now become a highly lucrative business, despite being labour-intensive and very slow. Oysters need constant cosseting from the moment of hatching. A single oyster produces up to a hundred million eggs every breeding season, of which only ten oysters will survive long enough to end up on your plate. It takes at least three years to produce an oyster of marketable size; natives take up to seven years and the giant "royals" take ten years to mature. The minuscule spats must first be caught and encouraged to settle on lime-soaked tiles or slates.

After about nine months, they are transferred to oyster parks, where they are enclosed in wire grilles and carefully nurtured while they feed on plankton. After being left to grow for two or three years, they are placed in nets and fattened for about a year in shallow beds or *claires*. The final stage of the lengthy process involves placing them in clean beds for several days under stringent hygiene conditions to expel any impurities. Small wonder that they are so expensive.

Left: Gigas oysters

Eastern/Atlantic oyster (Crassostrea virginica)

With rounded shells like those of the native oyster, these actually belong to the Portuguese oyster family and have a similar texture and flavour. In America, they are named after their place of origin; the best known is the Blue Point.

Native oyster (Ostrea edulis)

Considered the finest of all oysters, Natives are slow-growers, taking three years to reach their full size of 5–12cm/ 2–4½in. Their round shells vary in colour from greyish-green to beige, depending on their habitat, and they have a wonderful flavour. Native oysters are named after their place of origin. Among the best known are the French Belon, the English Whitstable, Colchester and Helford, the Irish Galway and the Belgian Ostendes. Native oysters are the most expensive of all oysters.
Other names The French call them *huitre plate* or *belon*, to the Italians they are *ostrica*, while in Spain, they are called *ostra plana*.

Pacific/Gigas oyster (Crassostrea gigas)

These large cupped bivalves with their craggy elongated shells are the most widely farmed oysters in the world. They are resistant to disease and can grow to 15cm/6in in the space of four years, which makes them comparatively economical to produce. Their texture is not as fine as that of native oysters, but their large size makes them more suitable for cooking than other oysters.
Other names The Pacific oyster is also known as the rock or Japanese oyster. In French, it is *creuse* (hollow); in Italian, *ostrica*; in Spanish *ostión*.

Portuguese cupped oyster (Crassostrea angulata)

These scaly greyish-brown oysters are considered finer than gigas, but not as good as natives. Their flesh is rather coarse and they are declining in popularity. In France, where

Portuguese cupped oysters are cultivated on a large scale, they are known as *fines de claires* after the fattening beds where they are farmed. Fatter, tastier (and, of course, more expensive) specimens are called *spéciales claires*.

Sydney rock oyster (Crassostrea commercialis)

This sex-changing cupped oyster is extremely fertile and is farmed in huge numbers on the coast of New South Wales. It grows quickly and has a good flavour, but has the disadvantage of being difficult to open.
Buying The age-old rule that oysters should not be bought when there is no "r" in the month still holds good in the northern hemisphere, not because they are poisonous as was once supposed, but because their flesh becomes unpleasantly soft and milky during the summer breeding season from May to August. Smoked oysters are available and you may also find frozen oysters.
Cooking Oysters are best eaten raw with just a squeeze of lemon or a dash of Tabasco. If you prefer to cook them, do so very briefly. They are good poached or steamed and served with a *beurre blanc* or Champagne sauce; stuffed and grilled; deep-fried in cornmeal batter; or as a luxurious addition to steak and kidney pie.

Left: Portuguese cupped oysters

SCALLOPS

Surely the most attractive of all shellfish, scallops (*Peeten maximus*) have two fan-shaped shells, one flat and the other curved, with grooves radiating out from the hinge to the outside edge. They are found on sandy seabeds in many parts of the world from Iceland to Japan. Unlike many bivalves, they do not burrow into the sand, but "swim" above the sea bed by opening and closing their shells, which gives them the appearance of leaping through the water. There are about three hundred species of scallop throughout the world, with shells ranging in colour from beige to brown, salmon pink, yellow and orange. The most common species is the common or great scallop, whose reddish-brown shell grows to a diameter of 5–6cm/2–2½in. Scallop shells contain a nugget of sweet, firm white flesh joined to the vibrant orange crescent-shaped roe or "coral", which is a delicacy in its own right.

Scallops are deeply symbolic and have long been associated with beauty. According to the legend depicted by Botticelli in one of his most famous paintings, the goddess Venus was born from a scallop shell; her Greek counterpart, Aphrodite, rode across the sea in a scallop shell pulled by six sea horses. Thanks to a miracle involving St James, scallop shells became the symbol of Christianity and the emblem of medieval pilgrims visiting the shrine at Santiago de Compostela in Spain.

Other names Sometimes known as "pilgrim shells", scallops are *coquille St Jacques* in French, *pettine* in Italian; *viera* in Spanish.

Buying Scallops are available almost all year round, but are best in winter when the roes are full and firm. The finest are individually hand-caught by divers; needless to say, they are also the most expensive. If you buy scallops in the shell, keep the shells to use as serving dishes for all sorts of fish recipes. Allow 4–5 large scallops per person as a main course, three times this number if they are small. Scallops are also available

Above: Queen scallops

shelled, which saves the effort of cleaning them. Always try to buy scallops with their delicious coral, although this is not always possible. Avoid frozen scallops, which have little or no taste.

Cooking The beard and all dark coloured parts of the scallop must be removed before they are cooked and eaten. If the scallops are large, slice the white flesh in half horizontally. Scallops require very little cooking and can be thinly sliced and eaten raw with a squeeze of lemon and a drizzle of olive oil. They need only the briefest of cooking to preserve their uniquely firm yet tender texture. Scallops can be poached for a couple of minutes in court-bouillon and served warm or cold in a salad with a tomato and basil vinaigrette or mayonnaise.

Whole scallops in the shell can be baked; seal the shells with a flour and water paste to trap the juices. They are equally delicious wrapped in bacon and grilled; coated in egg and breadcrumbs and deep-fried; pan-fried for about 30 seconds on each side; stir-fried with colourful vegetables or steamed with ginger and soy sauce. They make wonderful pâtés and mousses. A classic dish is *coquilles St Jacques*, in which poached scallops and corals are sliced, returned to the half shell and coated with Mornay (cheese) sauce, then grilled or baked until browned. A border of mashed potato is often piped round the edge of the shell.

Queen scallop (*Chlamys opercularis*)

These miniature scallops measure only about 3cm/1¼in across. Their cream-coloured shells are marked with attractive brown ridges and contain a small nugget of white flesh and a tiny pointed coral. Queen scallops are considerably cheaper than larger scallops, but have the same sweet flavour. They are often sold out of the shell; allow at least a dozen per person. "Queenies" as they are sometimes known, are commercially farmed. They are popular in Asia and are widely used in Chinese cooking.

Above: King scallops

CEPHALOPODS

Despite their appearance, cephalopods, which include cuttlefish, octopus and squid, are molluscs and are more closely related to snails than to fish. They are highly developed creatures with three-dimensional vision, memory and the ability to swim at high speeds. They can also change colour according to the environment. Their name derives from the Greek for "head with feet", which sums up their appearance very accurately. The bulbous head contains the mouth, which has two jaws, rather like a parrot's beak. This is surrounded by tentacles covered with suckers, which are used for crawling and for seizing their prey. The sack-shaped body contains a mantle cavity which houses the stomach, gills and sex organs. Although they developed from snail-like creatures, cephalopods no longer have an external shell; instead, most have an internal calcareous shell made from spongy material which they can inflate to make themselves buoyant. The most familiar of these is the cuttlebone, from the cuttlefish. Cuttlebones often wash up on beaches, and are used by bird-owners to provide calcium for budgerigars. In Roman times, ladies ground up cuttlebones and used the powder on their faces and to clean their teeth and their jewellery.

Most cephalopods also contain an ink sac which emits a blackish fluid designed to repel predators and provide a "smokescreen" for the creature when it is under attack. This fluid, or ink, is delicious and can be used for cooking.

Below: Baby cuttlefish

Right: Cuttlefish

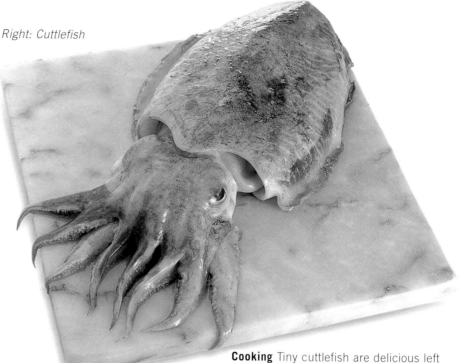

Cephalopods are found in almost all the world's oceans. Unlike many sea creatures, they have not yet suffered from overfishing and are still a sustainable food source.

Cuttlefish

The common cuttlefish *(Sepia officinalis)* has a flattened oval head with brownish camouflage stripes on the back and light coloration on the underside. It has eight stubby tentacles and two long tentacles for catching its prey. These are kept rolled up and hidden in openings near its mouth. Cuttlefish are comparatively small, with bodies measuring 25–30cm/10–12in. When unfurled, the catching tentacles double its length. As is the case with all cephalopods, the smaller the cuttlefish, the more tender the flesh. The smallest species is the Mediterranean little or dwarf cuttlefish *(sepiola)*, which grows to only 3–6cm/1¼–2½in. They are delicious, but time-consuming to prepare, as the tiny cuttlebones must be removed before cooking.
Other names The common cuttlefish is *seiche* in French, *seppia* in Italian, *sepia* in Spanish. Dwarf cuttlefish are *supion* or *chipiron* in French, *seppiolina* in Italian, and *chipirón* in Spanish.

Cooking Tiny cuttlefish are delicious left whole and either sautéed quickly in olive oil and garlic or deep-fried. They make an excellent addition to rice dishes. Larger specimens can be cooked like squid. A classic Spanish dish is *sepia en su tinta*, cuttlefish cooked in its own ink.

Octopuses *(Octopus vulgaris)*

Unlike cuttlefish and squid, the octopus has no internal shell, nor does it possess catching tentacles or fins. Octopuses spend their lives lurking in clefts in the rocks on the sea bed, blocking the entrance to their hidey-holes with shellfish and stones. Their eight equal-size tentacles each have two rows of suckers and can grow to a length of 5m/16¼ft. The larger an octopus grows, the tougher it becomes, so smaller specimens make the best eating. Octopus ink is contained in the liver and has a much stronger flavour than cuttlefish or squid ink.
Other names Octopus is *poulpe* or *pieuvre* in French; *polpo* in Italian; *pulpo* in Spanish.
Buying It is usually sold ready-prepared and frozen, although you may find whole fresh octopus in Mediterranean fish markets. Look for specimens with two rows of suckers on the tentacles; those with only a single row are curled octopus, which are inferior.

Right: Baby octopus

Cooking Octopus needs long, slow cooking. Before including it in a recipe, it is a good idea to blanch or marinate it. If the octopus has not been prepared already, cut off the tentacles and press out the beak from the head. Discard the head, turn the body inside out and discard the entrails. Rinse it thoroughly, then pound the body and tentacles with a mallet to tenderize them before cutting them into strips. Simmer the octopus in stock or salted water for at least 1 hour, until tender. Octopus can also be stewed with Mediterranean vegetables or robust red wine, or stuffed and baked slowly. Small specimens can be cut into rings and sautéed gently in olive oil. Octopus is best served warm as a salad, dressed with a simple olive oil and lemon vinaigrette. Whole octopus can be casseroled slowly in its own juices and ink, but be aware that the ink has a strong flavour which is not to everyone's taste. The Japanese are very fond of octopus and use the boiled tentacles for sushi.

Squid *(Loliginidae)*

These have elongated heads and slender, torpedo-shaped bodies, which end in a kite-shaped fin. Their internal shell is a transparent quill, which looks like a piece of clear acetate. They have ten tentacles, two of which are very long. Squid range from tiny creatures only 7.5cm/3in long to the giant squid which weighs several tons and can grow to a length of 17m/55¼ft. The most common squid is the calamary or long-finned squid *(Loligo vulgaris)*, which is found throughout Europe. It

has smooth, sandy-red spotted skin and weighs up to 2kg/4½lb. The so-called flying squid does not actually fly, but propels itself out of the water and glides through the air like a guided missile. Squid has firm, lean, white flesh that can be tender and delicious when properly cooked.

Other names In French squid is *encornet* or *calmar*; in Italian it is *calamaro*; in Spanish *calamar* or *puntilla*.

Buying Whole squid are sold fresh or frozen and are available all year round. Make sure they contain their ink sac. Some fishmongers and supermarkets also sell squid ink separately. Squid is also available ready-cleaned, which is very labour-saving. Whole tentacles and rings are available frozen, sometimes as part of a mixed *fruits de mer*. You can also buy ready-battered squid rings for deep-frying, but these are best avoided. Allow about 200g/7oz squid per person.

Cooking The cardinal rule with squid is to cook it either very briefly or for a long time; anything in between and it

Above: Squid

becomes tough and rubbery. The bodies can be stuffed and baked in tomato sauce, or braised with onions and tomatoes. Squid rings can be coated in batter and deep-fried, or boiled briefly and used for a salad. Tiny squid are delicious chargrilled, sautéed, or coated with egg and breadcrumbs and deep-fried. Squid can be added to pasta sauces and rice dishes such as paella. It goes well with such apparently unlikely ingredients as chorizo sausage and black pudding. Squid is frequently used in Oriental recipes and lends itself to flavourings such as ginger, chilli and lime. The ink can be used to colour and flavour home-made pasta and risotto.

Above: Octopus

OTHER EDIBLE SEA CREATURES

The sea is full of weird and wonderful creatures whose strange appearance belies their delicious taste. They may be soft and gelatinous like jellyfish, warty like sea cucumbers or menacingly spiny like sea urchins, but somewhere in the world, they will be regarded as a great delicacy.

Above: Dried jellyfish

Jellyfish *(Scyphoza)*

Jellyfish can strike terror into the hearts of those who have been stung by them. These strange, transparent creatures, with their dangling tentacles, look like open parachutes. They inhabit every ocean of the world, but are eaten almost exclusively in Asia, where they are dried and used to add texture and flavour to many seafood dishes.
Buying and using You will find dried jellyfish in any Oriental food store, together with jellyfish preserved in brine. Both types must be soaked in several changes of water before use. In China, slices of dried jellyfish are scalded in boiling water until they curl up, then drained and served in a dressing of soy sauce, sesame oil and rice vinegar. They are also added to shellfish or chicken stir-fries. In Japan, crisply fried strips of jellyfish are served with vinegar, and are sometimes combined with sea urchins.

Sea cucumber *(Holothurioidea)*

It is hard to imagine why anyone would wish to eat these repulsive-looking, warty, cucumber-shaped creatures, which rejoice in the alternative unattractive name of sea slugs, but they are considered a great delicacy in Japan and China, where they are reputed to be an aphrodisiac. The plethora of prickles along their backs are actually feet, which enable them to crawl along the sea bed. Sea cucumber is known in the Orient as *trepang* or *balatin*. In Japan, it is sliced and eaten raw as sashimi. Sea cucumber is available dried, but requires many hours of soaking to make it palatable. It is used in soup and in several complicated recipes which take so long to prepare that one feels it must have charms which are not apparent to Western palates.

Sea squirt *(Ascidiacea)*

There are over a thousand species of sea squirts, small invertebrates whose bodies are enclosed in thick

Above: Sea cucumber

leathery "tunics". They have two orifices or spouts through which they siphon water in and squirt it out, and attach themselves to the sea bed or rocks and crevices. They are found in the Mediterranean, where they are a popular if esoteric food, particularly in Spain and the south of France, where the local name, violet, refers to the sea squirt's resemblance to a large purple fig. Enthusiasts eat them by splitting them in half, then scooping out the soft yellow part inside and eating it raw, despite the strong aroma of iodine. Sea squirts can accumulate

Right: Sea squirt

Opening sea urchins

1 Hold the sea urchin on a board (wear gloves if the spines are especially prickly) and cut around the soft tissue on the underside, using a special knife or sharp, pointed scissors.

2 Lift off the top of the sea urchin and remove the mouth and innards, which are inedible. Keep the juices to flavour shellfish sauces, egg dishes or soup.

3 Use a teaspoon to scoop out the bright orange coral.

Right: Prickly sea urchins

toxins, so should never be eaten if they come from polluted waters.
Other names In French, sea squirt is *violet* or *figue de mer;* in Italian, *ovo di mare.*

Sea urchin *(Echinoidea)*

One of the most unpleasant experiences a holidaymaker can have is to tread on the long, poisonous spines of a sea urchin. To lovers of seafood, however, eating these marine creatures is one of life's great gastronomic pleasures. There are over eight hundred species of sea urchin, found all over the world, but only a few are edible. The most common European variety is the *Paracentrotus lividus*, a greenish or purplish-black hemispherical creature which measures about 7.5cm/3in across, and whose shell is covered with long spines, rather like those of a hedgehog. The females are slightly larger than the males and are said to taste better. Only the orange or yellow ovaries or gonads (known as the coral) are eaten; these have a pungent taste reminiscent of iodine.
Other names In French, sea urchins are variously known as *oursin, châtaigne de mer* (sea chestnut) and *hérisson de mer* (sea hedgehog); in Italian, they are *riccio di mare;* in Spanish *erizo de mar.*
Buying Overfishing has made sea urchins rare and expensive. The best

are the purple or green urchins with long spines; short-spined, whitish species have an extremely strong flavour and are best used in cooked dishes. Look for urchins with firm spines and a tightly closed mouth (on the underside). If you find a source of fresh sea urchins, they can be kept in the fridge for up to three days.
Preparing The best implement for opening sea urchins is a purpose-made *coupe oursin.* Failing this, use very sharp scissors. Wearing gloves, cut into the soft tissue around the mouth and lift off the top to reveal the coral. Alternatively, slice off the top like a boiled egg.
Cooking Sea urchins can be eaten raw or used to flavour sauces, pasta, omelettes and scrambled eggs. They make wonderful soup, which can be served in small portions in the shell and eaten with a teaspoon. The shells can also be used as containers for other seafood such as langoustines in a sea urchin sauce.

FISH AND SHELLFISH RECIPES

Fish and shellfish are both nutritious and enticing, and when properly cooked, can be among the most delicious foods imaginable. Every fish and shellfish has its own unique flavour, offering something for all tastes. In this collection of inspirational recipes there is a host of stunning contemporary creations as well as time-honoured classic dishes. With the increasingly wide range of fish and shellfish available in fishmongers and supermarkets, you can allow yourself the pleasure of experimenting and enjoying these wonderful dishes.

SOUPS

From light, spicy broths to hearty one-pot meals, fish and shellfish soups

are a delight. Chilled Cucumber and Prawn Soup is perfect for

summer eating, while Scallop and Jerusalem Artichoke Soup and

substantial Bouillabaisse make wonderful winter warmers along with

Clam Chowder from New England. For real luxury,

treat yourself and your guests to creamy Lobster Bisque, or travel to

the Orient with spicy Malaysian Prawn Laksa and the

wonderfully fragrant Thai Fish Broth.

CHILLED CUCUMBER AND PRAWN SOUP

IF YOU'VE NEVER SERVED A CHILLED SOUP BEFORE, THIS IS THE ONE TO TRY. DELICIOUS AND LIGHT, IT'S THE PERFECT WAY TO CELEBRATE SUMMER.

2 Stir in the milk, bring almost to boiling point, then lower the heat and simmer for 5 minutes. Tip the soup into a blender or food processor and purée until very smooth. Season to taste.

3 Pour the soup into a large bowl and leave to cool. When cool, stir in the prawns, chopped herbs and cream. Cover, transfer to the fridge and chill for at least 2 hours.

4 To serve, ladle the soup into four individual bowls and top each portion with a dollop of crème fraîche or soured cream, if using, and place a prawn over the edge of each dish. Scatter a little extra chopped dill over each soup and tuck two or three chives under the prawns on the edge of the bowls to garnish. Serve at once.

SERVES FOUR

INGREDIENTS

25g/1oz/2 tbsp butter
2 shallots, finely chopped
2 garlic cloves, crushed
1 cucumber, peeled, seeded and diced
300ml/½ pint/1¼ cups milk
225g/8oz cooked peeled prawns
15ml/1 tbsp each finely chopped fresh mint, dill, chives and chervil
300ml/½ pint/1¼ cups whipping cream
salt and ground white pepper
For the garnish
30ml/2 tbsp crème fraîche or soured cream (optional)
4 large, cooked prawns, peeled with tail intact
fresh dill and chives

1 Melt the butter in a saucepan and cook the shallots and garlic over a low heat until soft but not coloured. Add the cucumber and cook gently, stirring frequently, until tender.

COOK'S TIP
If you prefer hot soup, reheat it gently until hot but not boiling. Do not boil, or the delicate flavour will be spoilt.

VARIATION
If you like, you can use other cooked shellfish in place of the peeled prawns – try fresh, frozen or canned crab meat, or cooked, flaked salmon fillet.

SCALLOP AND JERUSALEM ARTICHOKE SOUP

THE SUBTLE SWEETNESS OF SCALLOPS COMBINES WELL WITH THE FLAVOUR OF JERUSALEM ARTICHOKES IN THIS ATTRACTIVE GOLDEN SOUP. FOR AN EVEN MORE COLOURFUL VERSION, SUBSTITUTE PUMPKIN FOR THE ARTICHOKES AND USE EXTRA STOCK INSTEAD OF THE MILK.

SERVES SIX

INGREDIENTS
  1kg/2¼lb Jerusalem artichokes
  juice of ½ lemon
  115g/4oz/½ cup butter
  1 onion, finely chopped
  600ml/1 pint/2½ cups fish stock
  300ml/½ pint/1¼ cups milk
  generous pinch of saffron threads
  6 large or 12 small scallops, with
    their corals
  150ml/¼ pint/⅔ cup whipping
    cream
  salt and ground white pepper
  45ml/3 tbsp flaked almonds and
    15ml/1 tbsp finely chopped
    fresh chervil, to garnish

1 Working quickly, scrub and peel the Jerusalem artichokes, cut them into 2cm/¾in chunks and drop them into a bowl of cold water, which has been acidulated with the lemon juice. This will prevent the artichokes from discolouring.

2 Melt half the butter in a saucepan, add the onion and cook over a low heat until softened. Drain the artichokes and add them to the pan. Cook gently for 5 minutes, stirring frequently. Pour in the stock and milk, add the saffron and bring to the boil. Lower the heat and simmer until the artichokes are tender but not mushy.

3 Meanwhile, carefully separate the scallop corals from the white flesh. Prick the corals and slice each scallop in half horizontally. Heat half the remaining butter in a frying pan, add the scallops and corals and cook very briefly (for about 1 minute) on each side. Dice the scallops and corals, keeping them separate, and set them aside until needed.

4 When the artichokes are cooked, tip the contents of the pan into a blender or food processor. Add half the white scallop meat and purée until very smooth. Return the soup to the clean pan, season with salt and white pepper and keep hot over a low heat while you prepare the garnish.

5 Heat the remaining butter in a frying pan, add the almonds and toss over a medium heat until golden brown. Add the diced corals and cook for about 30 seconds. Stir the cream into the soup and add the remaining diced white scallop meat. Ladle the soup into individual bowls and garnish each serving with the almonds, scallop corals and a sprinkling of chervil.

MATELOTE

Traditionally this fishermen's chunky soup is made from freshwater fish, including eel. Any firm fish can be used, but try to include at least some eel, and use a robust dry white or red wine for extra flavour.

SERVES SIX

INGREDIENTS

    1kg/2¼lb mixed fish, including
      450g/1lb conger eel if possible
    50g/2oz/¼ cup butter
    1 onion, thickly sliced
    2 celery sticks, thickly sliced
    2 carrots, thickly sliced
    1 bottle dry white or red wine
    1 fresh bouquet garni containing
      parsley, bay leaf and chervil
    2 cloves
    6 black peppercorns
    beurre manié for thickening, see
      Cook's Tip
    salt and cayenne pepper
For the garnish
    25g/1oz/2 tbsp butter
    12 baby onions, peeled
    12 button mushrooms
    chopped flat leaf parsley

1 Cut all the fish into thick slices, removing any obvious bones. Melt the butter in a large saucepan, put in the fish and sliced vegetables and stir over a medium heat until lightly browned. Pour in the wine and enough cold water to cover. Add the bouquet garni and spices and season. Bring to the boil, lower the heat and simmer gently for 20–30 minutes, until the fish is tender, skimming the surface occasionally.

2 Meanwhile, prepare the garnish. Heat the butter in a deep frying pan and sauté the baby onions until golden and tender. Add the mushrooms and fry until golden. Season and keep hot.

3 Strain the soup through a large sieve placed over a clean pan. Discard the herbs and spices in the sieve, then divide the fish among deep soup plates (you can skin the fish if you wish, but this is not essential) and keep hot.

4 Reheat the soup until it boils. Lower the heat and whisk in the *beurre manié* little by little until the soup thickens. Season it and pour over the fish. Garnish each portion with the fried baby onions and mushrooms and sprinkle with chopped parsley.

COOK'S TIP
To make the *beurre manié* for thickening, mix 15g/½oz/1 tbsp softened butter with 15ml/1 tbsp plain flour. Add to the boiling soup a pinch at a time, whisking all the time.

FISH SOUP WITH ROUILLE

. MAKING THIS SOUP IS SIMPLICITY ITSELF, YET THE FLAVOUR SUGGESTS IT IS THE PRODUCT OF PAINSTAKING PREPARATION AND COOKING.

SERVES SIX

INGREDIENTS
    1kg/2¼lb mixed fish
    30ml/2 tbsp olive oil
    1 onion, chopped
    1 carrot, chopped
    1 leek, chopped
    2 large ripe tomatoes, chopped
    1 red pepper, seeded and chopped
    2 garlic cloves, peeled
    150g/5oz/⅔ cup tomato purée
    1 large fresh bouquet garni,
        containing 3 parsley sprigs, 3 celery
        sticks and 3 bay leaves
    300ml/½ pint/1¼ cups dry
        white wine
    salt and ground black pepper
For the rouille
    2 garlic cloves, roughly chopped
    5ml/1 tsp coarse salt
    1 thick slice of white bread, crust
        removed, soaked in water and
        squeezed dry
    1 fresh red chilli, seeded and
        roughly chopped
    45ml/3 tbsp olive oil
    salt and cayenne pepper
For the garnish
    12 slices of baguette, toasted in
        the oven
    50g/2oz Gruyère cheese,
        finely grated

1 Cut the fish into 7.5cm/3in chunks, removing any obvious bones. Heat the oil in a large saucepan, then add the fish and chopped vegetables. Stir until these begin to colour.

2 Add all the other soup ingredients, then pour in just enough cold water to cover the mixture. Season well and bring to just below boiling point, then lower the heat to a bare simmer, cover and cook for 1 hour.

3 Meanwhile, make the rouille. Put the garlic and coarse salt in a mortar and crush to a paste with a pestle. Add the soaked bread and chilli and pound until smooth, or purée in a food processor. Whisk in the olive oil, a drop at a time, to make a smooth, shiny sauce that resembles mayonnaise. Season with salt and add a pinch of cayenne if you like a fiery taste. Set the rouille aside.

4 Lift out and discard the bouquet garni from the soup. Purée the soup in batches in a food processor, then strain through a fine sieve placed over a clean pan, pushing the solids through with the back of a ladle.

5 Reheat the soup without letting it boil. Check the seasoning and ladle into individual bowls. Top each serving with two slices of toasted baguette, a spoonful of rouille and some grated Gruyère.

COOK'S TIP
Any firm fish can be used for this recipe. If you use whole fish, include the heads, which enhance the flavour of the soup.

LOBSTER BISQUE

BISQUE IS A LUXURIOUS, VELVETY SOUP, WHICH CAN BE MADE WITH ANY CRUSTACEANS.

SERVES SIX

INGREDIENTS
   500g/1¼lb fresh lobster
   75g/3oz/6 tbsp butter
   1 onion, chopped
   1 carrot, diced
   1 celery stick, diced
   45ml/3 tbsp brandy, plus extra for
      serving (optional)
   250ml/8fl oz/1 cup dry white wine
   1 litre/1¾ pints/4 cups fish stock
   15ml/1 tbsp tomato purée
   75g/3oz/scant ½ cup long grain rice
   1 fresh bouquet garni
   150ml/¼ pint/⅔ cup double cream,
      plus extra to garnish
   salt, ground white pepper and
      cayenne pepper

1 Cut the lobster into pieces. Melt half the butter in a large saucepan, add the vegetables and cook over a low heat until soft. Put in the lobster and stir until the shell on each piece turns red.

2 Pour over the brandy and set it alight. When the flames die down, add the wine and boil until reduced by half. Pour in the fish stock and simmer for 2–3 minutes. Remove the lobster.

3 Stir in the tomato purée and rice, add the bouquet garni and cook until the rice is tender. Meanwhile, remove the lobster meat from the shell and return the shells to the saucepan. Dice the lobster meat and set it aside.

COOK'S TIP
It is best to buy a live lobster, chilling it in the freezer until it is comatose and then killing it just before cooking. If you can't face the procedure, use a cooked lobster; take care not to over-cook the flesh. Stir for only 30–60 seconds.

4 When the rice is cooked, discard all the larger bits of shell. Tip the mixture into a blender or food processor and whizz to a purée. Press the purée through a fine sieve placed over the clean pan. Stir the mixture, then heat until almost boiling. Season with salt, pepper and cayenne, then lower the heat and stir in the cream. Dice the remaining butter and whisk it into the bisque. Add the diced lobster meat and serve at once. If you like, pour a small spoonful of brandy into each soup bowl and swirl in a little extra cream.

BOUILLABAISSE

AUTHENTIC BOUILLABAISSE COMES FROM THE SOUTH OF FRANCE AND INCLUDES RASCASSE (SCORPION FISH) AS AN ESSENTIAL INGREDIENT. IT IS, HOWEVER, PERFECTLY POSSIBLE TO MAKE THIS WONDERFUL MAIN-COURSE SOUP WITHOUT IT. USE AS LARGE A VARIETY OF FISH AS YOU CAN.

SERVES FOUR

INGREDIENTS

  45ml/3 tbsp olive oil
  2 onions, chopped
  2 leeks, white parts only, chopped
  4 garlic cloves, chopped
  450g/1lb ripe tomatoes, peeled
    and chopped
  3 litres/5 pints/12 cups boiling fish
    stock or water
  15ml/1 tbsp tomato purée
  large pinch of saffron threads
  1 fresh bouquet garni, containing
    2 thyme sprigs, 2 bay leaves and
    2 fennel sprigs
  3kg/6½lb mixed fish, cleaned and
    cut into large chunks
  4 potatoes, peeled and thickly sliced
  salt, pepper and cayenne pepper
  a bowl of rouille (see Fish Soup) and
    a bowl of aïoli (see Provençal Aïoli
    with Salt Cod), to serve
For the garnish
  16 slices of French bread, toasted
    and rubbed with garlic
  30ml/2 tbsp chopped parsley

2 Simmer the soup for 5–8 minutes, removing each type of fish as it becomes cooked. Continue to cook until the potatoes are very tender. Season well with salt, pepper and cayenne.

3 Divide the fish and potatoes among individual soup plates. Strain the soup and ladle it over the fish. Garnish with toasted French bread and parsley. Serve with rouille and aïoli.

1 Heat the oil in a large saucepan. Add the onions, leeks, garlic and tomatoes. Cook until slightly softened. Stir in the stock or water, tomato purée and saffron. Add the bouquet garni and boil until the oil is amalgamated. Lower the heat; add the fish and potatoes.

COOK'S TIP
Suitable fish for Bouillabaisse include rascasse, conger eel, monkfish, red gurnard and John Dory.

CLAM CHOWDER

If fresh clams are hard to find, use frozen or canned clams for this classic recipe from New England. Large clams should be cut into chunky pieces. Reserve a few clams in their shells for garnish, if you like. Traditionally, the soup is served with savoury biscuits called saltine crackers. You should be able to find these in any good delicatessen.

SERVES FOUR

INGREDIENTS

100g/3¾oz salt pork or thinly sliced
  unsmoked bacon, diced
1 large onion, chopped
2 potatoes, peeled and cut into
  1cm/½in cubes
1 bay leaf
1 fresh thyme sprig
300ml/½ pint/1¼ cups milk
400g/14oz cooked clams, cooking
  liquid reserved
150ml/¼ pint/⅔ cup double cream
salt, ground white pepper and
  cayenne pepper
finely chopped fresh parsley, to garnish

1 Put the salt pork or unsmoked bacon in a saucepan, and heat gently, stirring frequently, until the fat runs and the meat is starting to brown. Add the chopped onion and fry over a low heat until softened but not browned.

2 Add the cubed potatoes, the bay leaf and thyme sprig, stir well to coat with fat, then pour in the milk and reserved clam liquid and bring to the boil. Lower the heat and simmer for about 10 minutes, until the potatoes are tender but still firm. Lift out the bay leaf and thyme sprig and discard.

3 Remove the shells from most of the clams. Add all the clams to the pan and season to taste with salt, pepper and cayenne. Simmer gently for 5 minutes more, then stir in the cream. Heat until the soup is very hot, but do not allow it to boil. Pour into a tureen, garnish with the chopped parsley and serve.

CHINESE CRAB AND SWEETCORN SOUP

Frozen white crab meat works as well as fresh in this delicately flavoured soup.

SERVES FOUR

INGREDIENTS

600ml/1 pint/2½ cups fish or
  chicken stock
2.5cm/1in piece fresh root ginger,
  peeled and very finely sliced
400g/14oz can creamed sweetcorn
150g/5oz cooked white crab meat
15ml/1 tbsp arrowroot or cornflour
15ml/1 tbsp rice wine or dry sherry
15–30ml/1–2 tbsp light soy sauce
1 egg white
salt and ground white pepper
shredded spring onions, to garnish

COOK'S TIP

This soup is sometimes made with whole kernel corn, but creamed corn gives a better texture. If you can't find it in a can, use thawed frozen creamed sweetcorn instead; the result will be just as good.

1 Put the stock and ginger in a large saucepan and bring to the boil. Stir in the creamed sweetcorn and bring back to the boil.

2 Switch off the heat and add the crab meat. Put the arrowroot or cornflour in a cup and stir in the rice wine or sherry to make a smooth paste; stir this into the soup. Cook over a low heat for about 3 minutes until the soup has thickened and is slightly glutinous in consistency. Add light soy sauce, salt and white pepper to taste.

3 In a bowl, whisk the egg white to a stiff foam. Gradually fold it into the soup. Ladle the soup into heated bowls, garnish each portion with spring onions and serve.

VARIATION

To make prawn and sweetcorn soup, substitute 150g/5oz cooked peeled prawns for the crab meat. Chop the peeled prawns roughly and add to the soup at the beginning of step 2.

THAI FISH BROTH

LEMON GRASS, CHILLIES AND GALANGAL ARE AMONG THE FLAVOURINGS USED IN THIS FRAGRANT SOUP.

SERVES TWO TO THREE

INGREDIENTS
1 litre/1¾ pints/4 cups fish or light
   chicken stock
4 lemon grass stalks
3 limes
2 small fresh hot red chillies, seeded
   and thinly sliced
2cm/¾in piece fresh galangal,
   peeled and thinly sliced
6 coriander stalks, with leaves
2 kaffir lime leaves, coarsely
   chopped (optional)
350g/12oz monkfish fillet, skinned
   and cut into 2.5cm/1in pieces
15ml/1 tbsp rice vinegar
45ml/3 tbsp *nam pla* (Thai fish sauce)
30ml/2 tbsp chopped coriander
   leaves, to garnish

1 Pour the stock into a saucepan and bring it to the boil. Meanwhile, slice the bulb end of each lemon grass stalk diagonally into pieces about 3mm/⅛in thick. Peel off four wide strips of lime rind with a potato peeler, taking care to avoid the white pith underneath which would make the soup bitter. Squeeze the limes and reserve the juice.

2 Add the sliced lemon grass, lime rind, chillies, galangal and coriander stalks to the stock, with the kaffir lime leaves, if using. Simmer for 1–2 minutes.

VARIATIONS
Prawns, scallops, squid or sole can be substituted for the monkfish. If you use kaffir lime leaves, you will need the juice of only 2 limes.

3 Add the monkfish, rice vinegar and *nam pla*, with half the reserved lime juice. Simmer for about 3 minutes, until the fish is just cooked. Lift out and discard the coriander stalks, taste the broth and add more lime juice if necessary; the soup should taste quite sour. Sprinkle with the coriander leaves and serve very hot.

MALAYSIAN PRAWN LAKSA

THIS SPICY PRAWN AND NOODLE SOUP TASTES JUST AS GOOD WHEN MADE WITH FRESH CRAB MEAT OR ANY FLAKED COOKED FISH. IF YOU ARE SHORT OF TIME OR CAN'T FIND ALL THE SPICY PASTE INGREDIENTS, BUY READY-MADE LAKSA PASTE, WHICH IS AVAILABLE FROM ORIENTAL STORES.

SERVES TWO TO THREE

INGREDIENTS
  115g/4oz rice vermicelli or stir-fry
    rice noodles
  15ml/1 tbsp vegetable or
    groundnut oil
  600ml/1 pint/2½ cups fish stock
  400ml/14fl oz/1⅔ cups thin
    coconut milk
  30ml/2 tbsp *nam pla* (Thai fish sauce)
  ½ lime
  16–24 cooked peeled prawns
  salt and cayenne pepper
  60ml/4 tbsp fresh coriander sprigs
    and leaves, chopped, to garnish
For the spicy paste
  2 lemon grass stalks, finely chopped
  2 fresh red chillies, seeded
    and chopped
  2.5cm/1in piece fresh root ginger,
    peeled and sliced
  2.5ml/½ tsp *blachan* (dried
    shrimp paste)
  2 garlic cloves, chopped
  2.5ml/½ tsp ground turmeric
  30ml/2 tbsp tamarind paste

1 Cook the rice vermicelli or noodles in a large saucepan of boiling salted water according to the instructions on the packet. Tip into a large sieve or colander, then rinse under cold water and drain. Keep warm.

2 To make the spicy paste, place all the prepared ingredients in a mortar and pound with a pestle. Alternatively, put the ingredients in a food processor and whizz until a smooth paste is formed.

3 Heat the vegetable or groundnut oil in a large saucepan, add the spicy paste and fry, stirring constantly, for a few moments to release all the flavours, but be careful not to let it burn.

4 Add the fish stock and coconut milk and bring to the boil. Stir in the *nam pla*, then simmer for 5 minutes. Season with salt and cayenne to taste, adding a squeeze of lime. Add the prawns and heat through for a few seconds.

5 Divide the noodles among two or three soup plates. Pour over the soup, making sure that each portion includes an equal number of prawns. Garnish with coriander and serve piping hot.

STARTERS

Fish and shellfish make the perfect light start to any meal, whatever the main course. Titillate your tastebuds with refreshing Ceviche or that old favourite, Prawn Cocktail. Classic Oysters Rockefeller, and Gratin of Mussels with Pesto are as succulent as they are sophisticated, while deliciously crisp Devilled Whitebait provide piquancy and crunch. If you prefer fish to shellfish, Red Mullet Dolmades make an unusual appetizer.

CEVICHE

YOU CAN USE ALMOST ANY FIRM-FLESHED FISH FOR THIS SOUTH AMERICAN DISH, PROVIDED THAT IT IS PERFECTLY FRESH. THE FISH IS "COOKED" BY THE ACTION OF THE ACIDIC LIME JUICE. ADJUST THE AMOUNT OF CHILLI ACCORDING TO YOUR TASTE.

SERVES SIX

INGREDIENTS

675g/1½lb halibut, turbot, sea bass
  or salmon fillets, skinned
juice of 3 limes
1–2 fresh red chillies, seeded and
  very finely chopped
15ml/1 tbsp olive oil
salt

For the garnish

4 large firm tomatoes, peeled, seeded
  and diced
1 ripe avocado, peeled
  and diced
15ml/1 tbsp lemon juice
30ml/2 tbsp olive oil
30ml/2 tbsp fresh coriander leaves

1 Cut the fish into strips measuring about 5 × 1cm/2 × ½ in. Lay these in a shallow dish and pour over the lime juice, turning the fish strips to coat them all over in the juice. Cover with clear film and leave for 1 hour.

2 Mix all the garnish ingredients, except the coriander, together. Set aside.

3 Season the fish with salt and scatter over the chillies. Drizzle with the olive oil. Toss the fish in the mixture, then replace the cover. Leave to marinate in the fridge for 15–30 minutes more.

4 To serve, divide the garnish among six plates. Spoon on the ceviche, sprinkle with coriander and serve.

MARINATED SMOKED HADDOCK FILLETS

THIS SIMPLE DISH IS ALSO EXCELLENT MADE WITH KIPPER FILLETS; USE WHISKY INSTEAD OF THE RUM.
IF YOU PREFER, OMIT THE SPIRITS AND ADD A TEASPOON OF CASTER SUGAR TO THE MARINADE.

SERVES SIX

INGREDIENTS
    450g/1lb undyed smoked haddock
      fillet, skinned
    1 onion, very thinly sliced
      into rings
    5–10ml/1–2 tsp Dijon mustard
    30ml/2 tbsp lemon juice
    90ml/6 tbsp olive oil
    45ml/3 tbsp dark rum
    12 small new potatoes, scrubbed
    30ml/2 tbsp chopped fresh dill, plus
      6 dill sprigs to garnish
    ground black pepper

COOK'S TIP
Try to get a large, thick haddock fillet.
If all you can find are small pieces, you
can still make the dish, but serve the
pieces whole instead of slicing them.

1 Cut the fish fillet in half lengthways.
Arrange the pieces in a single layer in a
shallow non-metallic dish. Sprinkle the
onion rings evenly over the top.

2 Whisk together the mustard, lemon
juice and some pepper. Add the oil
gradually, whisking. Pour two-thirds of
the dressing over the fish. Cover the
dish with clear film and leave the fish
to marinate for 2 hours in a cool place.
Sprinkle on the rum and leave for
1 hour more.

3 Cook the potatoes in boiling salted
water until tender. Drain, cut in half and
tip into a bowl. Cool until warm, then
toss in the remaining dressing. Stir in
the dill, cover and set aside.

4 Slice the haddock thinly, as for
smoked salmon, or leave whole.
Arrange on small plates and spoon over
some marinade and onion rings. Pile
the potato halves on one side of each
plate and garnish each portion with dill.
Serve chilled or at room temperature.

MOULES PROVENÇALES

EATING THESE DELECTABLE MUSSELS IS A MESSY AFFAIR, WHICH IS PART OF THEIR CHARM. HAND ROUND PLENTY OF CRUSTY FRENCH BREAD FOR MOPPING UP THE JUICES AND DON'T FORGET FINGERBOWLS OF WARM WATER AND A PLATE FOR DISCARDED SHELLS.

SERVES FOUR

INGREDIENTS

30ml/2 tbsp olive oil
200g/7oz rindless unsmoked streaky
  bacon, cubed
1 onion, finely chopped
3 garlic cloves, finely chopped
1 bay leaf
15ml/1 tbsp chopped fresh mixed
  Provençal herbs; thyme, marjoram,
  basil, oregano and savory
15–30ml/1–2 tbsp sun-dried
  tomatoes in oil, chopped
4 large, very ripe tomatoes, peeled,
  seeded and chopped
50g/2oz/½ cup stoned black
  olives, chopped
105ml/7 tbsp dry white wine
2.25kg/5–5¼ lb live mussels,
  scrubbed and bearded
salt and ground black pepper
60ml/4 tbsp coarsely chopped
  fresh parsley, to garnish

1 Heat the oil in a large saucepan. Fry the bacon until golden and crisp. Remove with a slotted spoon; set aside. Add the onion and garlic to the pan and cook gently until softened. Add the herbs, with both types of tomatoes. Fry gently for 5 minutes, stirring frequently. Stir in the olives and season.

2 Put the wine and mussels in another pan. Cover and shake over a high heat for 5 minutes until the mussels open. Discard any which remain closed.

3 Strain the cooking liquid into the saucepan containing the tomato sauce and boil until reduced by about one-third. Add the mussels and stir to coat them thoroughly with the sauce. Take out the bay leaf.

4 Divide the mussels and sauce among four heated dishes. Scatter over the fried bacon and chopped parsley and serve piping hot.

OYSTERS ROCKEFELLER

THIS IS THE PERFECT DISH FOR THOSE WHO PREFER THEIR OYSTERS LIGHTLY COOKED. AS A CHEAPER ALTERNATIVE, FOR THOSE WHO ARE NOT "AS RICH AS ROCKEFELLER", GIVE MUSSELS OR CLAMS THE SAME TREATMENT; THEY WILL ALSO TASTE DELICIOUS.

SERVES SIX

INGREDIENTS
    450g/1lb/3 cups coarse salt, plus
      extra to serve
    24 oysters, opened
    115g/4oz/½ cup butter
    2 shallots, finely chopped
    500g/1¼lb spinach leaves,
      finely chopped
    60ml/4 tbsp chopped fresh parsley
    60ml/4 tbsp chopped celery leaves
    90ml/6 tbsp fresh white breadcrumbs
    Tabasco sauce or cayenne pepper
    10–20ml/2–4 tsp Pernod or Ricard
    salt and ground black pepper
    lemon wedges, to serve

COOK'S TIP
If you prefer a smoother stuffing whizz it
to a paste in a food processor or blender.

1 Preheat the oven to 220°C/425°F/
Gas 7. Make a bed of coarse salt on two
large baking sheets. Set the oysters in
the half-shell in the bed of salt to keep
them steady. Set aside.

2 Melt the butter in a frying pan. Add
the finely chopped shallots and cook
them over a low heat for 2–3 minutes
until they are softened. Stir in the
spinach and let it wilt.

3 Add the parsley, celery leaves and
breadcrumbs to the pan and fry gently
for 5 minutes. Season with salt, pepper
and Tabasco or cayenne.

4 Divide the stuffing among the oysters.
Drizzle a few drops of Pernod or Ricard
over each oyster, then bake for about
5 minutes, until bubbling and golden
brown. Serve on a heated platter on a
shallow salt bed with lemon wedges.

AROMATIC TIGER PRAWNS

THERE IS NO ELEGANT WAY TO EAT THESE AROMATIC PRAWNS — JUST HOLD THEM BY THE TAILS, PULL THEM OFF THE STICKS WITH YOUR FINGERS AND POP THEM INTO YOUR MOUTH.

SERVES FOUR

INGREDIENTS
16 raw tiger prawns or scampi tails
2.5ml/½ tsp chilli powder
5ml/1 tsp fennel seeds
5 Sechuan or black peppercorns
1 star anise, broken into segments
1 cinnamon stick, broken into pieces
30ml/2 tbsp groundnut or
  sunflower oil
2 garlic cloves, chopped
2cm/¾in piece fresh root ginger,
  peeled and finely chopped
1 shallot, chopped
30ml/2 tbsp water
30ml/2 tbsp rice vinegar
30ml/2 tbsp soft brown or palm sugar
salt and ground black pepper
lime slices and chopped spring
  onion, to garnish

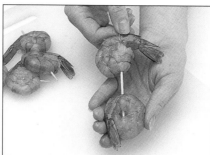

1 Thread the prawns or scampi tails in pairs on eight wooden cocktail sticks. Set aside. Heat a frying pan, put in all the chilli powder, fennel seeds, Sechuan or black peppercorns, star anise and cinnamon stick and dry fry for 1–2 minutes to release the flavours. Leave to cool, then grind the spices coarsely in a grinder or tip into a mortar and crush with a pestle.

2 Heat the groundnut or sunflower oil in a shallow pan, add the garlic, ginger and chopped shallot and then fry gently until very lightly coloured. Add the crushed spices and seasoning and cook the mixture gently for 2 minutes. Pour in the water and simmer, stirring, for 5 minutes.

3 Add the rice vinegar and soft brown or palm sugar, stir until dissolved, then add the prawns or scampi tails. Cook for 3–5 minutes, until the seafood has turned pink, but is still very juicy. Serve hot, garnished with lime slices and spring onion.

COOK'S TIP
If you buy whole prawns, remove the heads before cooking them.

PRAWN AND VEGETABLE CROSTINI

USE BOTTLED CARCIOFINI (TINY ARTICHOKE HEARTS PRESERVED IN OLIVE OIL) FOR THIS SIMPLE STARTER, WHICH CAN BE PREPARED VERY QUICKLY.

SERVES FOUR

INGREDIENTS
450g/1lb whole cooked prawns, in
  the shell
4 thick slices of ciabatta, cut
  diagonally across
3 garlic cloves, peeled and
  2 halved lengthways
60ml/4 tbsp olive oil
200g/7oz/2 cups small button
  mushrooms, trimmed
12 drained bottled *carciofini*
60ml/4 tbsp chopped flat leaf parsley
salt and ground black pepper

COOK'S TIP
Don't be tempted to use thawed frozen prawns, especially those that have been peeled; freshly cooked prawns in their shells are infinitely nicer.

1 Peel the prawns and remove the heads. Rub the ciabatta slices on both sides with the cut sides of the halved garlic cloves, drizzle with a little of the olive oil and toast in the oven or grill until lightly browned. Keep hot.

2 Finely chop the remaining garlic. Heat the remaining oil in a saucepan and gently fry the garlic until golden, but do not allow it to brown.

3 Add the mushrooms and stir to coat with oil. Season and sauté for about 2–3 minutes. Gently stir in the drained *carciofini*, then add the chopped flat leaf parsley.

4 Season again, then stir in the prawns and sauté briefly to warm through. Pile the prawn mixture on to the ciabatta, pour over any remaining cooking juices and serve immediately.

SCALLOPS WITH SAMPHIRE AND LIME

SAMPHIRE HAS A WONDERFUL TASTE AND AROMA OF THE SEA. IT IS THE PERFECT COMPLEMENT TO SCALLOPS AND HELPS TO CREATE A VERY ATTRACTIVE STARTER.

SERVES FOUR

INGREDIENTS
   225g/8oz fresh samphire
   12 large or 24 queen scallops, out of
      the shell
   300ml/½ pint/1¼ cups dry
      white wine
   juice of 2 limes
   15ml/1 tbsp groundnut or
      vegetable oil
   ½ cucumber, peeled, seeded
      and diced
   ground black pepper
   chopped fresh parsley, to garnish

1 Wash the fresh samphire in several changes of cold water. Drain, then trim off any woody ends. Bring a saucepan of water to the boil, then drop in the samphire and cook for 3–5 minutes, until tender but still crisp. Drain, refresh under cold water and drain again.

2 If the scallops are large, cut them in half horizontally. Detach the corals. In a shallow pan, bring the wine to the boil and cook until it is reduced by about one-third. Lower the heat and add the lime juice to the pan.

3 Add the scallops and corals and poach gently for 3–4 minutes until the scallops are just cooked, but still opaque. Using a slotted spoon, lift out the scallops and corals and set aside.

COOK'S TIP
Samphire grows wild in estuaries and salt marshes in Europe and North America. High-quality fishmongers sometimes stock it.

4 Leave the cooking liquid to cool until tepid, then whisk in the groundnut or vegetable oil. Add the samphire, cucumber, scallops and corals and toss lightly to mix. Grind over some black pepper, cover and leave at room temperature for about 1 hour to allow the flavours to develop. Divide the mixture among four individual dishes and then garnish with chopped fresh parsley. Serve the dish at room temperature.

GRATIN OF MUSSELS WITH PESTO

THIS IS THE PERFECT STARTER FOR SERVING WHEN TIME IS SHORT, AS BOTH THE PESTO AND THE MUSSELS CAN BE PREPARED IN ADVANCE, AND THE DISH ASSEMBLED AND GRILLED AT THE LAST MINUTE.

SERVES FOUR

INGREDIENTS
    36 large live mussels, scrubbed
      and bearded
    105ml/7 tbsp dry white wine
    60ml/4 tbsp finely chopped fresh
      flat leaf parsley
    1 garlic clove, finely chopped
    30ml/2 tbsp fresh white breadcrumbs
    60ml/4 tbsp olive oil
    chopped fresh basil, to garnish
    crusty bread, to serve
For the pesto
    2 fat garlic cloves, chopped
    2.5ml/½ tsp coarse salt
    100g/3¾ oz/3 cups basil leaves
    25g/1oz/⅓ cup pine nuts, chopped
    50g/2oz/⅔ cup freshly grated
      Parmesan cheese
    120ml/4fl oz/½ cup extra virgin
      olive oil

1 Put the mussels in a saucepan with the wine, clamp on the lid and shake over high heat for 3–4 minutes until the mussels have opened. Discard any which remain closed.

2 As soon as the mussels are cool enough to handle, strain the cooking liquid and keep it for another recipe. Discard the empty half-shells. Arrange the mussels in their half-shells in a single layer in four individual gratin dishes. Cover and set aside.

COOK'S TIP
Home-made pesto is best but when basil is out of season – or you are in a hurry – a jar may be used instead.

3 To make the pesto, put the chopped garlic and salt in a mortar and pound to a purée with a pestle. Then add the basil leaves and chopped pine nuts and crush to a thick paste. Work in the Parmesan cheese, and finally gradually drip in enough olive oil to make a smooth and creamy paste. Alternatively, use a food processor.

4 Spoon pesto over the mussels placed in gratin dishes. Mix the parsley, garlic and breadcrumbs. Sprinkle over the mussels. Drizzle with the oil.

5 Preheat the grill to high. Stand the dishes on a baking sheet and grill for 3 minutes. Garnish with chopped basil and serve with crusty bread.

PRAWN COCKTAIL

THERE IS NO NICER STARTER THAN A GOOD, FRESH PRAWN COCKTAIL — AND NOTHING NASTIER THAN ONE IN WHICH SOGGY PRAWNS SWIM IN A THIN, VINEGARY SAUCE EMBEDDED IN LIMP LETTUCE. THIS RECIPE SHOWS JUST HOW GOOD A PRAWN COCKTAIL CAN BE.

SERVES SIX

INGREDIENTS
60ml/4 tbsp double cream, lightly whipped
60ml/4 tbsp mayonnaise, preferably home-made
60ml/4 tbsp tomato ketchup
5–10ml/1–2 tsp Worcestershire sauce
juice of 1 lemon
½ cos lettuce or other very crisp lettuce
450g/1lb cooked peeled prawns
salt, ground black pepper and paprika
6 large whole cooked prawns in the shell, to garnish (optional)
thinly sliced brown bread with butter and lemon wedges, to serve

1 Place the lightly whipped cream, mayonnaise and tomato ketchup in a small bowl and whisk lightly to combine. Add Worcestershire sauce to taste, then whisk in enough of the lemon juice to make a really tangy sauce.

COOK'S TIP
Partly peeled prawns make a pretty garnish. To prepare, carefully peel the body shell from the prawns and leave the tail "fan" for decoration.

2 Finely shred the lettuce and fill six individual glasses one-third full.

3 Stir the prawns into the sauce, then check the seasoning and spoon the prawn mixture generously over the lettuce. If you like, drape a whole cooked prawn over the edge of each glass and sprinkle each of the cocktails with ground black pepper and/or paprika. Serve immediately, with thinly sliced brown bread with butter and lemon wedges.

CRAB SALAD WITH ROCKET

IF THE DRESSED CRABS ARE REALLY SMALL, PILE THE SALAD BACK INTO THE SHELLS FOR AN ATTRACTIVE ALTERNATIVE PRESENTATION.

SERVES FOUR

INGREDIENTS
white and brown meat from 4 small fresh dressed crabs, about 450g/1lb
1 small red pepper, seeded and finely chopped
1 small red onion, finely chopped
30ml/2 tbsp drained capers
30ml/2 tbsp chopped fresh coriander
grated rind and juice of 2 lemons
Tabasco sauce
salt and ground black pepper
lemon rind strips, to garnish
For the rocket salad
40g/1½oz rocket leaves
30ml/2 tbsp sunflower oil
15ml/1 tbsp fresh lime juice

1 Put the white and brown crab meat, red pepper, onion, capers and chopped coriander in a bowl. Add the lemon rind and juice and toss gently to mix together. Season with a few drops of Tabasco sauce, according to taste, and a little salt and pepper.

2 Wash the rocket leaves and pat dry on paper towels. Divide among four plates. Mix together the oil and lime juice in a small bowl. Dress the rocket leaves, then pile the crab salad on top and serve garnished with lemon rind strips.

RED MULLET DOLMADES

IF YOU CANNOT FIND PREPARED VINE LEAVES, USE BLANCHED CABBAGE OR LARGE SPINACH LEAVES INSTEAD. PLAICE OR LEMON SOLE CAN BE SUBSTITUTED FOR THE RED MULLET.

2 Remove the skin from the fish fillets and flake the flesh into a bowl. Gently stir in the cooked rice, pine nuts, the chopped parsley, and lemon rind and juice. Season the filling to taste with salt and ground black pepper.

3 Spoon 30–45ml/2–3 tbsp of the filling into the middle of each vine leaf. Roll up each filled leaf, tucking in the ends to make a secure package. Arrange the dolmades in an ovenproof dish, with the joins underneath. Then pour over the reserved cooking liquid and place the dolmades in the preheated oven for about 5 minutes, until they are heated through thoroughly.

SERVES FOUR

INGREDIENTS
   225g/8oz red mullet fillets, scaled
   45ml/3 tbsp dry white wine
   115g/4oz/1 cup cooked long
    grain rice
   25g/1oz/1/3 cup pine nuts
   45ml/3 tbsp chopped fresh parsley
   grated rind and juice of 1/2 lemon
   8 vine leaves in brine, rinsed
    and dried
   salt and ground black pepper
For the orange butter sauce
   grated rind and juice of 2 oranges
   2 shallots, very finely chopped
   25g/1oz/2 tbsp chilled butter, diced

1 Preheat the oven to 200°C/400°F/ Gas 6. Put the red mullet fillets in a shallow pan and season with salt and pepper. Pour over the wine, bring to the boil, then lower the heat and poach the fish gently for about 3 minutes, until it is just cooked. Strain, reserving the cooking liquid.

4 Meanwhile, make the sauce. Mix the orange rind and juice and the shallots in a small saucepan and boil vigorously for a few minutes until the mixture is reduced and syrupy.

5 Strain the sauce into a clean pan, discarding the shallots. Beat in the butter, one piece at a time. Reheat gently, but do not let the sauce boil. Drizzle the sauce over the hot dolmades and serve at once.

SALMON AND SCALLOP BROCHETTES

WITH THEIR DELICATE COLOURS AND SUPERB FLAVOUR, THESE SKEWERS MAKE THE PERFECT OPENER FOR A SOPHISTICATED MEAL.

SERVES FOUR

INGREDIENTS

8 lemon grass stalks
225g/8oz salmon fillet, skinned
8 queen scallops, with their corals
 if possible
8 baby onions, peeled
 and blanched
½ yellow pepper, cut into
 8 squares
25g/1oz/2 tbsp butter
juice of ½ lemon
salt, ground white pepper
 and paprika
For the sauce
30ml/2 tbsp dry vermouth
50g/2oz/¼ cup butter
5ml/1 tsp chopped fresh tarragon

1 Preheat the grill to medium-high. Cut off the top 7.5–10cm/3–4in of each lemon grass stalk. Reserve the bulb ends for another dish. Cut the salmon fillet into twelve 2cm/¾in cubes. Thread the salmon, scallops, corals if available, onions and pepper squares on to the lemon grass and arrange the brochettes in a grill pan.

2 Melt the butter in a small pan, add the lemon juice and a pinch of paprika and then brush all over the brochettes. Grill the skewers for about 2–3 minutes on each side, turning and basting the brochettes every minute, until the fish and scallops are just cooked, but are still very juicy. Transfer to a platter and keep hot while you make the tarragon butter sauce.

3 Pour the dry vermouth and all the leftover cooking juices from the brochettes into a small pan and boil quite fiercely to reduce by half. Add the butter and melt, always stirring. Stir in the chopped fresh tarragon and add salt and ground white pepper to taste. Pour the tarragon butter sauce over the brochettes and serve.

SOFT-SHELL CRABS WITH CHILLI AND SALT

IF FRESH SOFT-SHELL CRABS ARE UNAVAILABLE, YOU CAN BUY FROZEN ONES IN ORIENTAL SUPERMARKETS. ALLOW TWO SMALL CRABS PER SERVING, OR ONE IF THEY ARE LARGE. ADJUST THE QUANTITY OF CHILLI ACCORDING TO YOUR TASTE.

SERVES FOUR

INGREDIENTS
   8 small soft-shell crabs, thawed
      if frozen
   50g/2oz/½ cup plain flour
   60ml/4 tbsp groundnut or
      vegetable oil
   2 large fresh red chillies, or 1 green
      and 1 red, seeded and thinly sliced
   4 spring onions or a small bunch of
      garlic chives, chopped
   coarse sea salt and ground
      black pepper
To serve
   shredded lettuce, mooli and carrot
   light soy sauce

COOK'S TIP
The shredded vegetables make a colourful bed for the crabs. If you can't locate any mooli, use celeriac instead.

1 Pat the crabs dry with kitchen paper. Season the flour with pepper and coat the crabs lightly with the mixture.

2 Heat the oil in a shallow pan until very hot, then put in the crabs (you may need to do this in two batches). Fry for 2–3 minutes on each side, until the crabs are golden brown but still juicy in the middle. Drain the cooked crabs on kitchen paper and keep hot.

3 Add the sliced chillies and spring onions or garlic chives to the oil remaining in the pan and cook gently for about 2 minutes. Sprinkle over a generous pinch of salt, then spread the mixture on to the crabs.

4 Mix the shredded lettuce, mooli and carrot together. Arrange on plates, top each portion with two crabs and serve, with light soy sauce for dipping.

DEVILLED WHITEBAIT

SERVE THESE DELICIOUSLY CRISP LITTLE FISH WITH LEMON WEDGES AND THINLY SLICED BROWN BREAD AND BUTTER, AND EAT THEM WITH YOUR FINGERS.

SERVES FOUR

INGREDIENTS
   oil for deep-frying
   150ml/¼ pint/⅔ cup milk
   115g/4oz/1 cup plain flour
   450g/1lb whitebait
   salt, freshly ground black pepper and
      cayenne pepper

1 Heat the oil in a large saucepan or deep-fryer. Put the milk in a shallow bowl and spoon the flour into a paper bag. Season the flour with salt, pepper and a little cayenne.

COOK'S TIP
Most whitebait are sold frozen. Thaw them before use and dry them thoroughly on kitchen paper.

2 Dip a handful of the whitebait into the bowl of milk, drain them well, then pop them into the paper bag. Shake gently to coat them evenly in the seasoned flour. Repeat until all the fish have been coated. This is the easiest method of flouring whitebait, but don't add too many at once, or they will stick together.

3 Heat the oil for deep-frying to 190°C/375°F or until a cube of stale bread, dropped into the oil, browns in 20 seconds. Add a batch of whitebait, preferably in a chip basket, and fry for 2–3 minutes, until crisp and golden brown. Drain and keep hot while you fry the rest. Sprinkle with more cayenne and serve very hot.

MOUSSES, PÂTÉS AND TERRINES

Soft-textured fish and shellfish can be puréed to produce attractive light-textured mousses such as Smoked Fish and Asparagus Mousse. Hot Crab Soufflés make a substantial starter or light lunch or supper dish for a chilly day, and chunky Haddock and Smoked Salmon Terrine is ideal when the weather warms up. Celebrate summer with cold creamy Sea Trout Mousse. For the simplest of dishes, Smoked Mackerel Pâté takes only moments to prepare and is perennially popular.

SEA TROUT MOUSSE

THIS DELICIOUSLY CREAMY MOUSSE MAKES A LITTLE SEA TROUT GO A LONG WAY. IT IS EQUALLY GOOD MADE WITH SALMON IF SEA TROUT IS UNAVAILABLE.

SERVES SIX

INGREDIENTS
    250g/9oz sea trout fillet
    120ml/4fl oz/½ cup fish stock
    2 gelatine leaves, or 15ml/1 tbsp
        powdered gelatine
    juice of ½ lemon
    30ml/2 tbsp dry sherry or
        dry vermouth
    30ml/2 tbsp freshly grated Parmesan
    300ml/½ pint/1¼ cups whipping
        cream
    2 egg whites
    15ml/1 tbsp sunflower oil
    salt and ground white pepper
For the garnish
    5cm/2in piece of cucumber, with
        peel, thinly sliced and halved
    fresh dill or chervil

3 When the trout is cool enough to handle, remove the skin and flake the flesh. Pour the stock into a food processor or blender. Process briefly, then gradually add the flaked trout, lemon juice, sherry or vermouth and Parmesan through the feeder tube, continuing to process the mixture until it is smooth. Scrape into a large bowl and leave to cool completely.

4 Lightly whip the cream in a bowl; fold it into the cold trout mixture. Season to taste, then cover with clear film and chill until the mousse is just beginning to set. It should have the consistency of mayonnaise.

5 In a grease-free bowl, beat the egg whites with a pinch of salt until softly peaking. Using a large metal spoon, stir one-third into the trout mixture to slacken it, then fold in the rest.

6 Lightly grease six ramekins with the sunflower oil. Divide the mousse among the ramekins and level the surface. Place in the fridge for 2–3 hours, until set. Just before serving, arrange a few slices of cucumber and a small herb sprig on each mousse and add a little chopped dill or chervil.

1 Put the sea trout in a shallow pan. Pour in the fish stock and heat to simmering point. Poach the fish for about 3–4 minutes, until it is lightly cooked. Strain the stock into a jug and leave the trout to cool slightly.

2 Add the gelatine to the hot stock and stir until it has dissolved completely. Set aside until required.

COOK'S TIP
Serve the mousse with Melba toast, if you like. Toast thin slices of bread on both sides under the grill, then cut off the crusts and carefully slice each piece of toast in half horizontally. Return to the grill pan, untoasted sides up, and grill again. The thin slices will swiftly brown and curl, so watch them closely.

QUENELLES OF SOLE

TRADITIONALLY, THESE LIGHT FISH "DUMPLINGS" ARE MADE WITH PIKE, BUT THEY ARE EVEN BETTER MADE WITH SOLE OR OTHER WHITE FISH. IF YOU ARE FEELING EXTRAVAGANT, SERVE THEM WITH A CREAMY SHELLFISH SAUCE STUDDED WITH CRAYFISH TAILS OR PRAWNS.

SERVES SIX

INGREDIENTS
   450g/1lb sole fillets, skinned and cut
     into large pieces
   4 egg whites
   600ml/1 pint/2½ cups double cream
   salt, ground white pepper and
     grated nutmeg
For the sauce
   1 small shallot, finely chopped
   60ml/4 tbsp dry vermouth, such as
     Noilly Prat
   120ml/4fl oz/½ cup fish stock
   150ml/¼ pint/⅔ cup double cream
   50g/2oz/¼ cup butter, chilled
     and diced
   chopped fresh parsley, to garnish

1 Check the sole for stray bones, then put the pieces in a blender or food processor. Add a generous pinch of salt and a grinding of pepper. Switch on and, with the motor running, add the egg whites one at a time through the feeder tube to make a smooth purée. Press the purée through a metal sieve placed over a bowl. Stand the bowl of purée in a larger bowl and surround it with plenty of crushed ice or ice cubes.

2 Whip the cream until very thick and floppy, but not stiff. Gradually fold it into the fish mousse, making sure each spoonful has been absorbed completely before adding the next. Season with salt and pepper, then stir in nutmeg to taste. Cover the bowl of mousse and transfer it, still in its bowl of ice, to the fridge. Chill for several hours.

3 To make the sauce, combine the shallot, vermouth and fish stock in a small saucepan. Bring to the boil and cook until reduced by half. Add the cream and boil again until the sauce has the consistency of single cream. Strain, return to the pan and whisk in the butter, one piece at a time, until the sauce is very creamy. Season and keep hot, but do not let it boil.

4 Bring a wide shallow pan of lightly salted water to the boil, then reduce the heat so that the water surface barely trembles. Using two tablespoons dipped in hot water, shape the fish mousse into ovals. As each quenelle is shaped, slip it into the simmering water.

5 Poach the quenelles in batches for 8–10 minutes, until they feel just firm to the touch, but are still slightly creamy inside. As each is cooked, lift it out on a slotted spoon, drain on kitchen paper and keep hot. When all the quenelles are cooked, arrange them on heated plates. Pour the sauce around. Serve garnished with parsley.

COOK'S TIP
Keep the heat low when poaching; quenelles disintegrate in boiling water.

SMOKED MACKEREL PÂTÉ

SOME OF THE MOST DELICIOUS DISHES ARE ALSO THE SIMPLEST TO MAKE. SERVE THIS POPULAR PÂTÉ WITH WARMED MELBA TOAST AS A STARTER, OR FOR A LIGHT LUNCH WITH WHOLEMEAL TOAST.

SERVES SIX

INGREDIENTS
    4 smoked mackerel fillets, skinned
    225g/8oz/1 cup cream cheese
    1–2 garlic cloves, finely chopped
    juice of 1 lemon
    30ml/2 tbsp chopped fresh chervil,
        parsley or chives
    15ml/1 tbsp Worcestershire sauce
    salt and cayenne pepper
    fresh chives, to garnish
    warmed Melba toast, to serve

VARIATION
Use peppered mackerel fillets for a more piquant flavour. This pâté can be made with smoked haddock or kipper fillets.

1 Break up the mackerel and put it in a food processor. Add the cream cheese, garlic, lemon juice and herbs.

2 Process the mixture until it is fairly smooth but still has a slightly chunky texture, then add Worcestershire sauce, salt and cayenne pepper to taste. Whizz to mix, then spoon the pâté into a dish, cover with clear film and chill. Garnish with chives and serve with Melba toast.

BRANDADE OF SALT COD

THERE ARE ALMOST AS MANY VERSIONS OF THIS CREAMY SALT COD PURÉE AS THERE ARE REGIONS OF FRANCE. SOME CONTAIN MASHED POTATOES, OTHERS TRUFFLES. THIS COMPARATIVELY LIGHT RECIPE INCLUDES GARLIC, BUT YOU CAN OMIT IT AND SERVE THE BRANDADE ON TOASTED SLICES OF FRENCH BREAD RUBBED WITH GARLIC IF YOU PREFER.

SERVES SIX

INGREDIENTS
    200g/7oz salt cod
    250ml/8fl oz/1 cup extra virgin
        olive oil
    4 garlic cloves, crushed
    250ml/8fl oz/1 cup double or
        whipping cream
    freshly ground white pepper
    shredded spring onions, to garnish
    herbed crispbread, to serve

COOK'S TIP
You can purée the fish mixture in a mortar with a pestle. This gives a better texture, but is notoriously hard work.

1 Soak the fish in cold water for 24 hours, changing the water often. Drain. Cut into pieces, place in a shallow pan and pour in cold water to cover. Heat the water until simmering, then poach the fish for 8 minutes, until just cooked. Drain, then remove the skin and bones.

2 Combine the olive oil and garlic in a small saucepan and heat to just below boiling point. In another saucepan, heat the cream until it starts to simmer.

3 Put the cod into a food processor, process it briefly, then gradually add alternate amounts of the garlic-flavoured olive oil and cream, while continuing to process the mixture. The aim is to create a purée with the consistency of mashed potatoes.

4 Add pepper to taste, then scoop the brandade into a serving bowl. Garnish with shredded spring onions and serve warm with herbed crispbread.

HOT CRAB SOUFFLÉS

THESE DELICIOUS LITTLE SOUFFLÉS MUST BE SERVED AS SOON AS THEY ARE READY, SO SEAT YOUR GUESTS AT THE TABLE BEFORE TAKING THE SOUFFLÉS OUT OF THE OVEN.

SERVES SIX

INGREDIENTS
    50g/2oz/¼ cup butter
    45ml/3 tbsp fine wholemeal
        breadcrumbs
    4 spring onions, finely chopped
    15ml/1 tbsp Malaysian or mild
        Madras curry powder
    25g/1oz/2 tbsp plain flour
    105ml/7 tbsp coconut milk or milk
    150ml/¼ pint/⅔ cup whipping
        cream
    4 egg yolks
    225g/8oz white crab meat
    mild green Tabasco sauce
    6 egg whites
    salt and ground black pepper

VARIATION
Lobster or salmon can be used instead of crab in these soufflés.

1 Use some of the butter to grease six ramekins or a 1.75 litre/3 pint/7 cup soufflé dish. Sprinkle in the fine wholemeal breadcrumbs, roll the dishes or dish around to coat the base and sides completely, then tip out the excess breadcrumbs. Preheat the oven to 200°C/400°F/Gas 6.

2 Melt the remaining butter in a saucepan, add the spring onions and Malaysian or mild Madras curry powder and cook over a low heat for about 1 minute, until softened. Stir in the flour and cook for 1 minute more.

3 Gradually add the coconut milk or milk and cream, stirring constantly. Cook until smooth and thick. Off the heat, stir in the egg yolks, then the crab. Season with salt, black pepper and Tabasco sauce.

4 In a grease-free bowl, beat the egg whites stiffly with a pinch of salt. Using a metal spoon, stir one-third into the mixture to slacken it; fold in the rest. Spoon into the dishes or dish.

5 Bake until well-risen and golden brown, and just firm to the touch. Individual soufflés will be ready in about 8 minutes; a large soufflé will take 15–20 minutes. Serve at once.

SMOKED FISH AND ASPARAGUS MOUSSE

THIS ELEGANT MOUSSE LOOKS VERY SPECIAL WITH ITS STUDDING OF ASPARAGUS AND SMOKED SALMON.
SERVE A MUSTARD AND DILL DRESSING SEPARATELY IF YOU LIKE.

SERVES EIGHT

INGREDIENTS
 15ml/1 tbsp powdered gelatine
 juice of 1 lemon
 105ml/7 tbsp fish stock
 50g/2oz/¼ cup butter, plus extra
  for greasing
 2 shallots, finely chopped
 225g/8oz smoked trout fillets
 105ml/7 tbsp soured cream
 225g/8oz/1 cup low-fat cream cheese
  or cottage cheese
 1 egg white
 12 spinach leaves, blanched
 12 fresh asparagus spears,
  lightly cooked
 115g/4oz smoked salmon, cut into
  long strips
 salt
 shredded beetroot and leaves,
  to garnish

4 Grease a 1 litre/1¾ pint/4 cup loaf tin or terrine with butter, then line it with the spinach leaves. Carefully spread half the trout mousse over the spinach-covered base, arrange the asparagus spears on top, then cover with the remaining trout mousse.

5 Arrange the smoked salmon strips lengthways on the mousse and fold over the overhanging spinach leaves. Cover with clear film and chill for 4 hours, until set. To serve, remove the clear film, turn out on to a serving dish and garnish.

1 Sprinkle the gelatine over the lemon juice and leave until spongy. In a small saucepan, heat the fish stock, then add the soaked gelatine and stir to dissolve completely. Set aside. Melt the butter in a small pan, add the shallots and cook gently until softened but not coloured.

2 Break up the smoked trout fillets and put them in a food processor with the shallots, soured cream, stock mixture and cream or cottage cheese. Whizz until smooth, then spoon into a bowl.

3 In a clean bowl, beat the egg white with a pinch of salt to soft peaks. Fold into the fish. Cover the bowl; chill for 30 minutes or until starting to set.

STRIPED FISH TERRINE

*SERVE THIS ATTRACTIVE TERRINE COLD OR JUST WARM, WITH A HOLLANDAISE SAUCE IF YOU LIKE.
IT IS IDEAL AS A STARTER OR LIGHT LUNCH DISH.*

SERVES EIGHT

INGREDIENTS

15ml/1 tbsp sunflower oil
450g/1lb salmon fillet, skinned
450g/1lb sole fillets, skinned
3 egg whites
105ml/7 tbsp double cream
15ml/1 tbsp fresh chives,
  finely snipped
juice of 1 lemon
115g/4oz/scant 1 cup fresh or frozen
  peas, cooked
5ml/1 tsp chopped fresh mint leaves
salt, ground white pepper and
  grated nutmeg
thinly sliced cucumber, salad cress
  and chives, to garnish

1 Grease a 1 litre/1¾ pint/4 cup loaf tin
or terrine with the oil. Slice the salmon
thinly; cut it and the sole into long
strips, 2.5cm/1in wide. Preheat the
oven to 200°C/400°F/Gas 6.

2 Line the terrine neatly with alternate
slices of salmon and sole leaving the
ends overhanging the edge. You should
be left with about a third of the salmon
and half the sole.

3 In a grease-free bowl, beat the egg
whites with a pinch of salt until they
form soft peaks. Purée the remaining
sole in a food processor. Spoon into a
mixing bowl, season, then fold in two-
thirds of the egg whites, followed by
two-thirds of the cream. Put half the
mixture into a second bowl; stir in the
chives. Add nutmeg to the first bowl.

4 Purée the remaining salmon, scrape it
into a bowl; add the lemon juice. Fold
in the remaining whites, then cream.

5 Purée the peas with the mint. Season
the mixture and spread it over the base
of the terrine, smoothing the surface
with a spatula. Spoon over the sole with
chives mixture and spread evenly.

6 Add the salmon mixture, then finish
with the plain sole mixture. Cover with
the overhanging fish fillets and make a
lid of oiled foil. Stand the terrine in a
roasting tin and pour in enough boiling
water to come halfway up the sides.

7 Bake for 15–20 minutes, until the top
fillets are just cooked and the mousse
feels springy. Remove the foil, lay a wire
rack over the top of the terrine and
invert both rack and terrine on to a
lipped baking sheet to catch the
cooking juices that drain out. Keep
these to make fish stock or soup.

8 Leaving the tin in place, let the terrine
stand for about 15 minutes, then turn
the terrine over again. Invert it on to a
serving dish and lift off the tin carefully.
Serve warm, or chill in the fridge first
and serve cold. Garnish with thinly
sliced cucumber, salad cress and
chives before serving.

COOK'S TIPS
• Pop the salmon into the freezer about
an hour before slicing it. If it is almost
frozen, it will be much easier to slice.
• You can line the tin or terrine with
oven-safe clear film after greasing and
before adding the salmon and sole strips.
This makes it easier to turn out the
terrine but is not strictly necessary.

HADDOCK AND SMOKED SALMON TERRINE

THIS SUBSTANTIAL TERRINE MAKES A SUPERB DISH FOR A SUMMER BUFFET, ACCOMPANIED BY DILL MAYONNAISE OR A FRESH MANGO SALSA.

SERVES TEN TO TWELVE AS A STARTER,
SIX TO EIGHT AS A MAIN COURSE

INGREDIENTS
    15ml/1 tbsp sunflower oil,
      for greasing
    350g/12oz oak-smoked salmon
    900g/2lb haddock fillets, skinned
    2 eggs, lightly beaten
    105ml/7 tbsp crème fraîche
    30ml/2 tbsp drained capers
    30ml/2 tbsp drained soft green or
      pink peppercorns
    salt and ground white pepper
    crème fraîche, peppercorns and
      fresh dill and rocket, to garnish

3 Combine the eggs, crème fraîche, capers and green or pink peppercorns in a bowl. Season with salt and pepper; stir in the small pieces of haddock. Spoon the mixture into the mould until it is one-third full. Smooth the surface with a spatula.

6 Stand the terrine in a roasting tin and pour in boiling water to come halfway up the sides. Place in the oven and cook for 45 minutes–1 hour, until the filling is just set.

1 Preheat the oven to 200°C/400°F/ Gas 6. Grease a 1 litre/1¾ pint/4 cup loaf tin or terrine with the oil. Use some of the salmon to line the tin or terrine; let some of the ends overhang the mould. Reserve the remaining smoked salmon until needed.

4 Wrap the long haddock fillets in the reserved smoked salmon. Lay them on top of the layer of the fish mixture in the tin or terrine.

7 Take the terrine out of the roasting tin, but do not remove the foil cover. Place two or three large heavy tins on the foil to weight it and leave until cold. Chill in the fridge for 24 hours.

8 About an hour before serving, remove the terrine from the fridge, lift off the weights and remove the foil. Carefully invert the terrine on to a serving plate and lift off the tin or terrine.

9 Cut the terrine into thick slices using a sharp knife and serve, garnished with crème fraîche, peppercorns and fronds of dill and rocket leaves.

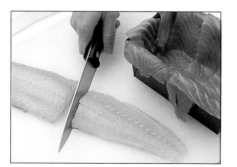

2 Cut two long slices of haddock the length of the tin or terrine and set aside. Cut the rest of the haddock into small pieces. Season all the haddock with salt and pepper.

5 Fill the tin or terrine with the rest of the fish mixture, smooth the surface and fold the overhanging pieces of smoked salmon over the top. Cover tightly with a double thickness of foil. Tap the terrine to settle the contents.

VARIATION
Use any thick white fish fillets for this terrine: try halibut or Arctic bass.

SMOKED HADDOCK AND AVOCADO MOUSSE

THE FRESH-TASTING SALSA COMPLEMENTS THE SMOOTH CREAMINESS OF THE MOUSSE.

SERVES SIX

INGREDIENTS
    225g/8oz undyed smoked haddock
        fillets, skinned
    ½ onion, cut into thick rings
    25g/1oz/2 tbsp butter
    1 bay leaf
    150ml/¼ pint/⅔ cup milk
    1 ripe avocado
    2 gelatine leaves, or 15ml/1 tbsp
        powdered gelatine
    30ml/2 tbsp dry white wine
    105ml/7 tbsp double cream
    1 egg white
    salt, ground white pepper and
        grated nutmeg
For the salsa
    3 tomatoes, peeled, seeded
        and diced
    1 avocado
    1 small red onion, finely chopped
    1–2 garlic cloves, finely chopped
    1 large fresh green chilli, seeded and
        finely chopped
    45ml/3 tbsp extra virgin olive oil
    juice of 1 lime
    12 lime slices, to garnish

1 Arrange the fish in a single layer in a large shallow pan and lay the onion rings on top. Dot with butter, season with pepper, add the bay leaf and pour over the milk. Poach gently over a low heat for 5 minutes, or until the fish flakes easily when tested with the tip of a sharp knife. Remove the fish using a slotted spoon and leave to cool.

VARIATION
Undyed smoked cod can be used instead of the smoked haddock.

2 Using a slotted spoon, lift out and discard the bay leaf and onion. Set the pan over a high heat and boil the milk until it has reduced by about two-thirds. Flake the fish into a food processor and strain over the reduced milk. Purée until smooth.

3 Spoon the fish mixture into a bowl. Peel the avocado and cut the flesh into 5mm/¼in dice. Fold into the fish purée.

4 In a small pan, soak the gelatine leaves in a little cold water until softened. If using powdered gelatine, sprinkle it over 30ml/2 tbsp cold water and leave until spongy. Add the wine to the softened gelatine and heat gently until completely dissolved, stirring constantly. Pour on to the fish mixture and mix well.

5 Lightly whip the cream in a bowl. In a second, grease-free bowl, beat the egg white with a pinch of salt until stiff. Fold the cream, then the egg white into the fish mixture. Season with salt and pepper and add a little nutmeg.

6 Pour the mixture into six ramekins or moulds, cover with clear film and place in the fridge for about 1 hour, until set.

7 Meanwhile, make the salsa. Put the diced tomatoes in a bowl. Peel and dice the avocado and add it to the tomatoes with the onion, garlic and chilli. Add the olive oil and lime juice, with salt and pepper to taste. Chill until needed.

8 To release the mousse, dip the moulds into hot water for a couple of seconds, invert on to individual plates and give each mould a sharp tap. Put a spoonful of salsa on each plate and a little on the top of each mousse. Make a cut to the centre of each slice of lime and twist a couple of slices on to each plate. Serve with the remaining salsa.

INSALATA DI MARE

You can vary the seafood in this Italian salad according to what is available, but try to include at least two kinds of shellfish and some squid. The salad is good warm or cold.

SERVES SIX AS A STARTER,
FOUR AS A MAIN COURSE

INGREDIENTS
   450g/1lb live mussels, scrubbed
     and bearded
   450g/1lb small clams, scrubbed
   105ml/7 tbsp dry white wine
   225g/8oz squid, cleaned
   4 large scallops, with their corals
   30ml/2 tbsp olive oil
   2 garlic cloves, finely chopped
   1 small dried red chilli, crumbled
   225g/8oz whole cooked prawns, in
     the shell
   6–8 large chicory leaves
   6–8 radicchio leaves
   15ml/1 tbsp chopped flat leaf
     parsley, to garnish
For the dressing
   5ml/1 tsp Dijon mustard
   30ml/2 tbsp white wine or
     cider vinegar
   5ml/1 tsp lemon juice
   120ml/4fl oz/½ cup extra virgin
     olive oil
   salt and ground black pepper

1 Put the mussels and clams in a large saucepan with the white wine. Cover and cook over a high heat, shaking the pan occasionally, for about 4 minutes, until they have opened. Discard any that remain closed. Use a slotted spoon to transfer the shellfish to a bowl, then strain and reserve the cooking liquid and set it aside.

2 Cut the squid into thin rings; chop the tentacles. Leave small squid whole. Halve the scallops horizontally.

3 Heat the oil in a frying pan, add the garlic, chilli, squid, scallops and corals, and sauté for about 2 minutes, until just cooked and tender. Lift the squid and scallops out of the pan; reserve the oil.

4 When the shellfish are cool enough to handle, shell them, keeping a dozen of each in the shell. Peel all but 6–8 of the prawns. Pour the shellfish cooking liquid into a small pan, set over a high heat and reduce by half. Mix all the shelled and unshelled mussels and clams with the squid and scallops, then add the prawns.

5 To make the dressing, whisk the mustard with the vinegar and lemon juice and season to taste. Add the olive oil, whisk vigorously, then whisk in the reserved cooking liquid and the oil from the frying pan. Pour the dressing over the seafood mixture and toss lightly to coat well.

6 Arrange the chicory and radicchio leaves around the edge of a large serving dish and pile the mixed seafood salad into the centre. Sprinkle with the chopped flat leaf parsley and serve immediately or chill first.

QUEEN SCALLOP AND FRENCH BEAN SALAD

IF YOU PREFER, USE LIGHTLY COOKED MANGETOUTS INSTEAD OF THE FINE FRENCH BEANS.

SERVES FOUR

INGREDIENTS
    115g/4oz fine French beans, trimmed
    2 good handfuls of frisée or batavia
      lettuce leaves, finely shredded
    15g/½oz/1 tbsp butter
    15ml/1 tbsp hazelnut oil
    20 shelled queen scallops, with
      corals if possible
    2 spring onions, very thinly sliced
    salt and ground black pepper
    4 fresh chervil sprigs, to garnish
For the dressing
    10ml/2 tsp sherry vinegar
    30ml/2 tbsp hazelnut oil
    15ml/1 tbsp finely chopped fresh
      mint leaves

1 Cook the beans in a pan of lightly salted boiling water for about 5 minutes, until crisp-tender. Drain, refresh under cold water, drain again and set aside.

2 Wash and dry the salad leaves; put in a bowl. Mix the dressing, season, pour over the salad and toss. Divide the salad among four serving plates.

3 Heat the butter and hazelnut oil in a frying pan until sizzling, then add the scallops and their corals and sauté for about 1 minute, tossing the scallops in the fat until they have just turned opaque. Stir in the French beans and spring onions. Spoon the vegetables over the salad and pile the scallops and corals into a tower. Garnish and serve.

RED MULLET WITH RASPBERRY DRESSING

THE COMBINATION OF RED MULLET AND RASPBERRY VINEGAR IS DELICIOUS IN THIS STARTER SALAD. KEEP TO THE "RED" THEME BY INCLUDING SALAD LEAVES SUCH AS RED OAKLEAF LETTUCE AND BABY RED-STEMMED CHARD. IF RED MULLET IS NOT AVAILABLE, USE SMALL RED SNAPPER FILLETS.

SERVES FOUR

INGREDIENTS
    8 red mullet fillets, scaled
    15ml/1 tbsp olive oil
    15ml/1 tbsp raspberry vinegar
    175g/6oz mixed dark green and red
      salad leaves, such as lamb's
      lettuce, radicchio, oakleaf lettuce
      and rocket
    salt and ground black pepper
For the raspberry dressing
    115g/4oz/1 cup raspberries, puréed
      and sieved
    30ml/2 tbsp raspberry vinegar
    60ml/4 tbsp extra virgin olive oil
    1.5–2.5ml/¼–½ tsp caster sugar

COOK'S TIP
To make the raspberry purée, whizz the fruit in a blender or food processor, then press it through a sieve placed over a bowl to remove the seeds.

1 Lay the red mullet fillets in a shallow dish. Whisk together the olive oil and raspberry vinegar, add a pinch of salt and drizzle the mixture over the fish. Cover and leave to marinate for 1 hour.

2 Meanwhile, whisk together the dressing ingredients and season to taste.

3 Wash and dry the salad leaves, put them in a bowl, pour over most of the dressing and toss lightly.

4 Heat a ridged grilling pan or frying pan until very hot, put in the red mullet fillets and fry for 2–3 minutes on each side, until just cooked. Cut the fillets diagonally in half to make rough diamond shapes.

5 Arrange a tall heap of salad in the middle of each serving plate. Prop up four red mullet fillet halves on the salad on each plate with the reserved dressing spooned around. Serve.

PIQUANT PRAWN SALAD

THE THAI-INSPIRED DRESSING ADDS A SUPERB FLAVOUR TO THE NOODLES AND PRAWNS. THIS
DELICIOUS SALAD CAN BE SERVED WARM OR COLD, AND WILL SERVE SIX AS A STARTER.

SERVES FOUR

INGREDIENTS
    200g/7oz rice vermicelli or stir-fry
        rice noodles
    8 baby corn cobs, halved
    150g/5oz mangetouts
    15ml/1 tbsp stir-fry oil
    2 garlic cloves, finely chopped
    2.5cm/1in piece fresh root ginger,
        peeled and finely chopped
    1 fresh red or green chilli, seeded
        and finely chopped
    450g/1lb raw peeled tiger prawns
    4 spring onions, very thinly sliced
    15ml/1 tbsp sesame seeds, toasted
    1 lemon grass stalk, thinly shredded,
        to garnish
For the dressing
    15ml/1 tbsp snipped chives
    15ml/1 tbsp *nam pla* (Thai fish sauce)
    5ml/1 tsp soy sauce
    45ml/3 tbsp groundnut oil
    5ml/1 tsp sesame oil
    30ml/2 tbsp rice vinegar

1 Put the rice vermicelli or noodles in a wide heatproof bowl, pour over boiling water and leave for 5 minutes. Drain, refresh under cold water and drain again. Tip back into the bowl and set aside until required.

2 Boil or steam the corn cobs and mangetouts for about 3 minutes; they should still be crunchy. Refresh under cold water and drain. Now make the dressing. Mix all the ingredients in a screw-top jar, close tightly and shake well to combine.

3 Heat the oil in a large frying pan or wok. Add the garlic, ginger and red or green chilli and cook for 1 minute. Add the tiger prawns and stir-fry for about 3 minutes, until they have just turned pink. Stir in the spring onions, corn cobs, mangetouts and sesame seeds, and toss lightly to mix.

4 Tip the contents of the pan or wok over the rice vermicelli or noodles. Pour the dressing on top and toss well. Serve, garnished with lemon grass, or chill for an hour before serving.

WARM MONKFISH SALAD

MONKFISH HAS A MATCHLESS FLAVOUR AND BENEFITS FROM BEING COOKED SIMPLY. TEAMING IT WITH WILTED BABY SPINACH AND TOASTED PINE NUTS IS INSPIRATIONAL.

3 Make the dressing by whisking all the ingredients together until smooth and creamy. Pour the dressing into a small saucepan, season to taste with salt and pepper and heat gently.

4 Heat the oil and butter in a ridged grilling pan or frying pan until sizzling. Add the fish; sauté for 20–30 seconds on each side.

SERVES FOUR

INGREDIENTS
   2 monkfish fillets, about
     350g/12oz each
   25g/1oz/⅓ cup pine nuts
   15ml/1 tbsp olive oil
   15g/½oz/1 tbsp butter
   225g/8oz baby spinach leaves,
     washed and stalks removed
   salt and ground black pepper
For the dressing
   5ml/1 tsp Dijon mustard
   5ml/1 tsp sherry vinegar
   60ml/4 tbsp olive oil
   1 garlic clove, crushed

VARIATION
Substitute salad leaves for the spinach.

1 Holding the knife at a slight angle, cut each monkfish fillet into 12 diagonal slices. Season lightly and set aside.

2 Heat an empty frying pan, put in the pine nuts and shake them about for a while, until golden brown. Do not burn. Transfer to a plate; set aside.

5 Put the spinach leaves in a large bowl and pour over the warm dressing. Sprinkle on the toasted pine nuts, reserving a few, and toss together well. Divide the dressed spinach leaves among four serving plates and arrange the monkfish slices on top. Scatter the reserved pine nuts on top and serve.

CRAB CAKES

UNLIKE FISH CAKES, CRAB CAKES ARE BOUND WITH EGG AND MAYONNAISE OR TARTARE SAUCE INSTEAD OF POTATOES, WHICH MAKES THEM LIGHT IN TEXTURE. IF YOU PREFER, THEY CAN BE GRILLED INSTEAD OF FRIED; BRUSH WITH A LITTLE OIL FIRST.

SERVES FOUR

INGREDIENTS
  450g/1lb mixed brown and white
    crab meat
  30ml/2 tbsp mayonnaise or
    tartare sauce
  2.5–5ml/½–1 tsp mustard powder
  1 egg, lightly beaten
  Tabasco sauce
  45ml/3 tbsp chopped fresh parsley
  4 spring onions, finely chopped
    (optional)
  50–75g/2–3oz/½–¾ cup dried
    breadcrumbs, preferably home-made
  sunflower oil, for frying
  salt, ground black pepper and
    cayenne pepper
  chopped spring onions, to garnish
  red onion marmalade, to serve

1 Put the crab meat in a bowl and stir in the mayonnaise or tartare sauce, with the mustard and egg. Season with Tabasco, salt, pepper and cayenne.

2 Stir in the parsley, spring onions, if using, and 50g/2oz/½ cup of the breadcrumbs. The mixture should be just firm enough to hold together; depending on how much brown crab meat there is, you may need to add some more breadcrumbs.

3 Divide the mixture into 8 portions, roll each into a ball and flatten slightly to make a thick flat disc. Spread out the crab cakes on a platter and put in the fridge for 30 minutes before frying.

4 Pour the oil into a shallow pan to a depth of about 5mm/¼in. Fry the crab cakes in two batches until golden brown all over. Drain on kitchen paper and keep hot. Serve with a spring onion garnish and red onion marmalade.

SARDINE FRITTATA

IT MAY SEEM ODD TO COOK SARDINES IN AN OMELETTE, BUT THEY ARE SURPRISINGLY DELICIOUS THIS WAY. FROZEN SARDINES ARE FINE FOR THIS DISH. SERVE THE FRITTATA WITH CRISP SAUTÉED POTATOES AND THINLY SLICED CUCUMBER CRESCENTS.

SERVES FOUR

INGREDIENTS
  4 fat sardines, cleaned, filleted and
    with heads removed, thawed
    if frozen
  juice of 1 lemon
  45ml/3 tbsp olive oil
  6 large eggs
  30ml/2 tbsp chopped fresh parsley
  30ml/2 tbsp snipped fresh chives
  1 garlic clove, chopped
  salt, ground black pepper
    and paprika

1 Open out the sardines and sprinkle the fish with lemon juice, a little salt and paprika. Heat 15ml/1 tbsp olive oil in a frying pan and fry the sardines for about 1–2 minutes on each side to seal them. Drain on kitchen paper, trim off the tails and set aside until required.

2 Separate the eggs. In a bowl, whisk the yolks lightly with the parsley, chives and a little salt and pepper. Beat the whites in a separate bowl with a pinch of salt until fairly stiff. Preheat the grill to medium-high.

3 Heat the remaining olive oil in a large frying pan, add the garlic and cook over a low heat until just golden. Gently mix together the egg yolks and whites and ladle half the mixture into the pan. Cook gently until just beginning to set on the base, then lay the sardines on the frittata and sprinkle lightly with paprika. Pour over the remaining egg mixture and cook gently until the frittata has browned underneath and is beginning to set on the top.

4 Put the pan under the grill and cook until the top of the frittata is golden. Cut into wedges and serve at once.

COOK'S TIP
It is important to use a frying pan with a handle that can safely be used under the grill. If your frying pan has a wooden handle, protect it with foil.

FISH PIE

FISH PIE CAN BE VARIED TO SUIT YOUR TASTE AND POCKET. THIS IS A SIMPLE VERSION, BUT YOU COULD ADD PRAWNS OR HARD-BOILED EGGS, OR MIX THE POTATO TOPPING WITH SPRING ONIONS.

SERVES FOUR

INGREDIENTS
   450g/1lb cod or haddock fillets
   225g/8oz smoked cod fillets
   300ml/½ pint/1¼ cups milk
   ½ lemon, sliced
   1 bay leaf
   1 fresh thyme sprig
   4–5 black peppercorns
   50g/2oz/¼ cup butter
   25g/1oz/¼ cup plain flour
   30ml/2 tbsp chopped fresh parsley
   5ml/1 tsp anchovy essence
   150g/5oz/2 cups shiitake or chestnut
      mushrooms, sliced
   salt, ground black pepper and
      cayenne pepper
For the topping
   450g/1lb potatoes, cooked and
      mashed with milk
   50g/2oz/¼ cup butter
   2 tomatoes, sliced
   25g/1oz/¼ cup grated Cheddar
      cheese (optional)

1 Put the fish skin-side down in a shallow pan. Add the milk, lemon slices, bay leaf, thyme and peppercorns. Bring to the boil, then lower the heat and poach gently for about 5 minutes, until just cooked. Strain off and reserve the milk. Remove the fish skin and flake the flesh, discarding any bones.

2 Melt half the butter in a small saucepan, stir in the flour and cook gently for 1 minute. Add the milk and boil, whisking, until smooth and creamy. Stir in the parsley and anchovy essence and season to taste.

3 Heat the remaining butter in a frying pan, add the sliced mushrooms and sauté until tender. Season and add to the flaked fish. Mix the sauce into the fish and stir gently to combine. Transfer the mixture to an ovenproof casserole.

4 Preheat the oven to 200°C/400°F/ Gas 6. Beat the mashed potato with the butter until very creamy. Season, then spread the topping evenly over the fish. Fork up the surface and arrange the sliced tomatoes around the edge. Sprinkle the exposed topping with the grated cheese, if using.

5 Bake for 20–25 minutes, until the topping is lightly browned. If you prefer, finish the browning under a hot grill.

VARIATION
Instead of using plain mashed potatoes, try a mixture of mashed potato and mashed swede or sweet potato.

SALMON AND PRAWN FLAN

THIS FLAN IS UNUSUAL BECAUSE IT IS MADE WITH RAW SALMON, WHICH MEANS THAT THE FISH STAYS MOIST. COOKING IT THIS WAY GIVES A LOVELY SUCCULENT RESULT. THIS VERSATILE DISH MAY BE SERVED HOT WITH VEGETABLES OR COOLED WITH MIXED SALAD LEAVES AND TOMATO WEDGES.

SERVES SIX

INGREDIENTS
    350g/12oz shortcrust pastry, thawed
       if frozen
    225g/8oz salmon fillet, skinned
    225g/8oz cooked peeled prawns
    2 eggs, plus 2 egg yolks
    150ml/¼ pint/⅔ cup whipping
       cream
    200ml/7fl oz/scant 1 cup milk
    15ml/1 tbsp chopped fresh dill
    salt, ground black pepper
       and paprika
    lime slices, tomato wedges and sprigs
       of dill, to garnish

VARIATION
For a more economical version of this
flan, omit the prawns and use some
extra salmon instead, or use a mixture
of salmon and white fish.

1 Roll out the pastry on a floured work
surface and use it to line a 20cm/8in
flan dish or tin. Prick the base all over
and mark the edges with the tines of
the fork. It need not be too neat. Chill
in the fridge for about 30 minutes.
Meanwhile, preheat the oven to 180°C/
350°F/Gas 4. Bake the pastry case for
about 30 minutes, until golden brown.
Reduce the oven temperature to 160°C/
325°F/Gas 3.

2 Cut the salmon into 2cm/¾in cubes.
Arrange the salmon and prawns evenly
in the pastry case. Dust with paprika.

3 In a bowl, beat together the eggs and
yolks, cream, milk and dill and season
to taste. Pour over the salmon and
prawns. Bake for about 30 minutes,
until the filling is just set. Serve hot or
at room temperature, garnished with
lime slices, tomato wedges and dill.

COCONUT BAKED SNAPPER

ADDING A COUPLE OF FRESH RED CHILLIES TO THE MARINADE GIVES THIS DISH A REALLY SPICY FLAVOUR. SERVE THE BAKED SNAPPER WITH PLAIN BOILED RICE.

SERVES FOUR

INGREDIENTS
    1 snapper, about 1kg/2¼lb, scaled
       and cleaned
    400ml/14fl oz/1⅔ cups coconut milk
    105ml/7 tbsp dry white wine
    juice of 1 lime
    45ml/3 tbsp light soy sauce
    1–2 fresh red chillies, seeded and
       finely sliced (optional)
    60ml/4 tbsp chopped fresh parsley
    45ml/3 tbsp chopped fresh coriander
    salt and ground black pepper

COOK'S TIP
Any type of snapper or trout can be used
for this recipe. If you prefer, use one
small fish per person, but be aware that
small snapper can be very bony.

1 Lay the snapper in an ovenproof
shallow dish and season with a little salt
and plenty of pepper. Mix together the
coconut milk, wine, lime juice, soy
sauce and chillies, if using. Stir in the
herbs and pour over the fish. Cover with
clear film and marinate in the fridge for
about 4 hours, turning the fish over
halfway through.

2 Preheat the oven to 190°C/375°F/
Gas 5. Take the fish out of the marinade
and wrap loosely in foil, spooning over
the marinade before sealing the parcel.
Support the fish on a clean dish and
bake for 30–40 minutes, until the flesh
comes away easily from the bone.

FRIED PLAICE WITH TOMATO SAUCE

This simple dish is perennially popular with children. It works equally well with lemon sole or dabs (these do not need skinning), or fillets of haddock and whiting.

SERVES FOUR

INGREDIENTS

25g/1oz/¼ cup plain flour
2 eggs, beaten
75g/3oz/¾ cup dried breadcrumbs,
  preferably home-made
4 small plaice, black skin removed
15g/½oz/1 tbsp butter
15ml/1 tbsp sunflower oil
salt and ground black pepper
1 lemon, quartered, to serve
fresh basil leaves, to garnish

For the tomato sauce

30ml/2 tbsp olive oil
1 red onion, finely chopped
1 garlic clove, finely chopped
400g/14oz can chopped tomatoes
15ml/1 tbsp tomato purée
15ml/1 tbsp torn fresh basil leaves

1 First make the tomato sauce. Heat the olive oil in a large saucepan, add the finely chopped onion and garlic and cook gently for about 5 minutes, until softened and pale golden. Stir in the chopped tomatoes and tomato purée and simmer for 20–30 minutes, stirring occasionally. Season with salt and pepper and stir in the basil.

2 Spread out the flour in a shallow dish, pour the beaten eggs into another and spread out the breadcrumbs in a third. Season the plaice with salt and pepper.

3 Hold a fish in your left hand and dip it first in flour, then in egg and finally in the breadcrumbs, patting the crumbs on with your dry right hand.

4 Heat the butter and oil in a frying pan until foaming. Fry the fish one at a time in the hot fat for about 5 minutes on each side, until golden brown and cooked through, but still juicy in the middle. Drain on kitchen paper and keep hot while you fry the rest. Serve with lemon wedges and the tomato sauce, garnished with basil leaves.

COD CARAMBA

THIS COLOURFUL MEXICAN DISH, WITH ITS CONTRASTING CRUNCHY TOPPING AND TENDER FISH FILLING, CAN BE MADE WITH ANY ECONOMICAL WHITE FISH SUCH AS COLEY OR HADDOCK.

SERVES FOUR TO SIX

INGREDIENTS
    450g/1lb cod fillets
    225g/8oz smoked cod fillets
    300ml/½ pint/1¼ cups fish stock
    50g/2oz/¼ cup butter
    1 onion, sliced
    2 garlic cloves, crushed
    1 green and 1 red pepper, seeded
        and diced
    2 courgettes, diced
    115g/4oz/⅔ cup drained canned or
        thawed frozen sweetcorn kernels
    2 tomatoes, peeled and chopped
    juice of 1 lime
    Tabasco sauce
    salt, ground black pepper and
        cayenne pepper
For the topping
    75g/3oz tortilla chips
    50g/2oz/½ cup grated
        Cheddar cheese
    coriander sprigs, to garnish
    lime wedges, to serve

1 Lay the fish in a shallow pan and pour over the fish stock. Bring to the boil, lower the heat, cover and poach for about 8 minutes, until the flesh flakes easily when tested with the tip of a sharp knife. Leave to cool slightly, then remove the skin and separate the flesh into large flakes. Keep hot.

2 Melt the butter in a saucepan, add the onion and garlic and cook over a low heat until soft. Add the peppers, stir and cook for 2 minutes. Stir in the courgettes and cook for 3 minutes more, until all the vegetables are tender.

3 Stir in the sweetcorn and tomatoes, then add lime juice and Tabasco to taste. Season with salt, black pepper and cayenne. Cook for a couple of minutes to heat the corn and tomatoes, then stir in the fish and transfer to a dish that can safely be used under the grill.

4 Preheat the grill. Make the topping by crushing the tortilla chips, then mixing in the grated cheese. Add cayenne pepper to taste and sprinkle over the fish. Place the dish under the grill until the topping is crisp and brown. Garnish with coriander sprigs and lime wedges.

HERRINGS IN OATMEAL WITH BACON

THIS TRADITIONAL SCOTTISH DISH IS CHEAP AND NUTRITIOUS. FOR EASE OF EATING, BONE THE HERRINGS BEFORE COATING THEM IN THE OATMEAL. IF YOU DON'T LIKE HERRINGS, USE TROUT OR MACKEREL INSTEAD. FOR EXTRA COLOUR AND FLAVOUR, SERVE WITH GRILLED TOMATOES.

SERVES FOUR

INGREDIENTS
  115–150g/4–5oz/1–1¼ cups
    medium oatmeal
  10ml/2 tsp mustard powder
  4 herrings, about 225g/8oz each,
    cleaned, boned, heads and
    tails removed
  30ml/2 tbsp sunflower oil
  8 rindless streaky bacon rashers
  salt and ground black pepper
  lemon wedges, to serve

COOK'S TIPS
• Use tongs to turn the herrings so as not to dislodge the oatmeal.
• Cook the herring two at a time.
• Don't overcrowd the frying pan.

1 In a shallow dish, mix together the oatmeal and mustard powder with salt and pepper. Press the herrings into the mixture one at a time to coat them thickly on both sides. Shake off the excess oatmeal mixture and set the herrings aside.

2 Heat the oil in a large frying pan and fry the bacon until crisp. Drain on kitchen paper and keep hot.

3 Put the herrings into the pan and fry them for 3–4 minutes on each side, until crisp and golden brown. Serve the herrings with the streaky bacon rashers and lemon wedges.

SKATE WITH BLACK BUTTER

SKATE CAN BE QUITE INEXPENSIVE, AND THIS CLASSIC DISH IS PERFECT FOR A FAMILY SUPPER. SERVE IT WITH STEAMED LEEKS AND PLAIN BOILED POTATOES.

SERVES FOUR

INGREDIENTS
  4 skate wings, about
    225g/8oz each
  60ml/4 tbsp red wine vinegar
    or malt vinegar
  30ml/2 tbsp drained capers in
    vinegar, chopped if large
  30ml/2 tbsp chopped fresh parsley
  150g/5oz/⅔ cup butter
  salt and ground black pepper

COOK'S TIP
Despite the title of the recipe, the butter should be a rich golden brown. It should never be allowed to blacken, or it will taste unpleasantly bitter.

1 Put the skate wings in a large, shallow pan, cover with cold water and add a pinch of salt and 15ml/1 tbsp of the red wine or malt vinegar.

2 Bring to the boil, skim the surface, then lower the heat and simmer gently for about 10–12 minutes, until the skate flesh comes away from the bone easily. Carefully drain the skate and peel off the skin.

3 Transfer the skate to a warmed serving dish, season with salt and pepper and sprinkle over the capers and parsley. Keep hot.

4 In a small saucepan, heat the butter until it foams and turns a rich nutty brown. Pour it over the skate. Pour the remaining vinegar into the pan and boil until reduced by about two-thirds. Drizzle over the skate and serve.

TROUT <u>WITH</u> TAMARIND <u>AND</u> CHILLI SAUCE

*TROUT IS A VERY ECONOMICAL FISH, BUT CAN TASTE RATHER BLAND. THIS SPICY THAI-INSPIRED
SAUCE REALLY GIVES IT A ZING. IF YOU LIKE YOUR FOOD VERY SPICY, ADD AN EXTRA CHILLI.*

<u>SERVES FOUR</u>

INGREDIENTS

   4 trout, about 350g/12oz each,
     cleaned
   6 spring onions, sliced
   60ml/4 tbsp soy sauce
   15ml/1 tbsp stir-fry oil
   30ml/2 tbsp chopped fresh coriander
For the sauce
   50g/2oz tamarind pulp
   105ml/7 tbsp boiling water
   2 shallots, roughly chopped
   1 fresh red chilli, seeded
     and chopped
   1cm/½in piece fresh root ginger,
     peeled and chopped
   5ml/1 tsp soft brown sugar
   45ml/3 tbsp *nam pla* (Thai fish sauce)

1 Slash the trout diagonally four or five times on each side with a sharp knife and place in a shallow dish.

2 Fill the cavities with spring onions and douse each fish with soy sauce. Carefully turn the fish over to coat both sides with the sauce. Sprinkle on any remaining spring onions and set aside until required.

3 Make the sauce. Put the tamarind pulp in a small bowl and pour on the boiling water. Mash with a fork until soft. Tip into a food processor or blender, add the shallots, fresh chilli, ginger, sugar and *nam pla* and whizz to a coarse pulp.

4 Heat the stir-fry oil in a large frying pan or wok and fry the trout, one at a time if necessary, for about 5 minutes on each side, until the skin is crisp and browned and the flesh cooked. Put on warmed plates and spoon over some sauce. Sprinkle with the coriander and serve with the remaining sauce.

GREEN FISH CURRY

ANY FIRM-FLESHED FISH CAN BE USED FOR THIS DELICIOUS CURRY, WHICH GAINS ITS RICH COLOUR FROM A MIXTURE OF FRESH HERBS; TRY EXOTICS SUCH AS MAHI MAHI, HOKI OR SWORDFISH OR HUMBLER FISH SUCH AS COLEY. SERVE IT WITH BASMATI OR THAI FRAGRANT RICE AND LIME WEDGES.

SERVES FOUR

INGREDIENTS

    4 garlic cloves, roughly chopped
    5cm/2in piece fresh root ginger,
      peeled and roughly chopped
    2 fresh green chillies, seeded and
      roughly chopped
    grated rind and juice of 1 lime
    5–10ml/1–2 tsp shrimp
      paste (optional)
    5ml/1 tsp coriander seeds
    5ml/1 tsp five-spice powder
    75ml/5 tbsp sesame oil
    2 red onions, finely chopped
    900g/2lb hoki fillets, skinned
    400ml/14fl oz/1⅔ cups coconut milk
    45ml/3 tbsp *nam pla* (Thai fish sauce)
    50g/2oz fresh coriander leaves
    50g/2oz fresh mint leaves
    50g/2oz fresh basil leaves
    6 spring onions, chopped
    150ml/¼ pint/⅔ cup sunflower or
      groundnut oil
    sliced fresh green chilli and finely
      chopped fresh coriander, to garnish
    cooked Basmati or Thai fragrant rice
      and lime wedges, to serve

2 Heat a wok or large shallow pan, and pour in the remaining sesame oil. When it is hot, stir-fry the red onions over a high heat for 2 minutes. Add the fish and stir-fry for 1–2 minutes to seal the fillets on all sides.

3 Lift out the red onions and fish and put them on a plate. Add the curry paste to the wok or pan and fry for 1 minute, stirring. Return the hoki fillets and red onions to the wok or pan, pour in the coconut milk and bring to the boil. Lower the heat, add the *nam pla* (fish sauce) and simmer for 5–7 minutes, until the fish is cooked through.

4 Meanwhile, process the herbs, spring onions, lime rind and oil in a food processor to a coarse paste. Stir into the fish curry. Garnish with chilli and coriander and serve with rice and lime wedges.

1 First make the curry paste. Combine the garlic, fresh root ginger, green chillies, the lime juice and shrimp paste (if using) in a food processor. Add the coriander seeds and five-spice powder, with half the sesame oil. Whizz to a fine paste, then set aside until required.

KEDGEREE

THIS CLASSIC DISH ORIGINATED IN INDIA. IT IS BEST MADE WITH BASMATI RICE, WHICH GOES WELL WITH THE MILD CURRY FLAVOUR, BUT LONG GRAIN RICE WILL DO. FOR A COLOURFUL GARNISH, ADD SOME FINELY SLICED RED ONION AND A LITTLE RED ONION MARMALADE.

SERVES FOUR

INGREDIENTS
450g/1lb undyed smoked
    haddock fillet
750ml/1¼ pints/3 cups milk
2 bay leaves
½ lemon, sliced
50g/2oz/¼ cup butter
1 onion, chopped
2.5ml/½ tsp ground turmeric
5ml/1 tsp mild Madras curry powder
2 green cardamom pods
350g/12oz/1¾ cups basmati or long
    grain rice, washed and drained
4 hard-boiled eggs (not *too* hard),
    roughly chopped
150ml/¼ pint/⅔ cup single cream or
    Greek yogurt (optional)
30ml/2 tbsp chopped fresh parsley
salt and ground black pepper

1 Put the haddock in a shallow pan and add the milk, bay leaves and lemon slices. Poach gently for 8–10 minutes, until the haddock flakes easily when tested with the tip of a sharp knife. Strain the milk into a jug, discarding the bay leaves and lemon slices. Remove the skin from the flesh of the haddock, and flake the flesh into large pieces. Keep hot until required.

2 Melt the butter in the pan, add the onion and cook over a low heat for about 3 minutes, until softened. Stir in the turmeric, the curry powder and cardamom pods and fry for 1 minute.

3 Add the rice, stirring to coat it well with the butter. Pour in the reserved milk, stir and bring to the boil. Lower the heat and simmer the rice for 10–12 minutes, until all the milk has been absorbed and the rice is tender. Season to taste, going easy on the salt.

4 Gently stir in the fish and hard-boiled eggs, with the cream or yogurt, if using. Sprinkle with the parsley and serve.

VARIATION
Use smoked and poached fresh salmon for a delicious change from haddock.

PAPPARDELLE, SARDINE AND FENNEL BAKE

PAPPARDELLE ARE WIDE, FLAT NOODLES. THEY ARE PERFECT FOR THIS SICILIAN RECIPE. IF YOU CAN'T FIND THEM, ANY WIDE PASTA SUCH AS MACCHERONCINI OR BUCATINI WILL DO INSTEAD. THE DISH IS ALSO DELICIOUS MADE WITH FRESH ANCHOVIES.

SERVES SIX

INGREDIENTS

2 fennel bulbs, trimmed
a large pinch of saffron threads
12 sardines, backbones and
  heads removed
60ml/4 tbsp olive oil
2 shallots, finely chopped
2 garlic cloves, finely chopped
2 fresh red chillies, seeded and
  finely chopped
4 drained canned anchovy fillets, or
  8–12 stoned black olives, chopped
30ml/2 tbsp capers
75g/3oz/1 cup pine nuts
450g/1lb pappardelle
butter, for greasing
30ml/2 tbsp grated Pecorino cheese
salt and ground black pepper

1 Preheat the oven to 200°C/400°F/ Gas 6. Cut the fennel bulbs in half and cook them in a pan of lightly salted boiling water with the saffron threads for about 10 minutes, until tender. Drain, reserving the cooking liquid, and cut into small dice. Then finely chop the sardines, season with salt and ground black pepper and set aside until required.

2 Heat the olive oil in a saucepan, add the shallots and garlic and cook until lightly coloured. Add the chillies and sardines; fry for 3 minutes. Stir in the fennel and cook gently for 3 minutes. If the mixture seems dry, add a little of the reserved fennel water.

3 Add the anchovies or olives and cook for 1 minute; stir in the capers and pine nuts, and season. Simmer for 3 minutes more, then turn off the heat.

4 Meanwhile, pour the reserved fennel liquid into a saucepan and top it up with enough water to cook the pasta. Stir in a little salt, bring to the boil and add the pappardelle. Cook dried pasta for about 12 minutes; fresh pasta until it rises to the surface of the water. When the pasta is just tender, drain it.

5 Grease a shallow ovenproof dish and put in a layer of pasta then make a layer of the sardine mixture. Continue until all the pasta and sardine mixture have been used, finishing with the fish. Sprinkle over the Pecorino; bake for 15 minutes, until bubbling and golden brown.

LOBSTER RAVIOLI

IT IS ESSENTIAL TO USE HOME-MADE PASTA TO OBTAIN THE DELICACY AND THINNESS THAT THIS SUPERB FILLING DESERVES. BEFORE YOU START THE RECIPE, MAKE A WELL-FLAVOURED FISH STOCK, INCLUDING THE LOBSTER SHELL AND HEAD.

SERVES SIX AS A STARTER,
FOUR AS A MAIN COURSE

INGREDIENTS
    1 lobster, about 450g/1lb, cooked
       and taken out of the shell
    2 soft white bread slices, about
       50g/2oz, crusts removed
    200ml/7fl oz/scant 1 cup fish stock,
       made with the lobster shell
    1 egg
    250ml/8fl oz/1 cup double cream
    15ml/1 tbsp snipped fresh chives,
       plus extra to garnish
    15ml/1 tbsp finely chopped
       fresh chervil
    salt and ground white pepper
    fresh chives, to garnish
For the pasta dough
    225g/8oz/2 cups strong plain flour
       (Italian tipo 00 if possible)
    2 eggs, plus 2 egg yolks
For the mushroom sauce
    a large pinch of saffron threads
    25g/1oz/2 tbsp butter
    2 shallots, finely chopped
    200g/7oz/3 cups white button
       mushrooms, finely chopped
    juice of ½ lemon
    200ml/7fl oz/scant 1 cup
       double cream

1 Make the pasta dough. Sift the flour with a good pinch of salt. Put into a food processor with the eggs and extra yolks; whizz until the mixture resembles coarse breadcrumbs. Turn out on to a floured surface; knead to make a smooth, dryish dough. Wrap in clear film and leave to rest in the fridge for an hour.

2 Meanwhile, make the lobster filling. Cut the lobster meat into large chunks and place in a bowl. Tear the white bread into small pieces and soak them in 45ml/3 tbsp of the fish stock. Place in a food processor with half the egg and 30–45ml/2–3 tbsp of the double cream and whizz until smooth. Stir the mixture into the lobster meat, then add the fresh chives and chervil and season to taste with salt and white pepper.

3 Roll the ravioli dough to a thickness of 3mm/⅛in, preferably using a pasta machine. The process can be done by hand with a rolling pin but is quite hard work. Divide the dough into four rectangles and dust each rectangle lightly with flour.

4 Spoon six equal heaps of filling on to one sheet of pasta, leaving about 3cm/1¼in between each pile of filling. Lightly beat the remaining egg with a tablespoon of water and brush it over the pasta between the piles of filling. Cover with a second sheet of pasta. Repeat with the other two sheets of pasta and remaining filling.

5 Using your fingertips, press the top layer of dough down well between the piles of filling, making sure each is well sealed. Cut between the heaps with a 7.5cm/3in fluted pastry cutter or a pasta wheel to make twelve ravioli.

6 Place the ravioli in a single layer on a baking sheet, cover with clear film or a damp cloth, and put in the fridge while you make the sauces.

7 Make the mushroom sauce. Soak the saffron in 15ml/1 tbsp warm water. Melt the butter in a saucepan and cook the shallots over a low heat until they are soft but not coloured.

8 Add the chopped mushrooms and lemon juice and continue to cook over a low heat until almost all the liquid has evaporated. Stir in the saffron, with its soaking water, and the cream, then cook gently, stirring occasionally, until the sauce has thickened. Keep warm while you cook the ravioli.

SEAFOOD RISOTTO

MOST SUPERMARKETS NOW STOCK PACKS OF READY-PREPARED MIXED SEAFOOD SUCH AS PRAWNS, SQUID AND MUSSELS, WHICH ARE IDEAL FOR MAKING THIS QUICK AND EASY RISOTTO.

SERVES FOUR

INGREDIENTS

1 litre/1¾ pints/4 cups fish or
  shellfish stock
50g/2oz/¼ cup butter
2 shallots, chopped
2 garlic cloves, chopped
350g/12oz/1¾ cups risotto rice
150ml/¼ pint/⅔ cup dry white wine
2.5ml/½ tsp powdered saffron, or a
  pinch of saffron threads
400g/14oz mixed prepared seafood
30ml/2 tbsp freshly grated
  Parmesan cheese
30ml/2 tbsp chopped fresh
  flat leaf parsley, to garnish
salt and ground black pepper

1 Pour the fish or shellfish stock into a large saucepan. Bring it to the boil, then reduce the heat and keep it at a gentle simmer. The water needs to be hot when it is added to the rice.

2 Melt the butter in a heavy-based saucepan, add the shallots and garlic and cook over a low heat until soft but not coloured. Add the rice, stir well to coat the grains with butter, then pour in the wine. Cook over a medium heat, stirring occasionally, until the wine has been absorbed by the rice.

COOK'S TIP
It is essential to use risotto rice for this dish. You can buy arborio or carnaroli risotto rice in an Italian delicatessan, or a large supermarket.

3 Add a ladleful of hot stock and the saffron, and cook, stirring continuously, until the liquid has been absorbed. Add the seafood and stir well. Continue to add stock a ladleful at a time, waiting until each quantity has been absorbed before adding more. Stir the mixture for about 20 minutes, until the rice is swollen and creamy, but still with a little bite in the middle.

VARIATION
Use peeled prawns, or cubes of fish such as cod or salmon in place of the mixed prepared seafood.

4 Vigorously mix in the freshly grated Parmesan cheese and season to taste, then sprinkle over the chopped parsley and serve at once.

LIGHT AND HEALTHY DISHES

What could be healthier than a meal based on simply cooked fish and shellfish?

We should all include fish in our diet at least twice a week, particularly the oily fish

that are so beneficial to health. Here are vibrant, attractive dishes certain to inspire, such as

Roast Cod with Pancetta and Butter Beans, Moroccan Spiced Mackerel, and Hoki

Stir-Fry. All are quick to prepare and so full of fresh, natural flavours that

healthy eating becomes pure pleasure.

STEAMED LETTUCE-WRAPPED SOLE

IF YOU CAN AFFORD IT, USE DOVER SOLE FILLETS FOR THIS RECIPE; IF NOT, LEMON SOLE, TROUT, PLAICE AND BRILL ARE ALL EXCELLENT COOKED THIS WAY.

SERVES FOUR

INGREDIENTS

2 large sole fillets, skinned
15ml/1 tbsp sesame seeds
15ml/1 tbsp sunflower or
  groundnut oil
10ml/2 tsp sesame oil
2.5cm/1in piece fresh root ginger,
  peeled and grated
3 garlic cloves, finely chopped
15ml/1 tbsp soy sauce or *nam pla*
  (Thai fish sauce)
juice of 1 lemon
2 spring onions, thinly sliced
8 large soft lettuce leaves
12 large fresh mussels, scrubbed
  and bearded

1 Cut the sole fillets in half lengthways. Season; set aside. Prepare a steamer.

2 Heat a heavy-based frying pan until hot. Toast the sesame seeds lightly but do not allow them to burn. Set aside in a bowl until required.

3 Heat the oils in the frying pan over a medium heat. Add the ginger and garlic and cook until lightly coloured; stir in the soy sauce or *nam pla*, lemon juice and spring onions. Off the heat, stir in the toasted sesame seeds.

4 Lay the pieces of fish on baking parchment, skinned-side up; spread each evenly with the ginger mixture. Roll up each piece, starting at the tail end. Place on a baking sheet.

5 Plunge the lettuce leaves into the boiling water you have prepared for the steamer and immediately lift them out with tongs or a slotted spoon. Lay them out flat on kitchen paper and gently pat them dry. Wrap each sole parcel in two lettuce leaves, making sure that the filling is well covered to keep it in place.

6 Arrange the fish parcels in a steamer basket, cover and steam over simmering water for 8 minutes. Add the mussels and steam for 2–4 minutes, until opened. Discard any that remain closed. Put the parcels on individual warmed plates, halve and garnish with mussels. Serve immediately.

SMOKED HADDOCK WITH MUSTARD CABBAGE

THIS SIMPLE DISH TAKES LESS THAN TWENTY MINUTES TO MAKE AND IS QUITE DELICIOUS. SERVE IT WITH NEW POTATOES.

2 Meanwhile put the haddock in a large shallow pan with the milk, onion and bay leaves. Add the lemon slices and peppercorns. Bring to simmering point, cover and poach until the fish flakes easily when tested with the tip of a sharp knife. This will take 8–10 minutes, depending on the thickness of the fillets. Take the pan off the heat and set aside until needed. Preheat the grill.

3 Cut the tomatoes in half horizontally, season them with salt and pepper and grill until lightly browned. Drain the cabbage, refresh under cold water and drain again.

4 Melt the butter in a shallow pan or wok, add the cabbage and toss over the heat for 2 minutes. Mix in the mustard and season to taste, then tip the cabbage into a warmed serving dish.

SERVES FOUR

INGREDIENTS
1 Savoy or pointu cabbage
675g/1½lb undyed smoked
   haddock fillet
300ml/½ pint/1¼ cups milk
½ onion, peeled and sliced into rings
2 bay leaves
½ lemon, sliced
4 white peppercorns
4 ripe tomatoes
50g/2oz/¼ cup butter
30ml/2 tbsp wholegrain mustard
juice of 1 lemon
salt and ground black pepper
30ml/2 tbsp chopped fresh parsley,
   to garnish

1 Cut the cabbage in half, remove the central core and thick ribs, then shred the cabbage. Cook in a pan of lightly salted boiling water, or steam over boiling water for about 10 minutes, until just tender. Leave in the pan or steamer until required.

5 Drain the haddock. Skin and cut the fish into four pieces. Place on top of the cabbage with some onion rings and grilled tomato halves. Pour on the lemon juice, then sprinkle with chopped parsley and serve.

BAKED SEA BASS WITH FENNEL

SEA BASS HAS A WONDERFUL FLAVOUR, BUT CHEAPER ALTERNATIVES, SUCH AS SNAPPER OR BREAM CAN BE USED. SERVE WITH CRISPLY COOKED FRENCH BEANS TOSSED IN OLIVE OIL AND GARLIC.

SERVES FOUR

INGREDIENTS

    4 fennel bulbs, trimmed
    4 tomatoes, peeled and diced
    8 drained canned anchovy fillets,
      halved lengthways
    a large pinch of saffron threads,
      soaked in 30ml/2 tbsp hot water
    150ml/¼ pint/⅔ cup chicken or
      fish stock
    2 red or yellow peppers, seeded and
      each cut into 12 strips
    4 garlic cloves, chopped
    15ml/1 tbsp chopped fresh marjoram
    45ml/3 tbsp olive oil
    1 sea bass, about 1.75kg/4–4½lb,
      scaled and cleaned
    salt and ground black pepper
    chopped parsley, to garnish

1 Preheat the oven to 200°C/400°F/ Gas 6. Quarter the fennel bulbs length- ways. Cook in lightly salted boiling water for 5 minutes, until barely tender. Drain and arrange in a shallow ovenproof dish. Season with pepper; set aside.

2 Spoon the diced tomatoes and anchovy strips on top of the fennel. Stir the saffron and its soaking water into the stock and pour the mixture over the tomatoes. Lay the strips of pepper alongside the fennel and sprinkle with the garlic and marjoram. Drizzle 30ml/ 2 tbsp of the olive oil over the peppers and season with salt and pepper.

VARIATION
If you prefer, use large pieces of thick- cut halibut or turbot for this dish.

3 Bake the vegetables for 15 minutes. Season the prepared sea bass inside and out and lay it on top of the fennel and pepper mixture. Drizzle the remaining olive oil over the fish and bake for 30–40 minutes more, until the sea bass flesh comes away easily from the bone when tested with the point of a sharp knife. Serve at once, garnished with parsley.

MOROCCAN SPICED MACKEREL

MACKEREL IS EXTREMELY GOOD FOR YOU, BUT SOME PEOPLE FIND ITS HEALTHY OILINESS TOO MUCH TO TAKE. THE MOROCCAN SPICES IN THIS RECIPE COUNTERACT THE RICHNESS OF THE FISH.

SERVES FOUR

INGREDIENTS

    150ml/¼ pint/⅔ cup sunflower oil
    15ml/1 tbsp paprika
    5–10ml/1–2 tsp harissa or
      chilli powder
    10ml/2 tsp ground cumin
    10ml/2 tsp ground coriander
    2 garlic cloves, crushed
    juice of 2 lemons
    30ml/2 tbsp chopped fresh
      mint leaves
    30ml/2 tbsp chopped fresh coriander
    4 mackerel, cleaned
    salt and ground black pepper
    lemon wedges, to serve
    mint sprigs, to garnish

1 In a bowl, whisk together the oil, spices, garlic and lemon juice. Season, then stir in the mint and coriander to make a spicy marinade.

2 Make two or three diagonal slashes on either side of each mackerel so that they may absorb the marinade. Pour the marinade into a shallow non-metallic dish that is large enough to hold the fish in a single layer.

3 Put in the mackerel and turn them over in the marinade, spooning it into the slashes. Cover the dish with clear film and place in the fridge for at least 3 hours or more if you wish.

4 When you are ready to cook the mackerel, preheat the grill to medium- high. Transfer the fish to a rack set over a grilling pan and grill for 5–7 minutes on each side until just cooked, turning the fish once and basting them several times with the marinade. Serve hot or cold with lemon wedges, garnished with mint. Herb-flavoured couscous or rice make good accompaniments.

COOK'S TIP
These spicy mackerel can be cooked on a barbecue. Make sure the coals are very hot before you begin cooking. Arrange the fish on a large hinged rack to make turning easier and barbecue for 5–7 minutes, turning once.

VARIATION
Trout, bonito, trevally or bluefish are also good cooked this way.

ORIENTAL FISH EN PAPILLOTE

THE AROMATIC SMELL THAT WAFTS OUT OF THESE FISH PARCELS AS YOU OPEN THEM IS DELICIOUSLY TEMPTING. IF YOU DON'T LIKE ORIENTAL FLAVOURS, USE WHITE WINE, HERBS AND THINLY SLICED VEGETABLES, OR MEDITERRANEAN INGREDIENTS SUCH AS TOMATOES, BASIL AND OLIVES.

SERVES FOUR

INGREDIENTS
2 carrots
2 courgettes
6 spring onions
2.5cm/1in piece fresh root
   ginger, peeled
1 lime
2 garlic cloves, thinly sliced
30ml/2 tbsp teriyaki marinade or *nam
   pla* (Thai fish sauce)
5–10ml/1–2 tsp clear sesame oil
4 salmon fillets, about
   200g/7oz each
ground black pepper
rice, to serve

VARIATION
Thick fillets of hake, halibut, hoki and fresh or undyed smoked haddock and cod can all be used for this dish.

1 Cut the carrots, courgettes and spring onions into matchsticks and set them aside. Cut the ginger into matchsticks and put these in a small bowl. Using a zester, pare the lime thinly. Add the pared rind to the ginger, with the garlic. Squeeze the lime juice.

2 Place the teriyaki marinade or *nam pla* into a bowl and stir in the lime juice and sesame oil.

3 Preheat the oven to 220°C/425°F/ Gas 7. Cut out four rounds of baking parchment, each with a diameter of 40cm/16in. Season the salmon with pepper. Lay a fillet on one side of each paper round, about 3cm/1¼in off centre. Scatter a quarter of the ginger mixture over each and pile a quarter of the vegetable matchsticks on top. Spoon a quarter of the teriyaki or *nam pla* mixture over the top.

4 Fold the bare side of the baking parchment over the salmon and roll the edges of the parchment over to seal each parcel very tightly.

5 Place the salmon parcels on a baking sheet and cook in the oven for about 10–12 minutes, depending on the thickness of the fillets. Put the parcels on plates and serve with rice.

ROAST COD WITH PANCETTA AND BUTTER BEANS

THICK COD STEAKS WRAPPED IN PANCETTA AND ROASTED MAKE A SUPERB SUPPER DISH WHEN SERVED ON A BED OF BUTTER BEANS, WITH SWEET AND JUICY CHERRY TOMATOES ON THE SIDE.

SERVES FOUR

INGREDIENTS
   200g/7oz/1 cup butter beans, soaked
      overnight in cold water to cover
   2 leeks, thinly sliced
   2 garlic cloves, chopped
   8 fresh sage leaves
   90ml/6 tbsp fruity olive oil
   8 thin slices of pancetta
   4 thick cod steaks, skinned
   12 cherry tomatoes
   salt and ground black pepper

1 Drain the beans, tip into a pan and cover with cold water. Bring to the boil and skim off the foam on the surface. Lower the heat, then stir in the leeks, garlic, 4 sage leaves and 30ml/2 tbsp of the olive oil. Simmer for 1–1½ hours until the beans are tender, adding more water if necessary. Drain, return to the pan, season, stir in 30ml/2 tbsp olive oil and keep warm.

2 Preheat the oven to 200°C/400°F/ Gas 6. Wrap two slices of pancetta around the edge of each cod steak, tying it on with kitchen string or securing it with a wooden cocktail stick. Insert a sage leaf between the pancetta and the cod. Season the fish with salt and pepper.

VARIATION
You can use cannellini beans for this recipe, and streaky bacon instead of pancetta. It is also good made with halibut, hake, haddock or salmon.

3 Heat a heavy-based frying pan, add 15ml/1 tbsp of the remaining oil and seal the cod steaks two at a time for 1 minute on each side. Transfer them to an ovenproof dish and roast in the oven for 5 minutes.

4 Add the tomatoes to the dish and drizzle over the remaining olive oil. Roast for 5 minutes more, until the cod steaks are cooked but still juicy. Serve them on a bed of butter beans with the roasted tomatoes. Garnish with parsley.

HERBED CHARGRILLED SHARK STEAKS

SHARK IS VERY LOW IN FAT, WITH DENSE, WELL-FLAVOURED FLESH. OTHER CLOSE-TEXTURED FISH LIKE TUNA, BONITO AND MARLIN WORK EQUALLY WELL IN THIS RECIPE, WHICH IS IDEAL FOR A BARBECUE. SERVE THE FISH WITH A TANGY TOMATO SALAD.

SERVES FOUR

INGREDIENTS
45ml/3 tbsp olive oil
2 fresh bay leaves, chopped
15ml/1 tbsp chopped fresh basil
15ml/1 tbsp chopped fresh oregano
30ml/2 tbsp chopped fresh parsley
5ml/1 tsp finely chopped
　fresh rosemary
5ml/1 tsp fresh thyme leaves
2 garlic cloves, crushed
4 pieces drained sun-dried tomatoes
　in oil, chopped
4 shark steaks, about 200g/7oz each
juice of 1 lemon
15ml/1 tbsp drained small
　capers in vinegar (optional)
salt and ground black pepper

1 Whisk the oil, herbs, garlic and sun-dried tomatoes in a bowl, then pour the mixture into a shallow dish that is large enough to hold the shark steaks in a single layer. Season the shark steaks with salt and pepper and brush the lemon juice over both sides. Lay the fish in the dish, turning the steaks to coat them all over. Cover and marinate in the fridge for 1–2 hours.

2 Heat a ridged grilling pan or barbecue until it is very hot. Lift the shark steaks out of the marinade, pat dry with kitchen paper and grill or barbecue for about 5 minutes on each side, until they are cooked through. Pour the marinade into a small saucepan and bring to the boil. Stir in the capers, if you are using them. Spoon over the grilled shark steaks and serve immediately.

CHINESE-STYLE SCALLOPS AND PRAWNS

SERVE THIS LIGHT, DELICATE DISH FOR LUNCH OR SUPPER ACCOMPANIED BY AROMATIC STEAMED RICE OR FINE RICE NOODLES AND STIR-FRIED PAK CHOI.

SERVES FOUR

INGREDIENTS
15ml/1 tbsp stir-fry or sunflower oil
500g/1¼lb raw tiger prawns, peeled
1 star anise
225g/8oz scallops, halved
　horizontally if large
2.5cm/1in piece fresh root ginger,
　peeled and grated
2 garlic cloves, thinly sliced
1 red pepper, seeded and cut into
　thin strips
115g/4oz/1¾ cups shiitake or button
　mushrooms, thinly sliced
juice of 1 lemon
5ml/1 tsp cornflour, mixed to a paste
　with 30ml/2 tbsp cold water
30ml/2 tbsp light soy sauce
snipped fresh chives, to garnish
salt and ground black pepper

1 Heat the oil in a wok until very hot. Put in the prawns and star anise and stir-fry over a high heat for 2 minutes. Add the scallops, ginger and garlic and stir-fry for 1 minute more, by which time the prawns should have turned pink and the scallops opaque. Season with a little salt and plenty of pepper and then remove from the wok using a slotted spoon. Discard the star anise.

2 Add the red pepper and mushrooms to the wok and stir-fry for 1–2 minutes. Pour in the lemon juice, cornflour paste and soy sauce, bring to the boil and bubble for 1–2 minutes, stirring all the time, until the sauce is smooth and slightly thickened.

3 Stir the prawns and scallops into the sauce, cook for a few seconds until heated through, then season with salt and ground black and serve garnished with snipped chives.

VARIATIONS
Use other prepared shellfish in this dish; try thinly sliced rings of squid, or mussels or clams, or substitute chunks of firm white fish, such as monkfish fillet, for the scallops.

FILO FISH PIES

THIS LIGHT FILO-WRAPPED FISH PIES CAN BE MADE WITH ANY FIRM WHITE FISH FILLETS, SUCH AS ORANGE ROUGHY, COD, HALIBUT OR HOKI. SERVE WITH SALAD LEAVES AND MAYONNAISE ON THE SIDE.

2 Brush the inside of six 13cm/5in tartlet tins with a little of the melted butter. Fit a piece of filo pastry into the tins, draping it so that it hangs over the sides. Brush with butter, then add another sheet at right angles to the first. Brush with butter. Continue to line the tins in this way.

3 Spread the spinach evenly over the pastry. Add the diced fish and season well. Stir the chives into the crème fraîche and spread the mixture over the top of the fish. Scatter the dill over.

4 Draw the overhanging pieces of pastry together and scrunch lightly to make a lid. Brush with butter. Bake for about 15–20 minutes, until golden brown.

SERVES SIX

INGREDIENTS
400g/14oz spinach, trimmed
1 egg, lightly beaten
2 garlic cloves, crushed
450g/1lb orange roughy or other
  white fish fillet
juice of 1 lemon
50g/2oz/¼ cup butter, melted
8–12 filo pastry sheets, thawed
  if frozen, quartered
15ml/1 tbsp finely snipped
  fresh chives
200ml/7fl oz/scant 1 cup half-fat
  crème fraîche
15ml/1 tbsp chopped fresh dill
salt and ground black pepper

VARIATION
If you prefer to make one large pie, use a 20cm/8in tin and cook for 45 minutes.

1 Preheat the oven to 190°C/375°F/ Gas 5. Wash the spinach, then cook it in a lidded heavy-based pan with just the water that clings to the leaves. As soon as the leaves are tender, drain, squeeze as dry as possible and chop. Put the spinach in a bowl, add the egg and garlic, season with salt and pepper and set aside. Dice the fish and place it in a bowl. Stir in the lemon juice. Season with salt and pepper and toss lightly.

ELEGANT DISHES FOR ENTERTAINING

For sheer elegance, fish and shellfish are hard to beat and so quick to prepare that they make light work of entertaining. A whole fish baked in a salt crust looks intriguing and tastes superb. For breathtaking elegance and taste, treat your guests to Lobster Thermidor, Vegetable-stuffed Squid or Fillets of Turbot with Oysters. Whatever the occasion, delight your guests with these superb party dishes.

HAKE AU POIVRE WITH RED PEPPER RELISH

THIS PISCINE VERSION OF THE CLASSIC STEAK AU POIVRE CAN BE MADE WITH MONKFISH OR COD INSTEAD OF HAKE. VARY THE QUANTITY OF PEPPERCORNS ACCORDING TO YOUR PERSONAL TASTE.

SERVES FOUR

INGREDIENTS
    30–45ml/2–3 tbsp mixed peppercorns
       (black, white, pink and green)
    4 hake steaks, about 175g/6oz each
    30ml/2 tbsp olive oil
For the red pepper relish
    2 red peppers
    15ml/1 tbsp olive oil
    2 garlic cloves, chopped
    4 ripe tomatoes, peeled, seeded
       and quartered
    4 drained canned anchovy
       fillets, chopped
    5ml/1 tsp capers
    15ml/1 tbsp balsamic vinegar
    12 fresh basil leaves, shredded, plus
       a few extra to garnish
    salt and ground black pepper

1 Put the peppercorns in a mortar and crush them coarsely with a pestle. Alternatively, put them in a plastic bag and crush them with a rolling pin. Season the hake fillets lightly with salt, then coat them evenly on both sides with the crushed peppercorns. Set the coated fish steaks aside while you make the red pepper relish.

2 Make the relish. Cut the red peppers in half lengthways, remove the core and seeds from each and cut the flesh into 1cm/½in wide strips. Heat the olive oil in a wok or a shallow pan that has a lid. Add the peppers and stir them for about 5 minutes, until they are slightly softened. Stir in the chopped garlic, tomatoes and the anchovies, then cover the pan and simmer the mixture very gently for about 20 minutes, until the peppers are very soft.

3 Tip the contents of the pan into a food processor and whizz to a coarse purée. Transfer to a bowl and season to taste. Stir in the capers, balsamic vinegar and basil. Keep the relish hot.

4 Heat the olive oil in a shallow pan, add the hake steaks and fry them, in batches if necessary, for 5 minutes on each side, turning them once or twice, until they are just cooked through.

5 Place the fish on individual plates and spoon a little red pepper relish on to each plate. Garnish with basil leaves and a little extra balsamic vinegar. Serve the rest of the relish separately.

MOROCCAN FISH TAGINE

THIS SPICY, AROMATIC DISH PROVES JUST HOW EXCITING AN INGREDIENT FISH CAN BE. SERVE IT WITH COUSCOUS FLAVOURED WITH CHOPPED MINT.

SERVES EIGHT

INGREDIENTS

1.4kg/3lb firm fish fillets, skinned
   and cut into 5cm/2in chunks
60ml/4 tbsp olive oil
4 onions, chopped
1 large aubergine, cut into
   1cm/½in cubes
2 courgettes, cut into 1cm/½in cubes
400g/14oz can chopped tomatoes
400ml/14fl oz/1⅔ cups passata
200ml/7fl oz/scant 1 cup fish stock
1 preserved lemon, chopped
90g/3½oz/scant 1 cup olives
60ml/4 tbsp chopped fresh coriander
salt and ground black pepper
coriander sprigs, to garnish
For the harissa
   3 large fresh red chillies, seeded
      and chopped
   3 garlic cloves, peeled
   15ml/1 tbsp ground coriander
   30ml/2 tbsp ground cumin
   5ml/1 tsp ground cinnamon
   grated rind of 1 lemon
   30ml/2 tbsp sunflower oil

1 Make the harissa. Whizz everything in a blender to a smooth paste.

2 Put the chunks of fish in a wide bowl and add 30ml/2 tbsp of the harissa. Toss to coat, cover and chill for at least 1 hour, or overnight.

3 Heat half the oil in a shallow, heavy-based pan. Cook the onions gently for 10 minutes, until golden brown. Stir in the remaining harissa; cook for 5 minutes, stirring occasionally.

4 Heat the remaining olive oil in a separate shallow frying pan. Add the aubergine cubes and fry for about 10 minutes, until they are golden brown. Add the cubed courgettes and fry for a further 2 minutes.

5 Tip the mixture into the shallow pan and combine with the onions, then stir in the chopped tomatoes, the passata and fish stock. Bring to the boil, then lower the heat and simmer the mixture for about 20 minutes.

6 Stir the fish chunks and preserved lemon into the pan. Add the olives and stir gently. Cover and simmer over a low heat for about 15–20 minutes until the fish is just cooked through. Season to taste. Stir in the chopped coriander. Serve with couscous, if you like, and garnish with coriander sprigs.

COOK'S TIP
To make the fish go further, you could add 225g/8oz/1¼ cups cooked chick-peas to the tagine.

GRILLED SQUID WITH CHORIZO

THE BEST WAY TO COOK THIS DISH IS ON A GRIDDLE OR IN A RIDGED GRILLING PAN. IF YOU HAVE NEITHER, USE AN OVERHEAD GRILL, MAKING SURE IT IS VERY HOT. IF YOU CAN ONLY FIND MEDIUM-SIZE SQUID, ALLOW TWO PER SERVING AND HALVE THEM LENGTHWAYS FROM THE TAIL END TO THE CAVITY.

SERVES SIX

INGREDIENTS
    24 small squid, cleaned
    150ml/¼ pint/⅔ cup extra
        virgin olive oil
    300g/11oz cooking chorizo, cut into
        12 slices
    3 tomatoes, halved and seasoned
        with salt and pepper
    juice of 1 lemon
    24 cooked new potatoes, halved
    a handful of fresh rocket leaves
    salt and ground black pepper
    lemon slices, to garnish

1 Separate the body and tentacles of the squid and cut the bodies in half lengthways if they are large.

2 Pour half the oil into a bowl, season with salt and pepper, then toss all the squid in the oil. Heat a ridged grilling pan or grill to very hot.

3 Grill the prepared squid bodies for about 45 seconds on each side until the flesh is opaque and tender. Then transfer to a plate and keep hot. Grill the tentacles for about 1 minute on each side, then place them on the plate. Grill the chorizo slices for about 30 seconds on each side, until golden brown, then set them aside with the squid. Grill the tomato halves for 1–2 minutes on each side, until they are softened and browned.

4 Place the potatoes and rocket in a large bowl.

5 Pour the lemon juice into a bowl and whisk in the remaining oil. Season. Reserve 30ml/2 tbsp of this dressing in a jug. Pour the dressing over the potatoes and rocket, toss lightly and divide among 6 plates. Pile a portion of the squid, tomatoes and chorizo on each salad, and drizzle over the reserved dressing. Garnish with lemon slices and serve at once.

SOLE WITH WILD MUSHROOMS

IF POSSIBLE, USE CHANTERELLES FOR THIS DISH; THEIR GLOWING ORANGE COLOUR COMBINES REALLY WONDERFULLY WITH THE INTENSELY GOLDEN SAUCE. OTHERWISE, USE ANY PALE-COLOURED OR OYSTER MUSHROOMS THAT YOU CAN FIND INSTEAD.

SERVES FOUR

INGREDIENTS
    4 Dover sole fillets, about 115g/4oz
        each, skinned
    50g/2oz/4 tbsp butter
    500ml/17fl oz/generous 2 cups
        fish stock
    150g/5oz/2 cups chanterelles
    a large pinch of saffron threads
    150ml/¼ pint/⅔ cup double cream
    1 egg yolk
    salt and ground white pepper
    finely chopped fresh parsley, and
        parsley sprigs to garnish
    boiled new potatoes, to serve

1 Preheat the oven to 200°C/400°F/Gas 6. Cut the sole fillets in half lengthways and place them on a board with the skinned side uppermost. Season them with salt and white pepper, then roll them up. Use a little of the butter to grease a baking dish just large enough to hold all the sole fillets in a single layer, arrange the sole rolls in it, then pour over the fish stock. Cover tightly with foil and bake for 12–15 minutes, until cooked through.

2 Meanwhile, pick off any bits of fern or twig from the chanterelles and wipe the mushrooms with a damp cloth. Halve or quarter any large ones. Heat the remaining butter in a frying pan until foaming, and sauté the mushrooms for 3–4 minutes, until just tender. Season with salt and pepper and keep hot.

3 Lift the cooked sole fillets out of the cooking liquid and place them on a heated serving dish. Keep hot. Strain the liquid into a small saucepan, add the saffron, set over a very high heat and boil down until reduced to about 250ml/8fl oz/1 cup. Stir in the cream and then let the sauce bubble gently once or twice.

4 Lightly beat the egg yolk in a small bowl, pour on a little of the hot sauce and stir well. Stir the mixture into the remaining sauce in the pan and cook over a very low heat for 1–2 minutes, until slightly thickened. Season to taste. Stir the chanterelles into the sauce and pour it over the sole fillets. Garnish with parsley sprigs and serve at once. Boiled new potatoes make the perfect accompaniment.

LOBSTER THERMIDOR

ONE OF THE CLASSIC FRENCH DISHES, LOBSTER THERMIDOR MAKES A LITTLE LOBSTER GO A LONG WAY. IT IS BEST TO USE ONE BIG RATHER THAN TWO SMALL LOBSTERS, AS A LARGER LOBSTER WILL CONTAIN A HIGHER PROPORTION OF FLESH AND THE MEAT WILL BE SWEETER. IDEALLY USE A LIVE CRUSTACEAN AND COOK IT YOURSELF, BUT A BOILED LOBSTER FROM THE FISHMONGER WILL DO.

SERVES TWO

INGREDIENTS

1 large lobster, about
   800g–1kg/1¾–2¼lb, boiled
45ml/3 tbsp brandy
25g/1oz/2 tbsp butter
2 shallots, finely chopped
115g/4oz/1½ cups white button
   mushrooms, thinly sliced
15ml/1 tbsp plain flour
105ml/7 tbsp fish or shellfish stock
120ml/4fl oz/½ cup double cream
5ml/1 tsp Dijon mustard
2 egg yolks, beaten
45ml/3 tbsp dry white wine
45ml/3 tbsp freshly grated
   Parmesan cheese
salt, ground black pepper and
   cayenne pepper

1 Split the lobster in half lengthways; crack the claws. Discard the stomach sac; keep the coral for another dish. Keeping each half-shell intact, extract the meat from the tail and claws, then cut into large dice. Place in a shallow dish; sprinkle over the brandy. Cover and set aside. Wipe and dry the half-shells and set them aside.

2 Melt the butter in a saucepan and cook the shallots over a low heat until soft. Add the mushrooms and cook until just tender, stirring constantly. Stir in the flour and a pinch of cayenne; cook, stirring, for 2 minutes. Gradually add the stock, stirring until the sauce boils and thickens.

3 Stir in the cream and mustard and continue to cook until the sauce is smooth and thick. Season to taste with salt, black pepper and cayenne. Pour half the sauce on to the egg yolks, stir well and return the mixture to the pan. Stir in the wine; adjust the seasoning, being generous with the cayenne.

4 Preheat the grill to medium-high. Stir the diced lobster and the brandy into the sauce. Arrange the lobster half-shells in a grill pan and divide the mixture among them. Sprinkle with Parmesan and place under the grill until browned. Serve with steamed rice and mixed salad leaves.

RED MULLET SALTIMBOCCA

THE RICH RED COLOUR OF THE MULLET IS INTENSIFIED BY RUBBING SAFFRON INTO THE SKIN, COMPLEMENTING THE PARMA HAM BEAUTIFULLY. SERVE WITH BRIGHTLY COLOURED ROASTED MEDITERRANEAN VEGETABLES AND CRISPLY COOKED FRENCH BEANS, IF YOU WISH.

SERVES FOUR

INGREDIENTS
   8 red mullet fillets, scaled but
     not skinned
   a pinch of saffron threads or
     powdered saffron
   15ml/1 tbsp olive oil
   8 fresh sage leaves
   8 thin slices of Parma ham
   25g/1oz/2 tbsp butter
   115g/4oz/²⁄₃ cup mixed olives
   salt and ground black pepper
For the dressing
   15ml/1 tbsp caster sugar
   105ml/7 tbsp balsamic vinegar
   300ml/½ pint/1¼ cups extra virgin
     olive oil
   5cm/2in slice red pepper, diced
   1 small courgette, very finely diced
   1 ripe tomato, peeled, seeded and
     very finely diced

1 Score the red mullet skin lightly in three or four places. Season both sides of each fillet with salt and ground black pepper. If you are using saffron threads, crumble them over the skin side of each red mullet fillet, or sprinkle the powdered saffron over the skin. Drizzle on a little olive oil and then rub the saffron in well with your fingertips. This will enhance the colour of the fish skin dramatically.

2 Heat a non-stick frying pan until very hot, then put in the fillets, skin side down, and cook over a high heat for 2 minutes. Turn the fillets over and cook them for 2 minutes more. Drain on kitchen paper and leave until cool enough to handle.

3 Place a sage leaf on each cooked red mullet fillet, then wrap the fillets in a slice of Parma ham to cover them completely. Melt the butter in the frying pan and continue to heat until it foams. Fry the ham and red mullet parcels over a high heat for 1–2 minutes on each side, until the ham is pale golden. Transfer to warmed serving plates and keep hot while you make the dressing.

4 Mix the sugar and vinegar in a small saucepan, set over a high heat and boil until syrupy.

5 Meanwhile, pour the olive oil into a bowl, stir in the diced vegetables and season. Stir the vinegar syrup into the dressing. Drizzle it over and around the ham-wrapped fish. Place the olives on the plates and serve immediately.

ROAST MONKFISH WITH GARLIC

MONKFISH TIED UP AND COOKED IN THIS WAY IS KNOWN IN FRENCH AS A "GIGOT", BECAUSE IT RESEMBLES A LEG OF LAMB. THE COMBINATION OF MONKFISH AND GARLIC IS SUPERB. FOR A CONTRAST IN COLOUR, SERVE IT WITH VIBRANT GREEN OR FRENCH BEANS.

SERVES FOUR TO SIX

INGREDIENTS

1kg/2¼lb monkfish tail, skinned
14 fat garlic cloves
5ml/1 tsp fresh thyme leaves
30ml/2 tbsp olive oil
juice of 1 lemon
2 bay leaves
salt and ground black pepper

1 Preheat the oven to 220ºC/425ºF/ Gas 7. Remove any membrane from the monkfish tail and cut out the central bone. Peel 2 garlic cloves and cut them into thin slivers. Scatter a quarter of these and half the thyme leaves over the cut side of the fish, then close it up and use fine kitchen string to tie it into a neat shape, like a boned piece of meat. Pat dry with kitchen paper.

2 Make incisions on either side of the fish and push in the remaining garlic slivers. Heat half the olive oil in a frying pan which can safely be used in the oven. When the oil is hot, put in the monkfish and brown it all over for about 5 minutes, until evenly coloured. Season with salt and pepper, sprinkle with lemon juice and scatter over the remaining thyme.

3 Tuck the bay leaves under the monkfish, arrange the remaining (unpeeled) garlic cloves around it and drizzle the remaining olive oil over the fish and the garlic. Transfer the frying pan to the oven and roast the monkfish for 20–25 minutes, until the flesh is cooked through.

4 Place on a warmed serving dish with the garlic and some green beans. To serve, remove the string and cut the monkfish into 2cm/¾in thick slices.

COOK'S TIPS
• The garlic heads can be used whole.
• When serving the monkfish, invite each guest to pop out the soft garlic pulp with a fork and spread it over the monkfish.

SEA BASS WITH GINGER AND LEEKS

YOU CAN USE WHOLE FISH OR THICK FILLETS FOR THIS RECIPE, WHICH IS ALSO EXCELLENT MADE WITH BREAM, SNAPPER, POMFRET AND TREVALLY. SERVE THE FISH WITH FRIED RICE AND STIR-FRIED CHINESE GREEN VEGETABLES SUCH AS PAK CHOI, IF YOU LIKE.

SERVES FOUR

INGREDIENTS

1 sea bass, about 1.4–1.5kg/
  3–3½lb, scaled and cleaned
8 spring onions
60ml/4 tbsp teriyaki marinade or
  dark soy sauce
30ml/2 tbsp cornflour
juice of 1 lemon
30ml/2 tbsp rice wine vinegar
5ml/1 tsp ground ginger
60ml/4 tbsp stir-fry or groundnut oil
2 leeks, shredded
2.5cm/1in piece fresh root ginger,
  peeled and grated
105ml/7 tbsp chicken or fish stock
30ml/2 tbsp rice wine or dry sherry
5ml/1 tsp caster sugar
salt and ground black pepper

1 Make several diagonal slashes on either side of the sea bass so it can absorb the flavours, then season the fish inside and out with salt and ground black pepper. Trim the spring onions, cut them in half lengthways, then slice them diagonally into 2cm/¾in lengths. Put half of the spring onions in the cavity of the fish and reserve the rest for later use.

2 In a shallow dish, mix together the teriyaki marinade or dark soy sauce, the cornflour, lemon juice, rice wine vinegar and ground ginger to make a smooth, runny paste. Turn the fish in the marinade to coat it thoroughly, working it into the slashes, then leave it to marinate for 20–30 minutes, turning it several times.

3 Heat a wok or frying pan that is large enough to hold the sea bass comfortably. Add the oil, then the leeks and grated ginger. Fry gently for about 5 minutes, until the leeks are tender. Remove the leeks and ginger with a slotted spoon, and drain on kitchen paper leaving the oil in the wok or pan.

4 Lift the sea bass out of the marinade and lower it carefully into the hot oil. Fry over a medium heat for 2–3 minutes on each side. Stir the stock, rice wine or sherry and sugar into the marinade, with salt and pepper to taste. Pour the mixture over the fish. Return the leeks and ginger to the wok, together with the reserved spring onions. Cover and simmer for about 15 minutes, until the fish is cooked through. Serve at once.

GRILLED LANGOUSTINES WITH HERBS

THIS SIMPLE COOKING METHOD ENHANCES BOTH THE DELICATE COLOUR AND FLAVOUR OF THE LANGOUSTINES. TRY TO FIND LIVE LANGOUSTINES FOR THIS RECIPE. CHOOSE THE LARGEST YOU CAN FIND (OR AFFORD) FOR THIS DISH, AND ALLOW 5–6 PER SERVING. LOBSTER AND CRAYFISH ARE ALSO DELICIOUS COOKED THIS WAY.

SERVES FOUR AS A MAIN COURSE,
SIX AS A STARTER

INGREDIENTS
    60ml/4 tbsp extra virgin olive oil
    60ml/4 tbsp hazelnut oil
    15ml/1 tbsp each finely chopped
        fresh basil, chives, chervil, parsley
        and tarragon
    pinch of ground ginger
    20–24 large langoustines,
        preferably live
    lemon wedges and rocket leaves,
        to garnish
    salt and ground black pepper

COOK'S TIPS
• Don't forget to provide your guests with fingerbowls of warm water and plenty of paper napkins.
• If you use cooked langoustines, then grill them for just 2–3 minutes to warm them through.

1 Preheat the grill to very hot. Mix together the olive and hazelnut oils in a small bowl. Add the herbs, a pinch of ground ginger and salt and pepper to taste. Whisk thoroughly until slightly thickened and emulsified.

2 If you are using live langoustines immerse them in a pan of boiling water for 1–2 minutes, then drain and leave them to cool.

3 Split the langoustines lengthways using a large sharp knife and arrange them on a foil-lined grill pan. Spoon over the herb-flavoured oil.

4 Grill for 8–10 minutes, basting the langoustines two or three times until they are cooked and lightly browned.

5 Arrange the langoustines on a warmed serving dish, pour the juices from the grill pan over and serve immediately garnished with lemon wedges and rocket leaves.

SEA BASS IN A SALT CRUST

BAKING FISH IN A CRUST OF SEA SALT ENHANCES THE FLAVOUR AND BRINGS OUT THE TASTE OF THE SEA. ANY FIRM FISH CAN BE COOKED IN THIS WAY. BREAK OPEN THE CRUST AT THE TABLE TO RELEASE THE GLORIOUS AROMA.

SERVES FOUR

INGREDIENTS
    1 sea bass, about 1kg/2¼lb, cleaned
        and scaled
    1 sprig each of fresh fennel,
        rosemary and thyme
    2kg/4½lb coarse sea salt
    mixed peppercorns
    seaweed or samphire, blanched, and
        lemon slices, to garnish

1 Preheat the oven to 240°C/475°F/ Gas 9. Fill the cavity of the sea bass with all the herbs and grind over some of the mixed peppercorns.

2 Spread half the salt on a shallow baking tray (ideally oval) and lay the sea bass on it. Cover the fish all over with a 1cm/½in layer of salt, pressing it down firmly. Moisten the salt lightly by spraying with water from an atomizer. Bake the fish in the hot oven for 30–40 minutes, until the salt crust is just beginning to colour.

3 Garnish the baking tray with seaweed or samphire and bring the fish to the table in its salt crust. Use a sharp knife to break open the crust. Serve the fish, adding lemon slices to each plate.

FILLETS OF BRILL IN RED WINE SAUCE

FORGET THE OLD MAXIM THAT RED WINE AND FISH DO NOT GO WELL TOGETHER. THE ROBUST SAUCE ADDS COLOUR AND RICHNESS TO THIS EXCELLENT DISH. TURBOT, HALIBUT AND JOHN DORY ARE ALSO GOOD COOKED THIS WAY.

SERVES FOUR

INGREDIENTS

    4 fillets of brill, about
        175–200g/6–7oz each, skinned
    150g/5oz/²⁄₃ cup chilled butter,
        diced, plus extra for greasing
    115g/4oz shallots, thinly sliced
    200ml/7fl oz/scant 1 cup robust
        red wine
    200ml/7fl oz/scant 1 cup fish stock
    salt and ground white pepper
    fresh chervil or flat leaf parsley
        leaves, to garnish

3 Using a fish slice, carefully lift the fish and shallots on to a serving dish, cover with foil and keep hot.

4 Transfer the casserole to the hob and bring the cooking liquid to the boil over a high heat. Cook it until it has reduced by half. Lower the heat and whisk in the chilled butter, one piece at a time, to make a smooth, shiny sauce. Season with salt and ground white pepper, set aside and keep hot.

5 Divide the shallots among four warmed plates and lay the brill fillets on top. Pour the sauce over and around the fish and garnish with the chervil or flat leaf parsley.

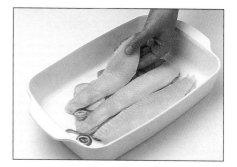

1 Preheat the oven to 180°C/350°F/ Gas 4. Season the fish on both sides with salt and pepper. Generously butter a flameproof dish, which is large enough to take all the brill fillets in a single layer without overlapping. Spread the shallots over the base and lay the fish fillets on top. Season.

2 Pour in the red wine and fish stock, cover the dish and bring the liquid to just below boiling point. Transfer the dish to the oven and bake for 6–8 minutes, until the brill is just cooked.

FILLETS OF TURBOT WITH OYSTERS

THIS LUXURIOUS DISH IS PERFECT FOR SPECIAL OCCASIONS. IT IS WORTH BUYING A WHOLE TURBOT AND ASKING THE FISHMONGER TO FILLET AND SKIN IT FOR YOU. KEEP THE HEAD, BONES AND TRIMMINGS FOR STOCK. SOLE, BRILL AND HALIBUT CAN ALL BE SUBSTITUTED FOR THE TURBOT.

SERVES FOUR

INGREDIENTS

    12 Pacific (rock) oysters
    115g/4oz/½ cup butter
    2 carrots, cut into julienne strips
    200g/7oz celeriac, cut into
      julienne strips
    the white parts of 2 leeks, cut into
      julienne strips
    375ml/13fl oz/generous 1½ cups
      Champagne or dry white sparkling
      wine (about ½ bottle)
    105ml/7 tbsp whipping cream
    1 turbot, about 1.75kg/4–4½lb,
      filleted and skinned
    salt and ground white pepper

1 Using an oyster knife, open the oysters over a bowl to catch the juices, then carefully remove them from their shells, discarding the shells, and place them in a separate bowl. Set aside until required.

2 Melt 25g/1oz/2 tbsp of the butter in a shallow pan, add the vegetable julienne and cook over a low heat until tender but not coloured. Pour in half the Champagne or sparkling wine and cook very gently until all the liquid has evaporated. Keep the heat low so that the vegetables do not colour.

3 Strain the oyster juices into a small saucepan and add the cream and the remaining Champagne or sparkling wine. Place over a medium heat until the mixture has reduced to the consistency of thin cream. Dice half the remaining butter and whisk it into the sauce, one piece at a time, until smooth. Season to taste, then pour the sauce into a blender and whizz until velvety smooth.

4 Return the sauce to the pan, bring it to just below boiling point, then drop in the oysters. Poach for about 1 minute, to warm but barely cook. Keep warm, but do not let the sauce boil.

5 Season the turbot fillets with salt and pepper. Heat the remaining butter in a large frying pan until foaming, then fry the fillets over a medium heat for about 2–3 minutes on each side until cooked through and golden.

6 Cut each turbot fillet into three pieces and arrange on individual warmed plates. Pile the vegetable julienne on top, place three oysters around the turbot fillets on each plate and pour the sauce around the edge.

JOHN DORY WITH LIGHT CURRY SAUCE

THIS EXCELLENT COMBINATION OF FLAVOURS ALSO WORKS WELL WITH OTHER FLAT FISH LIKE TURBOT, HALIBUT AND BRILL, OR MORE EXOTIC SPECIES LIKE MAHI-MAHI OR ORANGE ROUGHY. THE CURRY TASTE SHOULD BE VERY SUBTLE, SO USE A MILD CURRY POWDER. SERVE THE FISH WITH PILAU RICE AND MANGO CHUTNEY. IT LOOKS WONDERFUL ARRANGED ON BANANA LEAVES, IF YOU CAN FIND SOME.

SERVES FOUR

INGREDIENTS

    4 John Dory fillets, each about
      175g/6oz, skinned
    15ml/1 tbsp sunflower oil
    25g/1oz/2 tbsp butter
    salt and ground black pepper
    15ml/1 tbsp fresh coriander leaves,
      4 banana leaves (optional), and
      1 small mango peeled and diced,
      to garnish
For the curry sauce
    30ml/2 tbsp sunflower oil
    1 carrot, chopped
    1 onion, chopped
    1 celery stick, chopped
    white of 1 leek, chopped
    2 garlic cloves, crushed
    50g/2oz creamed coconut, crumbled
    2 tomatoes, peeled, seeded
      and diced
    2.5cm/1in piece fresh root
      ginger, grated
    15ml/1 tbsp tomato purée
    5–10ml/1–2 tsp mild curry powder
    500ml/17fl oz/generous 2 cups
      chicken or fish stock

1 Make the sauce. Heat the oil in a pan; add the vegetables and garlic. Cook gently until soft but not brown.

COOK'S TIP
The coconut sauce must be cooked over a very low heat, so use a heat diffuser if you have one.

2 Add the coconut, tomatoes and ginger. Cook for 1–2 minutes; stir in the tomato purée and curry powder to taste. Add the stock, stir and season.

3 Bring to the boil, then lower the heat, cover the pan and cook the sauce over the lowest heat for about 50 minutes. Stir once or twice to prevent burning. Leave the sauce to cool; pour into a food processor or blender and whizz until smooth. Return to a clean pan and reheat very gently, adding a little water if too thick.

4 Season the fish fillets with salt and pepper. Heat the oil in a large frying pan, add the butter and heat until sizzling. Put in the fish and fry for about 2–3 minutes on each side, until pale golden and cooked through. Drain on kitchen paper.

5 If you have banana leaves, place these on individual warmed plates and arrange the fillets on top. Pour the sauce around the fish and scatter on the finely diced mango. Decorate with coriander leaves and serve at once.

GRILLED HALIBUT WITH SAUCE VIERGE

ANY THICK WHITE FISH FILLETS CAN BE COOKED IN THIS VERSATILE DISH; TURBOT, BRILL AND JOHN DORY ARE ESPECIALLY DELICIOUS, BUT THE FLAVOURSOME SAUCE ALSO GIVES HUMBLER FISH LIKE COD, HADDOCK OR HAKE A REAL LIFT.

SERVES FOUR

INGREDIENTS

105ml/7 tbsp olive oil
2.5ml/½ tsp fennel seeds
2.5ml/½ tsp celery seeds
5ml/1 tsp mixed peppercorns
675–800g/1½–1¾lb middle cut of
  halibut, about 3cm/1¼in thick, cut
  into 4 pieces
coarse sea salt
5ml/1 tsp fresh thyme
  leaves, chopped
5ml/1 tsp fresh rosemary
  leaves, chopped
5ml/1 tsp fresh oregano or marjoram
  leaves, chopped
For the sauce
105ml/7 tbsp extra virgin olive oil
juice of 1 lemon
1 garlic clove, finely chopped
2 tomatoes, peeled, seeded
  and diced
5ml/1 tsp small capers
2 drained canned anchovy
  fillets, chopped
5ml/1 tsp snipped fresh chives
15ml/1 tbsp shredded fresh
  basil leaves
15ml/1 tbsp chopped fresh chervil

1 Heat a ridged grilling pan or preheat the grill to high. Brush the grilling pan or grill pan with a little of the olive oil. Mix the fennel and celery seeds with the peppercorns in a mortar. Crush with a pestle, and then stir in the coarse sea salt to taste. Spoon the mixture into a shallow dish and stir in the herbs and the remaining olive oil.

2 Add the halibut pieces to the olive oil mixture, turning them to coat them thoroughly, then arrange them with the dark skin uppermost in the oiled grilling pan or grill pan. Cook or grill for about 6–8 minutes, until the fish is cooked all the way through and the skin has browned.

3 Combine all the sauce ingredients except the fresh herbs in a saucepan and heat gently until warm but not hot. Stir in the chives, basil and chervil.

4 Place the halibut on four warmed plates. Spoon the sauce around and over the fish and serve immediately, with lightly-cooked green cabbage.

VEGETABLE-STUFFED SQUID

SHIRLEY CONRAN FAMOUSLY SAID THAT LIFE IS TOO SHORT TO STUFF A MUSHROOM. THE SAME MIGHT BE SAID OF SQUID, EXCEPT THAT THE RESULT IS SO DELICIOUS THAT IT MAKES THE EFFORT SEEM WORTHWHILE. SMALL CUTTLEFISH CAN BE PREPARED IN THE SAME WAY. SERVE WITH SAFFRON RICE.

SERVES FOUR

INGREDIENTS
   4 medium squid, or 12 small squid,
      skinned and cleaned
   75g/3oz/6 tbsp butter
   50g/2oz/1 cup fresh white
      breadcrumbs
   2 shallots, chopped
   4 garlic cloves, chopped
   1 leek, finely diced
   2 carrots, finely diced
   150ml/¼ pint/⅔ cup fish stock
   30ml/2 tbsp olive oil
   30ml/2 tbsp chopped fresh parsley
   salt and ground black pepper
   rosemary sprigs, to garnish
   saffron rice, to serve

1 Preheat the oven to 220°C/425°F/ Gas 7. Cut off the tentacles and side flaps from the squid and chop these finely. Set the squid aside. Melt half the butter in a large frying pan that can safely be used in the oven. Add the fresh white breadcrumbs and fry until they are golden brown, stirring to prevent them from burning. Using a slotted spoon, transfer the breadcrumbs to a bowl and set aside until required.

2 Heat the remaining butter in the frying pan and add the chopped and diced vegetables. Fry until softened but not browned, then stir in the fish stock and cook until the stock has reduced and the vegetables are very soft. Season to taste with salt and ground black pepper and transfer to the bowl with the breadcrumbs. Mix lightly together.

3 Heat half the olive oil in the frying pan, add the chopped squid and fry over a high heat for 1 minute. Remove the squid with a slotted spoon; stir into the vegetable mixture. Stir in the parsley.

4 Put the stuffing mixture into a piping bag, or use a teaspoon to stuff the squid tubes with the mixture. Do not overfill them, as the stuffing will swell lightly during cooking. Secure the openings with wooden cocktail sticks, or sew up with fine kitchen thread.

5 Heat the remaining olive oil in the frying pan, place the stuffed squid in the pan and fry until they are sealed on all sides and golden brown. Transfer the frying pan to the oven and roast the squid for 20 minutes.

6 Unless the squid are very small, carefully cut them into 3 or 4 slices and arrange on a bed of saffron rice. Spoon the cooking juices over and around the squid and serve immediately, with each serving garnished with sprigs of rosemary.

SAUCES FOR FISH AND SHELLFISH

MANY TYPES OF FISH ARE SO DELICIOUS THAT THEY DO NOT NEED TO BE COOKED IN A SAUCE, BUT A GOOD ACCOMPANYING SAUCE WILL CERTAINLY ENHANCE PLAINLY COOKED FISH.

NEVER-FAIL MAYONNAISE

Some people find classic mayonnaise difficult to make, but this simple version takes away the mystique. The essential thing is to have all the ingredients at room temperature before you start. Be aware that this recipe contains raw eggs. If this is a concern, use bought mayonnaise instead.

SERVES FOUR TO SIX

INGREDIENTS
    1 egg, plus 1 egg yolk
    5ml/1 tsp Dijon mustard
    juice of 1 large lemon
    175ml/6fl oz/¾ cup olive oil
    175ml/6fl oz/¾ cup grapeseed,
      sunflower or corn oil
    salt and ground white pepper

1 Put the whole egg and yolk in a food processor and whizz for 20 seconds. Add the mustard, half the lemon juice, and a generous pinch of salt and pepper. Process for about 30 seconds, until thoroughly mixed.

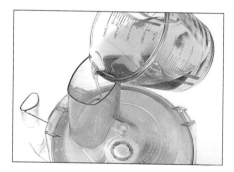

2 With the motor running, pour in the oils through the feeder tube in a thin, steady stream. Whizz until the oils are incorporated and the mayonnaise is pale and thick. Taste and add more lemon juice and seasoning if necessary.

VARIATIONS
Vary the oil according to the fish the mayonnaise is to accompany. Use all olive oil for robust fish such as salmon or tuna, a mixture of olive and light vegetable oil for more delicate fish.

BEURRE BLANC

Legend has it that this exquisite sauce was invented by a cook who forgot to put egg yolks into a béarnaise sauce. Whether or not this is true doesn't matter: this light sauce goes perfectly with poached or grilled fish.

SERVES FOUR

INGREDIENTS
    3 shallots, very finely chopped
    45ml/3 tbsp dry white wine or
      court-bouillon
    45ml/3 tbsp white wine or
      tarragon vinegar
    115g/4oz/½ cup chilled unsalted
      butter, diced
    lemon juice (optional)
    salt and ground white pepper

1 Put the shallots in a small saucepan with the wine or court bouillon and vinegar. Bring to the boil and cook over a high heat until only about 30ml/2 tbsp liquid remains. Remove the pan from the heat and leave to cool until the liquid is just lukewarm.

2 Whisk in the chilled butter, one piece at a time, to make a pale, creamy sauce. Taste the sauce, then season with salt and pepper and add a little lemon juice to taste if you like.

3 If you are not serving the sauce immediately, keep it warm in the top of a double boiler set over barely simmering water.

HOLLANDAISE SAUCE

This rich sauce goes well with any poached fish. Serve it warm. As the egg yolks are barely cooked, do not serve to children, the elderly or anyone with a compromised immune system.

SERVES FOUR

INGREDIENTS
    115g/4oz/½ cup unsalted butter
    2 egg yolks
    15–30ml/1–2 tbsp lemon juice or
      white wine or tarragon vinegar
    salt and ground white pepper

1 Melt the butter in a small saucepan Put the egg yolks and lemon juice or vinegar in a bowl. Add salt and pepper and whisk until completely smooth.

2 Pour the melted butter in a steady stream on to the egg yolk mixture, beating vigorously with a wooden spoon to make a smooth, creamy sauce. Alternatively, put the mixture in a food processor and add the butter through the feeder tube, with the motor running. Taste the sauce and add more lemon juice or vinegar if necessary.

PARSLEY SAUCE

Forget the pallid, lumpy parsley sauce of your youth; when this classic sauce is well made it is delicious. Serve it with poached cod, haddock or any white fish. If possible, use the poaching liquid to enhance the flavour of the sauce.

SERVES FOUR

INGREDIENTS
  50g/2oz/¼ cup butter
  45ml/3 tbsp plain flour
  300ml/½ pint/1¼ cups milk
  300ml/½ pint/1¼ cups poaching
    liquid from the fish (or an extra
    300ml/½ pint/1¼ cups milk)
  60ml/4 tbsp double cream
  lemon juice (see method)
  90ml/6 tbsp chopped fresh parsley
  salt and ground black pepper

1 Melt half the butter in a small saucepan, add the flour and stir for 2–3 minutes to make a smooth roux. Take the pan off the heat, add a couple of spoonfuls of milk and stir in until completely absorbed. Continue to add small quantities of milk and poaching liquid, if available, stirring until the sauce has the consistency of double cream. Add the rest of the milk and poaching liquid and whisk to break down any lumps.

2 Return the pan to the heat and bring the sauce to the boil. Lower the heat and simmer gently for about 5 minutes, stirring frequently. Stir in the cream and lemon juice to taste, and season with salt and pepper. If the sauce is at all lumpy at this stage, whisk it thoroughly with a hand-held blender or a balloon whisk.

3 Stir in the parsley, then whisk in the remaining butter and serve hot.

MUSTARD AND DILL SAUCE

Serve this fresh-tasting sauce with any cold, smoked or raw marinated fish. Note that it contains raw egg yolk.

SERVES FOUR

INGREDIENTS
  1 egg yolk
  30ml/2 tbsp brown French mustard
  2.5–5ml/½–1 tsp soft dark
    brown sugar
  15ml/1 tbsp white wine vinegar
  90ml/6 tbsp sunflower or
    vegetable oil
  30ml/2 tbsp finely chopped fresh dill
  salt and ground black pepper

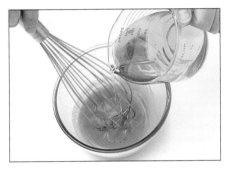

1 Put the egg yolk in a small bowl and add the mustard with a little soft brown sugar to taste. Beat with a wooden spoon until smooth. Stir in the white wine vinegar, then gradually whisk in the oil, a little at a time, mixing well after each addition.

2 When the oil has been completely amalgamated, season the sauce with salt and pepper, then stir in the finely chopped dill. Chill for an hour or more before serving.

CRAWFISH SAUCE

This sauce, also known as Nantua sauce, is perfect for using up the shells left over from seafood recipes. It can be made with other crustaceans, such as lobster or large prawns. Use it to enhance any white fish or shellfish.

SERVES FOUR

INGREDIENTS
  1 cooked crawfish (rock lobster),
    about 450g/1lb
  40g/1½oz/3 tbsp butter
  15ml/1 tbsp olive oil
  45ml/3 tbsp brandy
  500ml/17fl oz/generous 2 cups fish
    or shellfish stock
  15ml/1 tbsp plain flour
  45ml/3 tbsp double cream
  2 egg yolks
  salt and ground white pepper

1 Remove the tail meat from the crawfish and keep for another recipe. Break up the shells and legs and crush them coarsely in a food processor.

2 Melt 25g/1oz/2 tbsp of the butter in the oil in a pan, add the shells and cook for about 3 minutes, stirring frequently. Add the brandy and stock, bring to the boil, then simmer for 10 minutes.

3 Mash the remaining butter with the flour to make *beurre manié*. Whisk this into the sauce, a small piece at a time, and cook gently until thickened. Season the sauce and strain it through a fine sieve. Stir in the cream and bring back to just below boiling point.

4 Beat the egg yolks lightly in a bowl and mix in a couple of spoonfuls of the hot sauce. Return the mixture to the pan and cook gently until smooth. Adjust the seasoning and serve at once.

SHOPPING FOR FISH AND SHELLFISH

Fishmongers

Ashdown plc
Fish, Poultry and Game
23 Leadenhall Market
London EC3V 1LR
Tel: 020 7621 1365

B & M Seafoods
250 Kentish Town Road
London NW5 2AA
Tel: 020 7485 0346

Chalmers and Gray
67 Nottinghill Gate
London W11 3JS
Tel: 020 7221 6177

Corney, J. A. Ltd (kosher)
16 Hallswelle Parade
Finchley Road
London NW11 0DL
Tel: 020 8455 9588

Cornwall Fish
17 Station Approach
West Byfleet
Surrey KT14 6NF
Tel: 01932 355550/1

Covent Garden Fishmongers
Phil Diamond
37 Turnham Green Terrace
London W4 1RG
Tel: 020 8995 9273

Cutty Catering Supplies
Unit 4
57 Sandgate Street
London SE15 1LE
Tel: 020 7277 7759

Dagon's Ltd
16 Granvill Arcade
Brixton Market
London SW9 8PR
Tel: 020 7274 1665

Filipino Supermarket
1 Kenway Road
London SW5 0RP
Tel: 020 7244 0007

France Fresh Fish (tropical
   fish)
99 Stroud Green Road
London N4 3PX
Tel: 020 7263 9767

Good Harvest Fish and Meat
   Market (Chinese fish and
   shellfish)
14 Newport Place
London WC2H 7PR
Tel: 020 7437 0712

Harrods Food Hall
87 Brompton Road
Knightsbridge
London SW1X 7XL
Tel: 020 7730 1234

Harvey Nichols Food Hall
109–125 Knightsbridge
London SW1X 7RJ
Tel: 020 7235 5000

HM Seafoods Ltd
2 The Parade
Loxwood
West Sussex RH14 0SB
Tel: 01403 753250
Fax: 01403 753340

Jarvis
55 Coombe Road
Kingston
Surrey KT3 4QN
Tel: 020 8546 0989

John Blagdens
65 Paddington Street
London W1M 3RR
Tel: 020 7935 8321

John Nicholson Fishmongers
108 Manor Road
Wallington
Surrey SN6 0DW
Tel: 020 8647 3922

Loaves and Fishes
52 Thoroughfare
Woodbridge
Suffolk IP12 1AL
Tel: 01394 385650

Manta Ray Seafoods
24 Hildreth Street
London SW12 9RQ
Tel: 020 8673 4678

Newnes, C. J. (exotic fish)
73 Billingsgate Market
Trafalgar Way
London E14 5TQ
Tel: 020 7515 0793

Ramus Seafoods
Ocean House
132–136 Kings Road
Harrogate
North Yorkshire HG1 5HY
Tel: 01423 563271
Fax: 01423 531040

The Seafood Store
16 Downing Street
Farnham
Surrey GU9 7PB
Tel: 01252 715010

Selfridges
400 Oxford Street
London W1A 1AB
Tel: 020 7629 1234

Steve Hatt
88–90 Essex Road
London N1 8LU
Tel: 020 7226 3963

Information Services

Alaska Seafood Marketing
   Institute
P.O. Box 14
Guildford
Surrey GU1 2RH
Tel: 01483 416136
Fax: 01483 426662

British Trout Association
8–9 Lambton Place
London W11 2SH
Tel: 020 7221 6065

Fleetwood Fish Merchants
   Association Limited
6 Station Road
Fleetwood
Lancs FY7 6NW
Tel: 01253 873358

Herring Buyers Association
   Limited
36 Springfield Terrace
South Queensferry
Edinburgh EH30 9XF
Tel: 0131 331 1222
Fax: 0131 331 4646

New Zealand Trade
   Development Board
New Zealand House
80 Haymarket
London SW1Y 4TE
Tel: 020 7973 0380
Fax: 020 7973 0104

Northern Ireland Seafood
    Limited
Quay Gate House
19–23 Station Street
Belfast BT3 9DA
Tel: 028 9045 2829

Prepared Fish Products
    Association
6 Catherine Street
London WC2B 5JJ
Tel: 020 7836 2460
Fax: 020 7836 0580

Seafish Industry
    Authority
18 Logie Mill
Logie Green Road
Edinburgh EH7 4HG
Tel: 0131 558 3331
Fax: 0131 558 1442

Shellfish Association of
    Great Britiain
The Fishmongers' Hall
London Bridge
London EC4R 9EL
Tel: 020 7283 8305
Fax 020 7929 1389

Mail Order Companies

Atlantic Harvest Limited
Pennyburn Industrial
    Estate
Buncrana Road
Londonderry
Co Londonderry BT48 0LU
Tel: 028 7126 4275
Fax: 028 7126 2955

Atlantis Smoked Fish
Fore Street
Grampound
Truro
Cornwall TR2 4SB
Tel: 01726 883201

Bridfish (smoked fish)
Unit 1, The Old Laundry
    Industrial Estate
Sea Road North
Bridport
Dorset DT6 3BD
Tel: 01308 456306

Cornish Smoked Fish
    Company Limited
Charlestown
St Austell
Cornwall PL25 3NY
Tel: 01726 72356
Fax: 01726 72360

Rhydlewis Fishery
Rhydlewis
Llandysul
Ceredigion SA44 5QS
Tel/Fax: 01239 851224

Cooking Equipment

Divertimenti
45–47 Wigmore Street
London W1H 9LA
Tel: 0171 935 0689

and

139 Fulham Road
London SW3 6SD
Tel: 0171 581 8065

David Mellor
4 Sloane Square
London SW1W 8EE
Tel: 020 7730 4259

New Zealand

New Zealand Fishing Industry
    Board
Private Bag 24 901
Manners Street Post Office
Wellington
Tel: (04) 385 4005/8115
www.seafood.co.nz

Australia

De Costi Seafoods
Sydney Fish Markets
Gipps Street
Pyrmont NSW 2009
Tel: (02) 9692 9188

Sydney Fish Markets
Gipps Street
Pyrmont NSW 2009
Tel: (02) 9660 3652
www.sydneyfishmarket.com.au

Poulos Bros
21–29 Bank Street
Pyrmont NSW 2009
Tel: (02) 9692 8411
www.poulosbros.com.au

The Fish Factory
363 Lytton Road
Colmslie QLD 4170
Tel: (07) 3399 9888

Queen Victoria Markets
513 Elizabeth Street
Melbourne
VIC 3000
Tel: (03) 93205822
www.qvm.com.au

Angelakis Bros
30 Field Street
Adelaide SA 5000
Tel: (08) 8400 1300

Picture Acknowledgements

All photographs are by Willaim
Lingwood except those on the
following pages: p8bl Life
File/Barry Mayes, p8tr Life
file/Jeremy Hoare, p9 Tony
Stone/Joe Cornish; p51t New
Zealand Seafoods, p51b Kate
Whiteman, pp61tr and 72b
Food Features (fish supplied
by Tesco), p108 Sydney Fish
Markets, p112 Cephas/Alain
Proust, 122tl and tr Janine
Hosegood.

Publisher's
Acknowledgements

The publisher's would like to
thank the following companies
who kindly loaned equipment
for photography:
Divertimenti, Tel: 020 7581
8065 and Magimix, Tel: 01252
548976

INDEX